Time-Life
Old-Fashioned Christmas
Cookbook

TIME-LIFE

Old-Fashioned Christmas

COOKBOOK

TIME® LIFE BOOKS

Time-Life Books, Alexandria, Virginia

TIME-LIFE BOOKS IS A DIVISION OF TIME LIFE INC.

Time-Life Custom Publishing

Vice President and Publisher	Terry Newell
Project Manager	Teresa Graham
Director of Sales	Neil Levin
Director of Special Sales	Liz Ziehl
Director of Licensing and Permissions	Teresa Hartnett
Managing Editor	Donia Steele
Creative Director	Gary Stoiber
Production Manager	Carolyn Mills Bounds
Cover Photo	Renée Comet

Special thanks to Robin Bray, Peter Brett, Lisa Cherkasky, Dale M. Brown, Judith Harley, Don Sheldon, Paul Stewart, and Jack Weiser.

Produced by Storey Communications, Inc.

President	M. John Storey
Executive Vice President	Martha M. Storey
Vice President and Publisher	Pamela B. Art
Custom Publishing Director	Amanda R. Haar
Designer	Leslie Morris Noyes
Photographer	Richard Felber
Editor	Linda Glick Conway
Writer/Editor	Gwen Steege
Photo Stylist	Sara Barbaris
Food Stylist	Beverly Cox
Ornament Photographer	Nick Whitman

Editorial Staff: Angela Cardinali, Jessica Storey Dils, Roxanne Miller, Constance Oxley, and Edith Stovel.

Library of Congress Cataloging-in-Publication Data
The Time Life Old-Fashioned Christmas cookbook
     p. cm.
    Includes index.
    ISBN 0-7835-4831-1
    1. Christmas cookery. 2. Christmas decorations. 3. Christmas
I. Time-Life Books.
TX739.2C45T56   1996
641.5'68--dc20   96-17861
                                                      CIP

Books produced by Time-Life Custom Publishing are available
at special bulk discount for promotional and premium use.
Custom adaptations can also be created to meet
your specific marketing goals.
Call 1-800-323-5255.

Contents

Introduction

N TODAY'S BUSY world, the graceful images of an old-fashioned Christmas are more treasured than ever: A horse-drawn sleigh arriving on Christmas Eve, piled high with gifts . . . in the parlor, a fresh-scented pine tree gleaming with real candles, while a massive Yule log blazes on the hearth . . . aproned aunts and cousins bearing steaming platters of food to the holiday table.

Although most of this nostalgic picture lives on today only in memory, a festive Christmas dinner with family and friends is still the highlight of the season in countless households throughout the land. Indeed, thanks to modern shopping and kitchen conveniences, serving a sumptuous feast has never been easier!

To help you recreate the great food and good cheer of an old-fashioned holiday at home, we have brought together the best Christmas recipes from Time-Life Books and other publishers, including traditional favorites from every part of America and around the world. Along with recipes, you will find a variety of party menu suggestions, ideas for colorful decorations and special gifts from your kitchen, and—like plums in the pudding—occasional side notes on the intriguing origins of our cherished holiday customs. We hope these recipes and menus provide a dependable source for your own traditional favorites—or inspire you to adopt new Christmas traditions for your family.

THE BUSIEST TIME OF THE YEAR

The key to getting enjoyment out of your holiday cooking, baking, and entertaining is planning ahead. Here are some tried-and-true tips to help you organize for action.

❋ Make a list of the recipes you'd like to use, then stock up early on special ingredients for holiday baking and cooking: citron and candied fruit, raisins and dates, nuts, spices, chocolates, and mincemeat.

❋ Tuck away some special treats for spur-of-the-moment get-togethers: fancy crackers, tinned smoked salmon, artichoke hearts, candied ginger, flavored coffee, pistachios and macadamias, chutneys, mustards, pickled vegetables, and imported olives.

❋ Collect a supply of unusual vinegars —balsamic, wine, rice, herb, and spice *(see page 195)*—as well as of good-quality olive oil, flavored mustards, and other condiments.

❋ For busy-day meals, whether for family or guests, it never hurts to have some basic meal-starters in your freezer: tomato sauces, pie crusts, and interesting sweet and savory breads, for instance, along with homemade chicken, beef, and vegetable stocks.

❋ If you really believe in planning ahead, you can prepare gifts from the kitchen such as jellies, relishes, herbal vinegars, and flavored liqueurs in late summer.

STARS OF THE HOLIDAY KITCHEN: CHRISTMAS COOKIES

A Christmas cookie baking spree is an ideal way to usher in the holiday season.

Pick a cold, blustery day, turn on your favorite Christmas music, set the kettle on for tea, and mix up several different batches of cookies. The delicious smells alone will put you in a holiday mood. If you can set aside one afternoon or evening each December week for cookie baking, you'll have an impressive variety stored away by Christmas Day. Start early with Pfeffernüsse *(page 136)* and Springerle *(page 137)*, which require a period of aging at room temperature for the best flavor. Many other kinds of cookies may be baked ahead and frozen until needed. Package them in sturdy containers so they don't get crushed, taking care to arrange them in single layers separated by wax paper, and seal them airtight. Left in their freezer wrappings, baked cookies thaw within minutes at room temperature. To restore crispness, heat the cookies on baking sheets in a 350°F. oven for 2 to 3 minutes.

You can also freeze cookie dough, either before or after shaping the cookies. Package the dough, tightly sealed in plastic wrap and heavy-duty foil. If the cookies have been frozen preformed, bake them without thawing. Thaw bulk dough, covered, at room temperature, just until it can be manipulated and shaped.

If making batch after batch of cookies sounds like more work than fun, here's an alternate way to dazzle your family or guests with a spectacular trayful of a dozen or more different kinds of homemade Christmas cookies: Turn Christmas baking into a social event by organizing a cookie-swap luncheon. Invite guests to bring for trade two or three dozen of a single kind of Christmas cookie—their own specialties. Each guest will take home as many cookies as he or she brings, choosing one or two from every contribution. Begin the luncheon with a glass of wine and serve soup in mugs. An easy, festive way to serve the rest of the meal is to package it in individual bakery boxes tied with holiday ribbons and arranged under the Christmas tree.

CHRISTMAS IS FAMILY TIME

As the season really gets under way, you'll find that everyone will get more pleasure and satisfaction out of the festivities if they are included in pre-holiday menu planning and preparations. Small children love to help, and with supervision they are surprisingly capable in the kitchen, delighting in baking cookies or assembling such simple, uncooked dishes as Cranberry Orange Relish *(page 58)* or Ambrosia *(page 174)*.

A kids' Christmas cookie decorating party can be a highlight of the season, for both you and the younger crew—just don't forget to keep the numbers to what is comfortable for your energy level and the size of your kitchen. Make the dough for Sugar Cookie Cutouts or Ginger Shortbread *(pages 136 and 145)* ahead of time, provide colored icing, candies, and fruits, and let young imaginations take off. Small children also delight in stringing garlands of popcorn and cranberries *(page 209)* for both indoor and outdoor Christmas trees. For party refreshments, serve peanut-butter-and-jelly sandwiches cut in holiday shapes with cookie cutters along with apple wedges, seedless grapes, and nonalcoholic eggnog (plus a newly decorated cookie or two, of course!). For a special treat, invite your favorite Santa to make a surprise, pre-Christmas visit.

Introduction ❦

'TIS THE SEASON FOR FIRST-CLASS INGREDIENTS

Because cooking and baking so often take center stage during the holidays, it's natural to want to splurge on the best and freshest at Christmastime. All parts of the meal can benefit from the special attention you give to ingredients. Here are some ideas that may be useful.

❋ Fresh herbs usually contribute the most intense flavor to whatever sauce, stew, or entrée they are a part of, and today, fresh herbs are available year-round at most supermarkets. If you prefer to use dried herbs, you might consider using the holiday season as an excuse to replace and replenish your herb and spice shelf. When you purchase new spices for your baking needs, choose whole rather than ground, if possible. You can grind seeds with a mortar and pestle or in a blender, mini-food processor, or an electric coffee mill especially set aside for the purpose.

❋ It's surprising what a difference a pure extract, rather than an imitation, can make in all of your baked goods. It's easy (and inexpensive) to make your own vanilla extract: Split three vanilla beans lengthwise and pop them into a pint of rum—some cooks prefer dark rum, but light will also do. Allow the mixture to sit for about a month. You'll enjoy this for your own baking needs, and it makes a thoughtful gift for friends who like to cook, as well.

❋ If your cookie recipe calls for butter, the holidays are probably not the time to stint. Nothing beats the texture and flavor that real butter adds to the finished product. Some recipes call for salted butter (denoted simply as "butter" in ingredient lists in this book), while others specify unsalted butter. Because different brands of butter vary in saltiness, many cooks use unsalted butter to keep more control over the taste of the final product. Others prefer unsalted because of health concerns or simply because they like its fresh, sweet flavor. The choice is up to you. But if a recipe calls for unsalted butter and you decide to substitute salted butter, you may wish to reduce somewhat the amount of salt in the recipe.

❋ The vegetable shortening occasionally referred to in this book is pure, solid, all-vegetable shortening. It tends to produce softer, spongier, and flakier textures in baked goods. A cookie made with shortening can be described as a "short" cookie—one that breaks solidly and thickly, like a peanut butter cookie, rather than with a snap, like a ginger snap.

❋ Unless otherwise noted in a recipe, use large, room-temperature eggs in your baking.

❋ The word "flour" alone in a list of ingredients means sifted, all-purpose, unbleached white flour; "sugar" means granulated sugar.

❋ Prime grades of beef are aged, a process that improves both tenderness and flavor. Look for beef that is bright red outside and deep purple inside, with a springy feel to it.

❋ Pork should be grayish pink, with a minimum of fat. Since pork has a shorter storage life than other meats, purchase only the freshest cut, as close as possible to the time you will serve it.

❋ At Christmas you may wish to splurge on a farm-smoked ham, or even a Smithfield country ham. Because these hams are heavily salted, they require long soaking and simmering, after which they are usually baked in a hot oven, sometimes with a glaze, and served thinly sliced (for recipes see pages 70 and 71).

❋ Fresh poultry usually has a taste and texture superior to frozen. Whether they come fresh or from the freezer, the birds should have smooth skins and no discoloration. Though a large bird may not be as tender as a small one, with long, slow cooking and frequent basting, its meat will provide a richness of flavor that younger birds cannot match. Frozen birds should be thawed in the refrigerator to guard against bacterial growth, and cooked within two days of thawing.

❋ To be sure your meat or poultry is cooked to perfection, use an oven thermometer to monitor the temperature of your oven, calculate the amount of time needed for cooking, and then use a meat thermometer to check the meat's internal temperature while it is roasting. For birds, insert the thermometer into the fleshy part of the breast where it joins the leg. For all roasts, be sure the thermometer does not touch bone, which conducts heat and will yield a false reading.

❋ Because meats and poultry go on cooking after they come out of the oven, remove them a bit before the desired temperature has been registered. Let both meat and poultry rest for 15 to 30 minutes on the cutting board or platter before carving. They will retain more of their juices, and you'll find them easier to carve. You can use this time to make the gravy.

❋ You can make your meals more healthful by degreasing your meat and poultry dishes. During cooking, both juices and fats are released into the pan, and these often become the basis for gravies and sauces. Since the fat rises to the top of the heavier juices, you can carefully skim it off with a spoon or a bulb baster. If you have time, pour off all the liquid into a bowl and place it briefly in the freezer; when the fat has risen and congealed, remove it. Soups and stews may also require degreasing, and this, too, may be accomplished by drawing the fat off the hot liquid or by chilling the soup or stew and removing the fat after it solidifies.

WHEN TIME IS OF THE ESSENCE

Today's homemakers may have more hectic schedules than those of earlier generations, but we've also got some modern shortcuts that Great-Grandma never knew. Here are some tips that can save you precious minutes of holiday cooking and baking time.

❋ To melt chocolate in a microwave, unwrap and chop squares of chocolate into small (about ½-inch square) pieces of uniform size, and place the pieces in a microwaveable cup or bowl. Be sure to watch the melting process carefully, as chocolate easily hardens or burns if microwaved for too long. One 1-ounce square takes about 1 minute at high power, but check the melting progress often and be sure to stir the chocolate with a rubber spatula at 30-second intervals for even melting. When the chocolate is almost smooth, allow it to stand in the oven for a minute or two, then stir again. If unmelted lumps still remain, microwave it for additional 30-second periods. Melting butter or heating other liquids along with the chocolate reduces the risk of burning the chocolate.

❋ A microwave is particularly useful at parties for last-minute warm-ups: A minute or two in the microwave will produce piping-hot gravies and steamy breads. Warm homemade bread or rolls, wrapped in several layers of paper towel to prevent sogginess, for about 10 seconds per serving; take care not to leave the bread in too long or it will toughen. Heat appetizers, such as meatballs, stuffed mushrooms, and canapés, just before serving. With care, you can even take the chill off cheese or soften a wheel of Brie. The microwave also does an excellent job of toasting nuts and coconut.

❋ To chop citrus peel, remove the colored part of the peel with a vegetable peeler, taking care not to include the bitter white pith, and cut the strips into 1-inch pieces. Process with the steel blade of a food processor until finely chopped, about 1 minute. If sugar is called for in the recipe, whirl it in with the citrus pieces; this facilitates quick, even chopping.

❋ To prepare pastry dough in a food processor, cut well-chilled butter into ½-inch pieces. Put the dry ingredients and butter into the processor bowl, and process with the steel blade until the mixture resembles coarse meal. If sugar or nuts are included in the recipe, process them along with the butter mixture. Gradually add the liquid and process the mixture only until the dough begins to clump. Be careful not to overwork the dough or the pastry will be tough.

❋ To prepare yeast dough in a food processor, place all the dry ingredients, the butter or shortening, and the eggs in the processor bowl. With the machine running, pour the proofed yeast mixture (the yeast activated with warm water and sometimes sugar) and any other warm liquid through the feeder tube and process until the dough is smooth and elastic, about 30 seconds.

GETTING A GRIP ON PARTIES

Parties have always been an integral part of old-fashioned Christmas celebrations, and on these occasions planning really pays off. As soon as you complete the guest list, it's wise to make out your menu and recipe list. You'll find menu suggestions for a variety of parties for all ages on pages 214-219. It's thoughtful to remember the special needs of your guests. Offer nonalcoholic as well as alcoholic beverages, decaffeinated as well as regular coffee, and fresh fruits as a substitute for the rich desserts some people may decline.

Here are some additional tips for giving successful parties with minimum stress.

❋ Well before party time, take stock of your glassware, plates, flatware, and table linens, as well as serving dishes and utensils, cooking pots, pans, casseroles, and coffee maker. Survey your cupboards for ordinary containers to use in inventive ways: For instance, you might serve a colorful salad or an elegant ambrosia in a punch bowl. If you find you still do not have enough of certain items, you should make plans to borrow or rent them. And if you're skilled at sewing, you might buy gaily printed calico or plaid yard goods and make your own tablecloths and napkins.

❋ Even if you are not a natural-born list maker, your preparations will go more smoothly if you create a cooking schedule for yourself. Note which of your recipes can be prepared ahead and frozen, which should be made a few days in advance so that flavors can meld, and which must be done at the last minute. Be sure you have enough freezer or refrigerator space to store your dishes and ingredients. Include reminders to defrost or bring foods to room temperature before roasting or baking, and allow enough time for doubled or

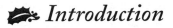

tripled quantities, which will take longer to reheat or cook.

❀ You'll avoid last-minute panic if you complete as many preparations as possible the day before. For example, if you set the table and notice something missing, you will still have a whole day left to take care of it.

❀ Plan for the traffic flow of your guests once the party is under way. If you are serving buffet-style, set beverages apart from the food, perhaps even in a different room, to avoid a logjam at the buffet table. For a transition from the table after a sit-down dinner, it's nice to serve dessert and coffee in the living room. And as a special holiday treat to yourself, hire a teenager or two to help serve and clean up.

❀ In spite of all the good party-planning advice you can gather, the fact is that some people love giving big parties and some are terrified at the very thought.

Entertain on a level you can afford—not just in terms of money, but of time and peace of mind. The purpose of a party, especially at Christmas, is to give your guests an opportunity to relax, enjoy each other's company, and have fun. If in spite of all your planning, things are less than perfect, take things in stride. Your family and guests will have a much better time if you are having a great time at your party, as well.

A MERRY CHRISTMAS TO ALL!

The best holiday cooking traditionally contains a generous sprinkling of love. As you lovingly select and create the old and new specialties that follow, may your kitchen be enriched and your family and guests delighted by the old-fashioned Christmas spirit of warmth and goodwill, throughout this season and many a season to come.

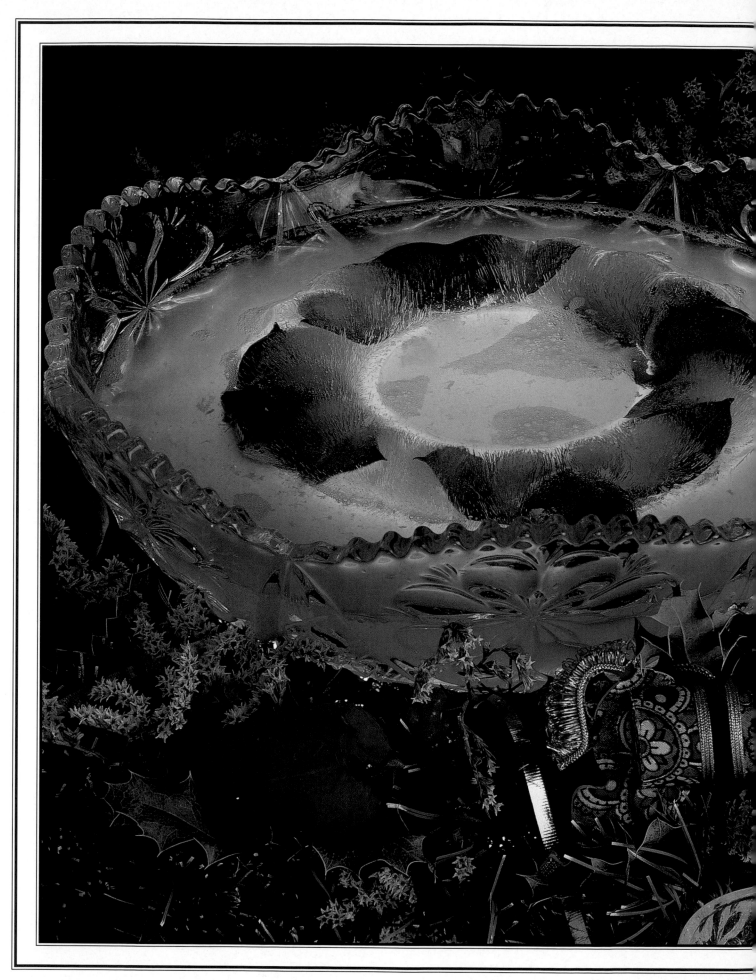

Appetizers & Beverages

HETHER YOU ARE PLANNING A FAMILY potluck or an elegant reception, you will want to offer an imaginative selection of appetizers and beverages to your holiday guests. Brisk, cold weather stimulates appetites, and in the pages that immediately follow you will find a variety of ideas for indulging those appetites, from a simple but delicious Potted Jack Cheese to an impressive Chicken Liver Terrine. Make your choices according to demands on your time, efforts to offer a balanced and varied selection, and attempts to complement the rest of your menu. The festive bowl is an age-old tradition, and both hot and cold Christmas punches can add an elegant touch to your holiday celebrations. Nothing gives a warmer welcome to guests than the rich, enticing aroma of Hot Spiced Cider or Mulled Wine on a cold night. Be sure to offer alternatives like Cardinal Punch or Mock Champagne Punch for those who prefer nonalcoholic beverages. And don't forget the slice of toast in the Wassail Bowl: Tradition says that the person who gets the toast in his or her cup and thus "drinks the toast" will have good luck all year.

Mock Champagne Punch

APPLE CHEESE SPREAD

Makes 2½ cups

8 ounces cream cheese, at room
temperature

1 cup grated Cheddar cheese, at room
temperature

2 tablespoons brandy or dry sherry

1 Granny Smith apple, peeled, cored,
and grated

¼ teaspoon freshly ground black
pepper

1 teaspoon dried thyme

1 teaspoon dried basil

1 teaspoon dried oregano

Crackers or toast rounds

1. In the large bowl of an electric mixer, combine the cream cheese, Cheddar
cheese, and brandy or sherry. Beat until
smooth.
2. Add the apple to the cheese mixture
and sprinkle with the pepper, thyme,
basil, and oregano. Stir the spread thoroughly until it is well combined.
3. Spoon the spread into a crock, cover
it, and chill it for approximately 1 hour.
Serve on crackers or toast rounds.

CHEESE STRAWS

Makes about 100

½ cup butter, softened

1 pound sharp Cheddar cheese, grated
(about 6 cups)

½ teaspoon salt

¼ teaspoon cayenne pepper

1¾ cups flour

1. Preheat the oven to 350°F.
2. In a large bowl, cream the butter.
Add the cheese, salt, and cayenne and
mix well. Add the flour and stir until
well combined. Use your hands for the
final mixing. Divide the dough into four
equal parts, and shape each into a ball.

3. On a lightly floured surface, roll out
one of the balls to a ¼-inch thickness.
Cut the dough into strips 4 inches by ½
inch and place them on an ungreased
baking sheet. Save the scraps.
4. Repeat this procedure with all of the
balls and then gather the scraps into a
ball, roll it out, and cut into strips.
5. Bake the cheese straws until golden
around the edges, 10 to 15 minutes. Do
not let them brown. With a spatula,
remove them from the baking sheets to
cool on wire racks. Serve the straws
warm or at room temperature.

BRIE WITH ROQUEFORT
AND HERBS

This is a great savory to serve at a buffet
supper or with aged port after dessert at
a formal dinner party. If you wish, decorate the top of the Brie with fresh fruit,
such as halved strawberries or kiwi, laid
in a pretty concentric pattern.

Serves about 6

1 round (8 inches) ripe Brie

1 cup Roquefort (or any blue-
veined cheese)

2 to 4 tablespoons crème fraîche
(see below)

4 tablespoons chopped fresh herbs
(such as chives, sage, parsley,
and basil)

Cracked black peppercorns, to taste

1. Place the Brie in the freezer for
about 15 minutes to make it firm. With
the knife blade parallel to the work surface, cut the Brie in half horizontally.
2. In a small bowl, combine the Roquefort with enough crème fraîche to make
it spreadable but not runny.
3. Place the bottom layer of Brie, cut
side up, on a serving dish. Spread the
Roquefort over the Brie. Sprinkle on a
liberal layer of chopped herbs and
cracked pepper. Cover with the top
layer of Brie. Seal the Brie in plastic

wrap and refrigerate it overnight. Bring it to room temperature before serving.

Crème Fraîche

    2 tablespoons buttermilk or
      1 tablespoon plain yogurt

    1 cup heavy cream

1. In a glass or earthenware bowl or jar, thoroughly stir the buttermilk or yogurt into the cream, using a wooden spoon.
2. Cover the container and let it stand in a warm place for 8 hours.
3. Refrigerate the cream to allow it to thicken, preferably overnight. It will keep, covered and refrigerated, for up to 2 weeks.

NOTE: For a group of twelve or more, buy a 12- to 14-inch Brie, and use about 2 cups of Roquefort, ¼ to ⅓ cup of crème fraîche, and ½ cup of chopped fresh herbs.

POTTED JACK CHEESE

Makes about 1½ cups

    ½ pound grated Monterey
      Jack cheese, at room temperature

    4 ounces chive cream cheese, at room
      temperature

    ¼ cup dry vermouth

    2 teaspoons Dijon mustard

    Crackers or toast rounds

1. In the large bowl of an electric mixer, combine the two cheeses, vermouth, and mustard and beat until the mixture is smooth.
2. Pack the cheese into a crock, cover, and refrigerate (it keeps well up to 3 weeks). Let the cheese stand at room temperature for 30 minutes before serving with crackers or toast rounds.

GARNISHING THE FESTIVE BOWL

Scarlet berries captured in a crystal wreath of ice will make an eye-catching, yet practical, decoration for your Christmas punch bowl. Choose perfect cranberries or cherries and the leaves of such plants as mint, verbena, or rose geranium, and freeze them in a ring mold filled with water or juice. (Use only edible fruits and leaves, never holly or mistletoe, which are poisonous.) To prevent the decorations from floating to the top while the liquid is freezing, make the ice in stages: First arrange the fruits and leaves on the bottom of the mold, and pour in only enough liquid to cover them; freeze this layer until firm. Then add another layer of liquid, and more decoration if you wish, continuing until the ring is full. Fruit punches will become less diluted if you use fruit juice instead of water for the wreath.

BENNE SEED WAFERS

In the South, benne seeds (sesame seeds) are a common ingredient for cookies and candies as well as cocktail biscuits.

Makes 2 to 3 dozen, depending on the size

⅔ cup sesame seeds

2 cups flour

Salt to taste

Cayenne pepper to taste

½ cup butter

¼ cup vegetable shortening

¼ cup ice water, approximately

1. Preheat the oven to 300°F.
2. Spread out the sesame seeds on a baking sheet and bake, stirring occasionally, until lightly browned, about 20 minutes.
3. In a large bowl, combine the flour, salt, and cayenne. Add the butter and shortening and cut in with two knives or a pastry blender until the mixture has the texture of coarse cornmeal. Add the water, a little at a time, using a two-pronged fork to toss the mixture. Add just enough water so that the dough will hold together.
4. To make the dough with a food processor, put the flour, salt, cayenne, butter, and vegetable shortening in the bowl and process with the steel blade attachment until the mixture resembles coarse cornmeal. Gradually add ice water until the dough forms a ball.
5. Knead in the sesame seeds, roll the dough to a ⅛-inch thickness on a lightly floured board, and cut it into small round wafers with a biscuit cutter. Place them on a baking sheet and bake 15 to 20 minutes. Remove the wafers from the oven and sprinkle, while hot, with a little salt.

CHICKEN LIVER TERRINE

Though originally the French word *terrine* referred to a ground meat mixture baked in an earthenware casserole, today the term is used interchangeably with pâté.

Serves 8 to 12

1¼ pounds chicken livers

6 tablespoons port wine

Pinch of dried thyme

2 bay leaves, crumbled

¼ pound boiled ham

¼ pound sausage meat

3 slices bread, soaked in a little milk

½ cup dry white wine

½ garlic clove, finely chopped

Freshly ground black pepper

8 slices bacon

2 bay leaves

Lard, melted, or clarified butter
(see page 157)

1. Place the chicken livers in a medium-size bowl with the port, thyme, and bay leaves. Cover the bowl and marinate the livers in the refrigerator for at least 2 hours.
2. Preheat the oven to 375°F.
3. Remove three quarters of the chicken livers from the bowl and coarsely chop them in a food processor or food chopper, with the ham, sausage, and bread.
4. Stir the wine, garlic, and pepper into the chicken liver mixture.

5. Line an ovenproof terrine or pâté mold with half of the bacon slices. Spread half of the liver-sausage mixture in the pan. Add the whole chicken livers and cover with the rest of the chopped mixture.

6. Top the terrine with the remaining strips of bacon and the 2 whole bay leaves.

7. Cover the mold, place it in a pan of boiling water, and bake the pâté for 1¼ to 1½ hours. Remove the terrine from the oven and uncover it.

8. Pour off the excess juices and place a weight directly on the terrine as it cools in the pan. You may do this by placing a bread pan filled with uncooked rice or legumes on top of the terrine.

9. Pour a thin layer of lard or clarified butter on top of the cooled terrine, making sure that the lard reaches the edges of the pan to seal the terrine. Chill it for 2 to 3 days before serving.

SAVORY STUFFED MUSHROOMS

Makes 18 mushrooms

12 ounces white button mushrooms, 1¼ to 1½ inches in diameter (about 18), wiped clean, stems separated from caps, and trimmed, 1 cup of the stems reserved for stuffing

3 tablespoons olive oil

⅛ teaspoon plus ¼ teaspoon salt

3 large garlic cloves, thinly sliced

¼ cup chopped shallots

2 tablespoons brandy

⅓ cup walnuts

1 bunch watercress, washed, trimmed, and patted dry

1. In a large skillet, heat 2 tablespoons of the olive oil over medium heat. Add the mushroom caps and sauté them until they are cooked but not soft, 2 to 3 minutes. With a slotted spoon, remove them from the skillet. Place the mushrooms round side up on a plate. Sprinkle them with ⅛ teaspoon salt. Set them aside.

2. In the same skillet, heat the remaining 1 tablespoon olive oil over medium heat. Add the garlic and sauté until it starts to turn golden, about 1 minute. Add the reserved mushroom stems and the shallots. Cook over medium heat until the mushroom stems are soft, 5 to 8 minutes. Be careful not to burn the garlic; it should be a golden color.

3. Add the brandy to the skillet and cook over low heat, stirring constantly, until all liquid has evaporated.

4. With a knife or food processor, finely chop the mushroom stem mixture and the walnuts. Stir in the remaining ¼ teaspoon salt.

5. Stuff each mushroom cap with about 1 teaspoon of walnut filling. Serve the mushrooms hot or cold on a bed of watercress. Garnish each cap with a watercress leaf.

TEXAS CAVIAR

Serves 6

1 15-ounce can black-eyed peas, drained

¼ cup red wine vinegar

½ cup thick picante sauce

1 small sweet red pepper, seeded, deribbed, and cut into thin strips

1 small green pepper, seeded, deribbed, and cut into thin strips

1 small yellow pepper, seeded, deribbed, and cut into thin strips

1 tablespoon chopped cilantro (fresh coriander) or parsley

½ teaspoon salt

½ teaspoon black pepper

1. Place the peas in a bowl and add the vinegar and picante sauce. Cover and refrigerate the mixture for several hours or overnight.

2. Add the peppers, cilantro, salt, and pepper to the marinated peas. Taste and adjust the seasoning. Serve chilled.

CHRISTMAS GUACAMOLE

Makes 1½ cups

   2 ripe avocados

   1 tablespoon grated onion

   1 tablespoon lemon juice

   Salt to taste

   Chili powder or cayenne pepper
      to taste

   1 ripe pomegranate, peeled and pulled
      apart, seeds separated from yellow
      membrane

   Nacho chips or crackers

1. Cut the avocados in half and remove the pits. Scoop the flesh into a medium-size bowl and mash it well with the back of a fork.
2. Season the mashed avocado with the onion, lemon juice, salt, and chili powder (use cayenne if you like your guacamole hot).
3. Place the guacamole in a serving dish and sprinkle the top with pomegranate seeds. Serve with nacho chips or crackers.

HOT CRAB MEAT APPETIZER

Makes 2 cups

   8 ounces cream cheese, softened

   2 tablespoons finely chopped onion

   ¼ teaspoon salt

   Freshly ground black pepper

   ½ pound fresh crab meat (carefully
      picked over) or 1 6-ounce can
      crab meat

   1 tablespoon milk

   ½ teaspoon horseradish

   ½ cup slivered almonds, toasted

   Crackers

1. Preheat the oven to 350°F.
2. In a medium-size bowl, place the cream cheese, onion, salt, pepper, crab meat, milk, and horseradish, and stir until well blended.
3. Place the mixture in a 1-quart shallow casserole or pie pan and sprinkle with the almonds.
4. Bake the appetizer until it bubbles around the edges, about 15 minutes. Serve the appetizer hot, with crackers.

RAW VEGETABLE PLATTER WITH CURRY DIP

Serves 12

   1 fennel bulb, cut into strips

   2 green or sweet red peppers, seeded,
      deribbed, and cut into strips

   ½ pound mushrooms, wiped clean
      and sliced

   1 head cauliflower, trimmed and cut
      into florets

   1 bunch broccoli, the florets trimmed
      from the stems and stems discarded

   1 Belgian endive, trimmed and leaves
      separated

   1 pint cherry tomatoes

   ½ pound fresh green beans, trimmed

Curry Dip

   1½ cups mayonnaise

   2 teaspoons curry powder

   1 tablespoon grated onion

   ½ teaspoon dry mustard

   ½ teaspoon salt

   Freshly ground black pepper

   Few drops of hot red-pepper sauce

1. Cover the vegetables and chill them until serving time. Then arrange them on two platters.
2. To make the curry dip, combine all the ingredients in a bowl and mix them together thoroughly. Add more curry powder if you like a spicy dip.
3. Cover and chill the dip for at least 2 hours before serving with the chilled raw vegetables.

SMOKED SALMON SPREAD

Makes 1½ cups

- 1½ cups yogurt cheese *(see below)*
- 3 tablespoons finely cut fresh chives or tops of green onions
- 1½ ounces smoked salmon, very finely chopped
- ¼ teaspoon white pepper
- ⅛ teaspoon paprika, preferably Hungarian
- 1 teaspoon lemon juice
- ⅛ teaspoon salt

Yogurt Cheese

- 3 cups plain low-fat yogurt

1. To make the yogurt cheese, line a large sieve with a double layer of cheesecloth or a large, round paper coffee filter. Place the lined sieve over a deep bowl so that the yogurt can effectively drain; spoon the yogurt into the sieve. Cover the bowl and sieve with plastic wrap. Put the bowl in the refrigerator and let the yogurt drain overnight.
2. Discard the liquid (whey) that has collected in the bowl and transfer the yogurt cheese to another bowl; the cheese should be very thick. Cover the bowl with plastic wrap and refrigerate the cheese until you are ready to use it. Yogurt cheese will keep in the refrigerator for 2 weeks.
3. In a medium-size bowl, combine the yogurt cheese with the chives, salmon, pepper, paprika, lemon juice, and salt and mix well to allow the flavors to meld; refrigerate the spread for at least 2 hours before serving it.

GRAVLAX WITH DILL MUSTARD SAUCE

Marinating the raw salmon "cooks" and tenderizes the fish. Gravlax is served as a part of a smorgasbord or as an appetizer, and is accompanied by mustard sauce.

Serves 30

- 3 to 3½ pounds fresh salmon, center cut, cleaned and scaled
- 1 large bunch fresh dill
- ¼ cup coarse (kosher) salt, or if unavailable, substitute regular salt
- ¼ cup sugar
- 2 tablespoons white peppercorns (or substitute black), crushed

1. Ask the fish dealer to cut the salmon in half lengthwise and to remove the backbone and the small bones as well.
2. Place half of the fish, skin side down, in a deep glass, enamel, or stainless-steel baking dish or casserole. Wash and shake dry the bunch of dill, and place it on the fish. (If the dill is of the hothouse variety and not very pungent, chop the herb coarsely to release its flavor and sprinkle it over the fish instead.)
3. In a small bowl, combine the salt, sugar, and crushed peppercorns. Sprinkle this mixture evenly over the dill. Top with the other half of the fish, skin side up. Cover the fish with plastic wrap and on it set a heavy platter slightly larger than the salmon. Pile the platter with 3 or 4 cans of food; these make convenient weights that are easy to distribute evenly.
4. Refrigerate for 48 hours (or up to 3 days). Turn the fish over every 12 hours, basting it with the liquid marinade that accumulates, and separating the halves a little to baste the salmon inside. Replace the platter and weights each time.
5. When the gravlax is finished, remove the fish from its marinade, scrape away the dill and seasonings, and pat it dry with paper towels. Place

the separated halves skin side down on a carving board and slice the salmon halves thinly on the diagonal, detaching each slice from the skin.

Dill Mustard Sauce

Makes about 1½ cups

  ½ cup Dijon mustard

  2 teaspoons dry mustard

  6 tablespoons sugar

  4 tablespoons white vinegar

  ⅔ cup vegetable oil

  6 tablespoons finely cut fresh dill

1. In a small, deep bowl, mix the Dijon mustard, dry mustard, sugar, and vinegar to a paste.
2. With a wire whisk, slowly beat in the oil until the mixture forms a thick, mayonnaise-like emulsion.
3. Stir in the chopped dill.

NOTE: The sauce may be stored in the refrigerator in a tightly covered jar for several days. Shake vigorously or beat with a whisk to remix the ingredients before serving.

SPICED PICKLED SHRIMP

Serves 8 to 10

  2 pounds cooked shrimp, peeled and deveined

  Bay leaves

  6 small white onions, thinly sliced

  1 cup olive oil

  ¼ cup tarragon vinegar

  2 teaspoons salt

  ½ teaspoon dry mustard

  1 teaspoon sugar

  1 teaspoon Worcestershire sauce

  Cayenne pepper to taste

  4 tablespoons mixed pickling spices

1. In a large crock, put a layer of shrimp, a layer of bay leaves (about 5 to

a layer), and a layer of sliced onions. Alternate layers until all the shrimp are used.
2. In a small bowl, mix together the oil, vinegar, salt, mustard, sugar, Worcestershire sauce, cayenne, and pickling spices, and pour the dressing over the shrimp.
3. Cover the crock and refrigerate for 24 hours, stirring occasionally.
4. Place the shrimp in a bowl over ice and pass with toothpicks.

NOTE: The shrimp may also be served on a bed of lettuce as a salad.

DILL SHRIMP DIP

Makes 2½ cups

  ½ pound cooked shrimp, peeled, deveined, and chopped

  8 ounces cream cheese, softened

  2 tablespoons sour cream

  1 tablespoon ketchup

  1 tablespoon mayonnaise

  1 tablespoon Dijon mustard

  1 unpeeled garlic clove, crushed

  2 dashes Worcestershire sauce

  1 cup finely chopped celery

  1 tablespoon finely chopped onion

  1 tablespoon finely minced fresh parsley

  3 tablespoons finely cut fresh dill or 1 tablespoon dried dill

  ½ teaspoon horseradish

  Crackers, chips, or raw vegetables

1. In a food processor or blender, purée all the ingredients (except the crackers, chips, or raw vegetables) until creamy.
2. Mound the mixture in a serving bowl, cover with plastic wrap, and chill before serving.
3. Serve the dip with assorted crackers, chips, or raw vegetables.

Wassail and lambs' wool

"Wes hal!" meaning, "Be whole!" is a toast for health and good fortune dating back to the Anglo-Saxons. Traditionally garnished with cored, roasted apples, hot, spiced Christmas Wassail is sometimes called "Lambs' Wool," for the puffed up, burst apples take on the appearance of fluffy white fleece. The basic Wassail recipe was poetically rendered in seventeenth-century England by Robert Herrick in his Twelfth Night:

> *Next crowne the bowle full*
> *With gentle Lambs' Wool,*
> *Add sugar, nutmeg, and ginger,*
> *With store of ale too;*
> *And thus ye must doe*
> *To make the Wassaile a swinger.*

Fish house punch

The peach brandy makes this punch especially mellow.

Makes about 7 quarts

   12 cups water

   2 cups firmly packed dark brown sugar

   12 to 18 lemons, the peel grated and the juice strained

   8 cups dark rum

   4 cups brandy

   ⅔ cup peach brandy

   Crushed ice

1. Combine the water and brown sugar in a large pot and heat until the sugar dissolves, stirring occasionally.
2. Put the lemon peel and juice in a large bowl, and pour in the hot syrup. Stir, then let the mixture cool.
3. Add the rum, brandy, and peach brandy.
4. Just before serving, fill a punch bowl with the crushed ice, and pour the punch over the ice.

Champagne punch

Makes 4 quarts

   1 grapefruit

   1 navel orange

   1 pint strawberries, washed and hulled

   1 cup brandy

   1 cup Benedictine

   ¾ cup maraschino cherry liqueur

   2 bottles champagne, chilled

   1 33.8-ounce (1 liter) bottle club soda, chilled

1. Peel the grapefruit and orange. Over a medium-size bowl, cut between the membranes to remove the sections and catch the juice. Place the sections in the bowl and add the strawberries.
2. Pour the brandy, Benedictine, and maraschino liqueur over the fruit and refrigerate it for 1 hour so the fruit can steep, or macerate, in the liqueurs.
3. Just before serving, fill a punch bowl with ice. Add the fruit and macerating liquid to the bowl. Pour the champagne and club soda over the fruit, stir gently with a punch ladle, and serve.

YULETIDE WASSAIL

Makes about 7 cups

> 6 apples, peeled and cored
>
> About 12 teaspoons plus
> ¾ cup sugar
>
> 1½ quarts ale or beer
>
> ½ teaspoon ground cinnamon
>
> ½ teaspoon ground ginger
>
> ¼ teaspoon grated nutmeg
>
> 2 teaspoons grated lemon zest
>
> ¾ cup medium sherry, or any
> sweet red or white wine

1. Preheat the oven to 350°F.
2. Place the apples in a buttered baking dish, and fill the center of each apple with about 2 teaspoons of sugar. Bake the apples until tender, about 30 minutes. Let the apples cool.
3. Pour ¾ cup of the ale or beer into a large pot and add the cinnamon, ginger, nutmeg, and the ¾ cup sugar. Heat over medium heat, stirring occasionally, but do not let the mixture boil. When the mixture is hot, add the lemon zest, the remaining ale or beer, and the wine. Keep the wassail over medium heat, stirring occasionally, until it is very hot. Place the baked apples in a small, heat-resistant punch bowl and pour over the hot wassail.

MULLED WINE

Makes about 1 quart

> 1 bottle dry, full-bodied red wine,
> such as Burgundy or Cabernet
> Sauvignon
>
> 12 whole cloves
>
> 2 pieces whole cinnamon
>
> Peel of 1 lemon, thinly pared to
> include yellow part only
>
> 2 tablespoons sugar

1. Pour the wine into an enameled or nonreactive pot; add the cloves, cinnamon, lemon peel, and sugar. Simmer the mixture over low heat for 10 minutes. Do not let it boil.
2. Strain the wine and serve hot.

EGGNOG

The "nog" in eggnog is short for "noggin," a small cup carved from a piece of birch. Tavernkeepers used noggins for table service in contrast to the large tankards reserved for patrons sitting by the fire.

Makes 2 quarts

> 6 eggs, separated
>
> ½ cup sugar
>
> 2 cups milk
>
> Dash of salt
>
> 2 cups heavy cream, whipped
>
> 2 cups brandy or rum
>
> Freshly grated nutmeg

1. In the large bowl of an electric mixer, beat the egg whites at high speed until stiff but not dry.
2. Place the egg yolks and sugar in a smaller bowl of the mixer and, using the same beaters, beat at high speed until the mixture is thick and lemon colored.
3. Add the milk and salt to the egg yolk mixture and blend well at low speed.
4. With a large spatula, gently fold the egg yolk mixture into the egg whites until blended. Fold in the whipped cream and gently stir in the brandy or rum.
5. Pour the eggnog into a large, chilled punch bowl. Sprinkle nutmeg on each serving.

NOTE: If you plan to serve the eggnog from a punch bowl, freeze about 2 cups of the mixture in ice cube trays before adding the egg whites and brandy or rum. Float the frozen eggnog cubes in the punch bowl to keep the punch chilled without diluting it.

HOT AND SPICY TOMATO JUICE

Makes 1 quart

> 28 ounces canned whole tomatoes, puréed in a food processor or a blender and sieved
>
> 3 tablespoons lime juice
>
> ⅛ teaspoon cayenne pepper
>
> 2 tablespoons chopped fresh mint, or 2 teaspoons dried mint
>
> 4 lime slices, for garnish (optional)

1. In a large enameled or nonreactive saucepan, combine the puréed tomatoes, lime juice, cayenne, and mint.
2. Heat the mixture over low heat and simmer it for 10 minutes.
3. Pour the hot tomato juice into mugs, garnish each serving with a slice of lime, if you like, and serve immediately.

SWEDISH GLÖGG

Makes 6 quarts

> 2 quarts dry red wine
>
> 2 quarts muscatel
>
> 1 pint sweet vermouth
>
> 2 tablespoons Angostura bitters
>
> 2 cups dark raisins
>
> Peel of 1 orange, removed with a vegetable peeler
>
> 12 whole cardamoms, bruised in a mortar with a pestle or covered with a towel and crushed with a rolling pin
>
> 10 whole cloves
>
> 1 2-inch piece fresh ginger (optional)
>
> 1 stick cinnamon
>
> 1½ cups aquavit or vodka
>
> 1½ cups sugar
>
> 2 cups whole blanched almonds

1. In a 6- to 8-quart enameled or nonreactive pot, mix together the red wine, muscatel, vermouth, bitters, raisins, orange peel, and the cardamoms, whole cloves, ginger, if you are using it, and

cinnamon. Cover the pot and let the mixture stand at least 12 hours so that the flavors will develop and mingle.
2. Shortly before serving, add the aquavit or vodka and the sugar. Stir well and bring the mixture to a full boil. Remove it at once from the heat, stir in the almonds, and serve the hot glögg in mugs. In Sweden, a small spoon is placed in each mug to scoop up the almonds and raisins.

NOTE: To make a simpler glögg, divide the quantities of spices in half and mix them with 2 bottles of dry red wine. Leave it overnight, then stir in ¾ cup of sugar and bring the mixture almost to a boil. Remove it from the heat, stir in 1 cup of whole, blanched almonds, and serve hot.

HOT BUTTERED RUM

Serves 16

> 2 cups butter, softened
>
> 4½ cups firmly packed dark brown sugar
>
> 1½ cups honey
>
> ¼ cup rum flavoring
>
> 2 tablespoons ground nutmeg
>
> 2 teaspoons ground cinnamon
>
> 1 teaspoon ground cloves
>
> Hot water
>
> 1½ cups warm rum (1½ ounces per serving)

1. To make the base, cream together the butter and the sugar in a large bowl. Add the honey, rum flavoring, nutmeg, cinnamon, and cloves, and mix well.
2. To serve, place 3 tablespoons of the butter base in each 10-ounce mug, add ¼ cup hot water, and stir until the base is dissolved.
3. Add 1½ ounces warm rum to each mug and stir. Fill the mug with hot water and serve hot.

PUNCH'S HUMBLE ORIGINS

Punch sparklingly bright and cold, or spiced and steamy, is a mainstay of Christmas buffets, but its origin was simple and somewhat lowly. A favorite beverage of seventeenth-century sailing men, punch originally consisted of only tea, water, sugar, lemon, and arrack (a highly alcoholic Eastern liquor, similar to rum in taste, and distilled from the fermented juice of coconut palm or from rice and molasses). Hindu-speaking peoples called it "punch," their word for "five," because of its five ingredients. Rum soon supplanted arrack as the spirit of choice.

CARDINAL PUNCH

Makes about 1¾ quarts

> 2½ cups boiling water
>
> 2 tablespoons black tea leaves
>
> ¼ teaspoon ground allspice
>
> ¼ teaspoon ground cinnamon
>
> ⅛ teaspoon ground nutmeg
>
> ¾ cup sugar
>
> 2 cups cranberry juice cocktail
>
> ½ cup orange juice
>
> ⅓ cup lemon juice
>
> 1½ cups cold water
>
> 1 lemon, thinly sliced

1. Place the tea in a large bowl, and pour the boiling water over it. Add the allspice, cinnamon, and nutmeg, cover the mixture, and let it steep for 5 minutes.
2. Strain the tea into another bowl and stir in the sugar.
3. Add the fruit juices and cold water and stir. Cover the bowl and chill for several hours. Serve cold. Float a slice of lemon in each glass.

NEW MEXICAN HOT CHOCOLATE

Traditionally, this beverage is beaten at the table with a *molinillo*—a specially carved wooden stirrer—just before pouring it into heavy earthenware mugs. A *molinillo* can be purchased at Mexican specialty stores and will add a bit of showmanship to your presentation.

Makes 1½ quarts

⅓ cup unsweetened cocoa

1 tablespoon flour

⅓ cup sugar

Pinch of salt

¾ teaspoon ground cinnamon

¼ teaspoon ground cloves

1 cup water

1 pint half-and-half

1 cup milk

1½ teaspoons pure vanilla extract

1 cup heavy cream, whipped

Freshly grated nutmeg

6 whole cinnamon sticks

1. In a heavy 2-quart saucepan, combine the cocoa, flour, sugar, salt, ground cinnamon, and cloves with the water. Whisk the mixture until it is very well blended. Place it over medium-high heat until it is just barely beginning to simmer.

2. Gradually add the half-and-half, then the milk, in a very fine stream, stirring all the time. Add the vanilla. Beat with the *molinillo*, a whisk, or a rotary beater. Heat the chocolate until it is hot but do not let it boil, and keep it warm for at least 5 minutes.

3. Whip the chocolate again just before serving, beating it until it is frothy. Serve in large earthenware mugs you have rinsed with hot water. Top each serving with a dollop of whipped cream and a shave of nutmeg, and poke a cinnamon stick into the cream.

Hot spiced cider

Makes 4 quarts

    1 gallon apple cider, beginning to harden

    2 4-inch cinnamon sticks, broken

    12 whole cloves

    ½ teaspoon allspice

    1 teaspoon freshly grated nutmeg

1. Pour the cider into a large enameled or nonreactive pot. Add the cinnamon, cloves, allspice, and nutmeg and let it stand for at least a half hour.

2. Place the pot over high heat and bring the cider to the boiling point, but do not let it boil. Strain and ladle it into mugs.

Mock champagne punch

Makes about 1½ quarts

    ⅓ cup sugar

    1 cup water

    1 cup white grape juice, chilled

    ½ cup orange juice

    1 quart ginger ale, chilled

1. In a medium-size saucepan, bring the sugar and water to a boil. Boil the mixture for 3 minutes. Remove the pan

from the heat and cool the sugar water. When it is cool, pour it into a punch bowl over ice cubes or an ice ring *(see page 16)*.

2. Add the grape juice and orange juice and stir. Just before serving, add the ginger ale.

Hot spiced cranberry punch

Makes 2 quarts

    2 lemons, thickly sliced

    24 whole cloves

    6 cups cranberry juice cocktail

    2 cups lemonade, fresh or made from frozen concentrate

    ½ teaspoon ground cloves

    ½ teaspoon ground cinnamon

    ½ teaspoon ground allspice

    1 cup sugar or honey

    12 cinnamon sticks (optional)

1. Stud the lemon slices with the whole cloves to float on top of the punch.

2. In a large enameled or nonreactive pot, combine the cranberry juice, lemonade, cloves, ground cinnamon, allspice, honey, and cinnamon sticks, if you are using them, and simmer the punch over low heat for 15 minutes.

3. Serve in a 2- to 3-quart punch bowl, or keep the punch warm in a deep chafing dish or an electric cooking pot. Offer the cinnamon sticks as swirlers, if desired.

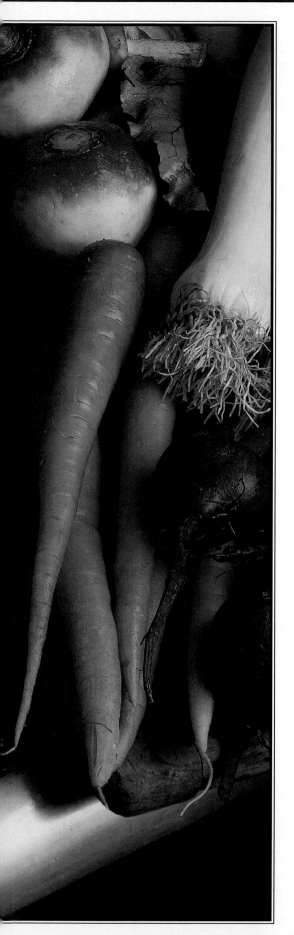

Soups & Salads

AS OPENERS FOR AN ELEGANT DINNER OR as meals in themselves, steamy, colorful soups never fail to please, and never are they more appreciated than during the Christmas season. Served with a salad of fresh greens and a basket of warm, crusty French bread, soup is a wonderfully satisfying and complete meal. The bright colors of such soups as Christmas Eve Borscht with Polish Mushroom Pockets and Tomato Purée with Yogurt-Ricotta Stars make them especially welcome. You might want to follow the tradition of many families and serve a rich Oyster Stew on Christmas Eve, or, to be different, a Spinach Soup—one legend tells that spinach was the only food Mary ate on that special night. Like the soups of the season, the salads of the winter table are often heartier than those of summer. Featuring raw or parboiled vegetables, these salads, unlike tossed green salads, have the added appeal of advance preparation. The Salad of the Good Night is an especially beautiful one of beets, fruits, and peanuts, traditionally eaten in Mexico on Christmas Eve.

Christmas Eve Borscht with Polish Mushroom Pockets

SPICY CREAM OF TOMATO SOUP

Serves 6

3 slices bacon, cut in ¼-inch dice

1 onion, chopped

4 large tomatoes, peeled, seeded, and chopped, or 4 cups drained canned tomatoes, seeded and chopped

4 whole cloves

6 black peppercorns

1 teaspoon dark brown sugar

1 teaspoon salt

4 parsley sprigs

3 tablespoons butter

3 tablespoons flour

1½ cups chicken stock

1 cup heavy cream

1. In a large saucepan, cook the bacon and onions over medium heat until the bacon is brown and crisp and the onions are soft.
2. Add the tomatoes, cloves, peppercorns, sugar, salt, and parsley to the pan and simmer for 10 minutes.
3. Remove the mixture from the heat and purée it in a food processor, blender, or food mill.
4. In a medium-size skillet, melt the butter over low heat, add the flour, and cook the mixture, stirring, until it is golden. Pour in the chicken stock and cook until the mixture is thickened, stirring frequently.
5. Add the thickened broth and the cream to the tomato purée, combine well, and heat thoroughly. Serve immediately.

TOMATO PURÉE WITH YOGURT-RICOTTA STARS

Serves 6

1 tablespoon olive oil

3 onions, chopped

1 carrot, sliced into thin rounds

1 teaspoon chopped fresh thyme, or ¼ teaspoon dried thyme

3 garlic cloves, chopped

Freshly ground black pepper

28 ounces canned tomatoes, seeded and coarsely chopped, with their juice

1¼ cups chicken or vegetable stock

¼ teaspoon salt

⅓ cup part-skim ricotta cheese

2 tablespoons plain low-fat yogurt

1½ cups watercress sprigs, stems trimmed

1. Heat the oil in a large, heavy pot over medium heat. Add the onions, carrot, thyme, garlic, and some pepper, and cook the mixture, stirring it often, until the onions are translucent, 7 to 10 minutes.
2. Add the tomatoes and their juice, the stock, and the salt. Reduce the heat and simmer the vegetables for 30 minutes.
3. While the soup is cooking, purée the cheese and yogurt together in a food processor, blender, or food mill. Set the purée aside.
4. Purée the soup in batches, processing each batch for about 1 minute. Return the puréed soup to the pot, bring it to a simmer over medium heat, and add the watercress. Simmer the soup just long enough to wilt the watercress—about 1 minute—then ladle the soup into warmed serving bowls.
5. Gently spoon 1 heaping tablespoon of the ricotta-yogurt mixture into the middle of each bowl. With the tip of a knife, make a star pattern by pushing a little of the mixture out from the center in several directions. Serve the soup at once.

CREAM OF CARROT SOUP

Serves 4 to 6

> 2 tablespoons butter
>
> ½ cup finely chopped onion
>
> 1 tablespoon flour
>
> 3½ cups chicken stock
>
> 1½ cups sliced carrots
>
> 1½ cups diced potatoes
>
> Dash of rosemary
>
> Salt and black pepper
>
> ½ cup plain yogurt
>
> 2 tablespoons finely chopped parsley

1. In a medium-size saucepan, melt the butter over low heat and sauté the onions until they are soft and translucent. Blend in the flour. Gradually stir in the chicken stock, carrots, potatoes, rosemary, and salt and pepper to taste.

2. Simmer the mixture until the vegetables are tender, remove from the heat, and allow the mixture to cool slightly.

3. Purée the carrot mixture in a food processor or blender, return it to the saucepan, and heat it over medium heat to just under a boil. Correct the seasoning.

4. Fold in the yogurt, reheat the soup over low heat, and serve at once, sprinkling each serving with some parsley.

SPINACH SOUP

— ◆ ◆ ◆ —

Make this colorful soup even more festive by passing a bowl of croutons cut from white bread with tiny star- or tree-shaped cutters.

Serves 6

6 large baking potatoes, peeled and sliced into ½-inch pieces

1 large Spanish onion, thinly sliced

1 large leek, sliced (about 1 cup)

2 stalks celery, sliced

½ cup unsalted butter

1 teaspoon salt

1 teaspoon freshly ground black pepper

4 cups water

1 pound fresh spinach, washed, stemmed, and coarsely chopped

1 cup heavy cream

¼ cup finely chopped sweet red pepper

Croutons (optional) *(see Note)*

1. Place the potatoes, onion, leek, celery, butter, salt, pepper, and water in a large pot. Bring the water to a boil, then reduce the heat and simmer the vegetables, covered, until they are quite tender, about 30 minutes.
2. Remove the pot from the heat and immediately add the spinach. Stir until the spinach wilts, about 3 minutes.
3. Purée the soup in a food processor, blender, or food mill.
4. Pour the purée into the pot, add the cream, and carefully reheat. Do not allow it to boil.
5. Serve hot, garnished with the red pepper.

NOTE: To make the croutons, cut the desired shapes from slices of fresh white bread. Sauté the cutouts in a mixture of 1 tablespoon olive oil and 1 tablespoon butter over medium heat. Drain the croutons on paper towels and pass separately, so they will remain crisp.

CHRISTMAS EVE BORSCHT WITH POLISH MUSHROOM POCKETS

— ◆ ◆ ◆ —

Serves 6 to 8

2 quarts water

2 onions, chopped

2 celery stalks with leaves, chopped

2 carrots, peeled and chopped

8 beets, left whole

1 extra beet, peeled

¼ head Savoy cabbage, chopped, and/or ½ cup chopped parsley root

1 white turnip and/or 1 medium potato, peeled and chopped

2 leeks, trimmed, split, washed thoroughly to remove all grit, and chopped (optional)

Dried or fresh mushrooms

1 small bunch fresh parsley, or parsley and dill, chopped

1 teaspoon salt

1 bay leaf

6 black peppercorns

1 tablespoon butter, softened (optional)

1 tablespoon flour

1 tablespoon lemon juice, or more, to taste

Vinegar

1. In a large pot, bring the water to a boil. Add all the soup vegetables (except the extra beet), the parsley, salt, bay leaf, and peppercorns. Reduce the heat to low and simmer until the vegetables are tender, about 1 hour. Remove the pot from the heat, and strain the broth.
2. Peel the beets, cut them into julienne strips, and return them to the stock. If you wish, grate part or all of the extra raw beet into the soup to intensify the red color.
3. Thicken the broth a little by stirring in little balls of *beurre manié* (pea-size balls of softened butter mixed with flour). Add the lemon juice and vinegar to taste, and taste for seasoning.

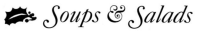
4. Borscht is often served with a generous dollop of sour cream, topped with horseradish, chopped hard-cooked eggs, or thick chunks of rye bread. However, at this special meal, Mushroom Pockets *(uszku)* are set afloat in the Borscht.

Dough for Mushroom Pockets

    2 cups flour

    Pinch of salt

    1 large egg

    Water

Filling

    2 tablespoons butter

    2 tablespoons finely chopped onions

    2 cups finely chopped mushrooms

    Salt and freshly ground black pepper
       to taste

    Chopped fresh dill and/or parsley

1. In a medium-size bowl, combine the flour with the salt and the egg, and add enough water to make a firm dough. Turn the mixture out onto a floured surface and knead it until the dough is smooth and elastic. Cover it well and let the dough rest for 10 minutes.
2. To make the filling, melt the butter in a medium-size skillet over medium heat, add the onions and mushrooms, and sauté them until they are golden brown, about 5 minutes. Add the salt, pepper, and dill or parsley. Set the mixture aside to cool.
3. Divide the dough into thirds and roll it out paper thin. Cut it into 2-inch or smaller squares.
4. Place ½ teaspoon of the filling a little to one side of the center of each square. Moisten the edges of the square with a little water, fold the empty side over the filling, and press the edges gently but firmly together, to form a triangle.
5. Drop the pockets into a large pot of boiling salted water and cook them until they rise to the top. Remove them with a slotted spoon and add them to the hot borscht. Serve immediately.

KEEPING THINGS HOT

A bowl of steamy soup is an ageless symbol of warmth and comfort, especially on the cold, damp days of early winter. Use your electric slow cooker to keep large quantities of soups and chilis piping hot for family or entertaining. It serves equally well as the perfect low-heat source for mulling cider or wine.

NOTE: To be completely authentic, borscht must be made with *kvas*, fermented beet juice. To make *kvas*, pour 5 cups boiling water over 3 peeled and sliced cooked beets. Stir in ½ cup vinegar. Let it stand at room temperature for 3 to 4 days. One cup *kvas* can be substituted for part of the water, and *kvas* can be added, to taste, instead of, or along with, the lemon juice and vinegar.

BLACK BEAN SOUP

Serves 6

1 pound black beans, rinsed and
    picked over

2 quarts water

1 ham bone

1 garlic clove, finely chopped

¼ teaspoon allspice

4 whole cloves

1 bay leaf

¼ teaspoon dried thyme

1 onion, sliced

1 stalk celery, finely chopped

3 tablespoons butter

1½ tablespoons flour

6 tablespoons medium sherry

2 lemons, sliced

3 hard-boiled eggs, chopped

1. Place the beans in a large soup pot
with the water and soak them
overnight. In the morning, add the ham
bone, garlic, allspice, cloves, bay leaf,
and thyme and bring to a boil.
2. In the meantime, sauté the onion
and celery in 1½ tablespoons of the
butter in a medium-size skillet over
medium heat. Add the vegetables to
the beans, lower the heat, and simmer
for 4 hours. Stir occasionally and add
hot water to prevent scorching.
3. When the beans are soft, drain them
and reserve the liquid. Add enough
water to the liquid to make 3 cups.
Remove the ham bone and cloves and
purée the bean mixture in batches in a
food processor or blender, until smooth.
4. Place the remaining butter in the
skillet, add the flour, and cook for 1
minute over medium heat. Slowly add
the reserved liquid, stirring well over
low heat until the mixture thickens.

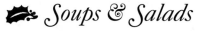

Cook for 2 minutes. Combine the thickened liquid with the bean purée in the soup pot. If you prefer a thinner soup, add an additional ½ cup water.
5. Gently heat the soup. Ladle into bowls. Add 1 tablespoon sherry to each serving and garnish each with 2 slices of lemon and some chopped egg.

LENTIL SOUP

Lentils, with their unique flavor and high protein and carbohydrate value, have been a staple food in many countries for centuries. Soups made from this colorful legume—lentils vary in color from yellow-orange to green-brown and even black—improve with age.

Serves 4 to 6

>   3 cups raw lentils, rinsed and picked over
>
>   7 cups water or beef stock
>
>   2 teaspoons salt
>
>   2 teaspoons finely chopped garlic
>
>   1 onion, chopped
>
>   2 stalks celery, finely chopped
>
>   2 carrots, chopped (1 cup)
>
>   Freshly ground black pepper
>
>   2 medium tomatoes, chopped (1½ cups)
>
>   2 tablespoons dry red wine
>
>   2 tablespoons lemon juice
>
>   1½ tablespoons molasses or brown sugar
>
>   1 tablespoon wine vinegar
>
>   Chopped green onions for garnish

1. In a large soup pot, place the lentils, the water or stock, and the salt. Bring the liquid to a boil, reduce the heat to low, and simmer, covered, for 3 to 4 hours. Stir the lentils occasionally.
2. Pour enough water into a large saucepan to fill it about 1 inch deep. Set a vegetable steamer in the pan and put the garlic, onion, celery, and carrots into it. Cover the pan and bring the

water to a boil. Steam the vegetables until they are tender, about 5 minutes. Set aside.
3. About 30 minutes before serving, add the pepper, tomatoes, wine, lemon juice, molasses or brown sugar, vinegar, and steamed vegetables.
4. Serve in individual bowls, sprinkled with chopped green onions and a few drops of vinegar. Serve immediately.

OYSTER STEW

Oyster stew may seem to be misnamed, since it is actually a creamy broth carrying only delectable plump oysters.

Serves 6

>   1 pint small oysters
>
>   ½ cup butter
>
>   6 cups half-and-half, scalded
>
>   ½ teaspoon salt
>
>   ⅛ teaspoon freshly ground pepper
>
>   Dash of paprika

1. In a large saucepan, sauté the oysters in the butter over low heat until the edges curl. Add the hot half-and-half and the seasonings.
2. Let the stew stand a few minutes over hot water before serving.

NOTE: Small raw shrimp may be substituted for the oysters. Sauté the shrimp until they turn pink, then add them to the liquid.

COUNTRY BEAN AND CABBAGE SOUP

Make this soup at least 1 or 2 days before it's needed, to assure a stronger and better flavor.

Serves 14

- 1 pound dried pea or navy beans, rinsed and picked over (about 2 cups)
- 2 quarts water
- 3 pounds smoked ham, with bone
- 1 stalk celery, sliced
- 2 carrots, quartered lengthwise and sliced
- 1 bouquet garni, composed of 5 parsley sprigs and 2 bay leaves *(see Note)*
- 1 onion, stuck with 2 whole cloves
- 2 onions, sliced
- 4 garlic cloves, crushed
- ½ teaspoon dried thyme
- ½ teaspoon black pepper
- 1 teaspoon salt
- 8 tomatoes (about 2 pounds), peeled
- 2 tablespoons tomato paste
- 3 pounds cabbage, halved, cored, and shredded
- 4 tablespoons lard or vegetable shortening
- 3 tablespoons flour

1. Place the beans in a large soup pot. Add the water and let them soak overnight. If you are pressed for time, bring the water to a boil, turn off the heat, and soak the beans for 1 hour, instead of overnight.
2. Add the ham to the pot. The water should cover at least half of the ham; if not, add more. Bring the water to a boil, reduce the heat to low, and simmer for 15 minutes, skimming off any foam that rises to the top. When the foam stops rising, add the celery, carrots, bouquet garni, onions, garlic, thyme, pepper, and salt. Cover the pot and simmer for 1½ hours.
3. Add the tomatoes and tomato paste and simmer for another ½ hour. Stir the soup occasionally, mashing the tomatoes against the side of the pot to break them into smaller pieces. Add the shredded cabbage and simmer for another ½ hour, stirring from time to time and mashing the tomatoes still further.
4. In a small skillet, make a very dark roux. Melt the lard or shortening over medium-high heat, add the flour, and stir constantly with a wooden spoon until the flour is well browned, 7 to 10 minutes. Be careful not to burn the roux. The color should be almost that of light chocolate. Add a ladleful of the soup to the roux and mix them quickly and thoroughly. Be careful: a lot of steam will rise when the hot liquid meets the hot skillet. Add a few more ladlefuls of soup to the skillet, mixing well after each addition. Then pour the contents of the skillet into the soup pot and stir well. Simmer the soup briskly for 15 minutes more.
5. With a long-handled slotted spoon, retrieve the whole onion and the bouquet garni and discard them. With two long forks, lift out the ham and bone. Remove the fat and bone from the ham. Cut the meat into bite-size pieces and return these to the pot. Correct the seasoning and serve the soup hot.

NOTE: To make the bouquet garni, lay the herbs on a small square of cheesecloth, gather it into a bag shape, and tie with clean white string.

NEW ENGLAND CLAM CHOWDER

Serves 4

3 dozen hard-shell or littleneck clams, each about 3 inches in diameter, shucked to produce about 3 cups, with their liquor or juices reserved

2 boiling potatoes, peeled, sliced ½ inch thick, and cut into ½-inch dice (about 2 cups)

2 ounces lean slab bacon with rind removed, sliced ¼ inch thick and cut into ¼-inch dice

1 tablespoon plus 4 teaspoons butter

1 large onion, finely chopped

2 cups milk

½ cup light cream

½ teaspoon dried thyme

½ teaspoon salt

Freshly ground black pepper

1. With a sharp knife, cut the tough meat away from the soft centers, or stomachs, of the clams. Chop the tough meat fine and set it aside. Cut the soft centers in half and reserve them. To remove any sand, strain the clam liquor through a fine sieve lined with a double thickness of dampened cheesecloth and set over a bowl. Measure and reserve 1 cup of the liquor.

2. In a 1-quart saucepan, bring 2½ cups water to a boil. Add the potatoes to the boiling water and cook them briskly until they are tender but still somewhat resistant to the bite, about 10 minutes. Drain the potatoes in a sieve set over a bowl or pan, and reserve ½ cup of the cooking liquid.

3. Meanwhile, in a small saucepan, drop the bacon dice into 1 cup of boiling water, enough to cover the pieces completely, and boil for 2 minutes. Drain the dice and pat them dry with paper towels.

4. In a heavy 2- to 3-quart saucepan, sauté the bacon and 1 tablespoon of the butter over medium heat, stirring frequently until the dice are crisp and brown and have rendered all their fat. With a slotted spoon, transfer the dice to paper towels to drain.

5. Add the onions to the fat remaining in the pan and, stirring frequently, cook over medium heat until they are soft and translucent but not brown, about 5 minutes. Watch carefully for any sign of burning and regulate the heat accordingly.

6. Stir in the reserved clam liquor, the reserved potato cooking liquid, and the finely chopped clams. Reduce the heat to low, cover tightly, and simmer for 10 minutes. Stir in the clam centers and the reserved potatoes and continue to simmer, covered, for 3 minutes more.

7. Meanwhile, in a separate saucepan, warm the milk and cream over medium heat until small bubbles appear around the edge of the pan.

8. Pour the hot milk and cream into the simmering clam mixture and mix well. Crumble in the thyme and add the salt, a few grindings of pepper, and the bacon. Taste the chowder and add more salt if needed. Ladle the chowder into 4 heated soup plates, place a teaspoon of butter on top of each serving, and serve at once.

NOTE: Some New England traditionalists insist that clam chowder improves in flavor if, after cooking, it is allowed to rest off the heat (unrefrigerated) for about an hour and then is reheated very briefly just before it is served.

THE BEAUTY OF SOUP

One of the many nice things about soup is that it usually can be made several days in advance, and improves in flavor as a result. What's more, it can be frozen and used when you need it. Defrosting is easy in a microwave oven. Bear in mind that if milk or cream is part of the recipe, you should include it after the soup has been defrosted. When you reheat the soup on the stove, add the milk toward the end, stirring the soup over a low flame and watching it carefully so that it does not boil and the milk curdle.

SWEET RED PEPPERS AND ENDIVE WITH SALSA VINAIGRETTE

Serves 6

    3 small white heads Belgian endive, rinsed, trimmed, and dried

    2 garlic cloves, finely chopped

    ½ cup olive oil, preferably virgin

    ¼ cup red wine vinegar

    ⅓ cup any red salsa

    1 small head Boston or red leaf lettuce, washed and dried

    2 large sweet red bell peppers, seeded, deribbed, and cut into julienne strips

1. Cut the endive in half lengthwise and slice, crosswise, ¼ inch thick.

2. In a small bowl, marinate the garlic in the olive oil for at least 30 minutes. Add the vinegar and the salsa to the oil and garlic and whisk.

3. To serve, place the lettuce leaves on chilled salad plates and evenly distribute the endive and peppers over them, then drizzle the dressing over all. Or serve buffet style in a lettuce-lined bowl.

CARROT AND ORANGE SALAD WITH DILL

Serves 4

    1 naval orange

    6 carrots (about 1¼ pounds), finely grated

    1 tablespoon red wine vinegar

    ½ cup freshly squeezed orange juice

    ½ teaspoon grated orange zest

    2 tablespoons finely cut fresh dill

1. Working over a bowl to catch the juice, cut away the peel, white pith, and outer membrane from the orange. To separate the segments from the inner membranes, slice down to the core with a sharp knife on either side of each segment and set the segments aside.

2. Combine the carrots, vinegar, orange juice, and zest in the bowl. Add the orange segments and 1 tablespoon of the dill and gently toss.

3. Refrigerate the salad for at least 15 minutes. Shortly before serving, garnish the top with the remaining dill.

WINTER SALAD

Serves 6 to 8

    4 cups water

    1 tablespoon salt

    3 stalks celery, peeled and sliced on the bias

    ½ small head cauliflower, trimmed and broken into florets

    1 pound fresh green beans, washed and trimmed, or two 10-ounce packages frozen green beans, thawed

    2 tomatoes, peeled, seeded, and chopped

    ¼ pound mushrooms, wiped clean and thinly sliced

    3 tablespoons chopped fresh parsley

    1 medium shallot, finely chopped, or 4 green onions, white part only, thinly sliced

    1 pound mild white cheese (such as Monterey Jack), cut into ¼-inch cubes

    2 bunches watercress, trimmed, washed, and dried

Vinaigrette

    ¼ cup tarragon vinegar

    2 teaspoons grainy mustard or Dijon mustard

    2 teaspoons lemon juice

    2 teaspoons salt

    Freshly ground black pepper

    ¾ cup olive oil, preferably virgin

1. In a large pot, bring the water to a boil and add the salt. Blanch the celery in the boiling water for 4 minutes. Remove the celery with a slotted spoon, plunge it into ice water to stop

the cooking, and drain it on paper towels. Using the same water, cook the cauliflower florets and the green beans in the same manner, separately, until they are barely tender, about 4 minutes for the cauliflower and 5 to 7 minutes for the green beans. Refresh and drain them as you did the celery.

2. To make the vinaigrette, whisk together in a medium-size bowl the vinegar, mustard, lemon juice, salt, and pepper. Slowly whisk in the olive oil. Set the dressing aside.

3. In a serving bowl, toss the cooked vegetables together. Add the tomatoes, mushrooms, parsley, shallot or green onions, and cheese, and toss again. Add enough vinaigrette to coat the vegetables and toss once more. Present the salad on a bed of watercress.

Holiday vegetable salad

Serves 12

- 1 10-ounce package frozen peas, thawed
- 1 head cauliflower, broken into small florets
- 1 bunch broccoli, florets chopped into bite-size pieces and stems discarded
- 2 small zucchinis, sliced
- 1 green pepper, seeded, deribbed, and coarsely chopped
- 2 sweet red peppers, seeded, deribbed, and coarsely chopped
- 1 cup diced celery
- 2 green onions, sliced
- Parsley sprigs
- Watercress, stemmed

Marinade

- 1 cup white vinegar
- ½ cup vegetable oil
- ½ cup sugar
- 1 teaspoon salt
- 1 teaspoon freshly ground black pepper

1. Place all the vegetables except the parsley sprigs and watercress in a deep bowl.
2. In a small bowl, whisk together the vinegar, oil, sugar, salt, and pepper. Pour the marinade over the vegetables and toss to coat them well. Cover tightly.
3. Refrigerate for about 24 hours, tossing the salad a couple of times to distribute the marinade evenly.
4. Serve in a glass bowl, garnished with the fresh parsley and watercress.

Cucumber, kiwi, and pomegranate salad

Here is a beautiful-looking, refreshing starter salad that is served plain—any vinegar or citrus-based dressing would destroy the subtle flavor of the kiwi fruit.

Serves 4

- 1 8-inch length of cucumber, peeled and thinly sliced
- Salt
- 4 kiwi fruit, peeled and thinly sliced
- 1 pomegranate, cut in half lengthwise and pulled apart

1. Place the cucumber rounds in a small bowl, sprinkle them lightly with salt, and put a heavy plate on top. Place the bowl in the refrigerator and leave for at least 30 minutes. Drain off any liquid.
2. Alternating cucumber rounds with kiwi rounds, decorate four small chilled salad plates in a spiral pattern. Loosely overlap the slices so that the beautiful center of the kiwi is not obscured.
3. Scatter the pomegranate seeds across each individual salad, taking care not to include any bitter yellow membrane.

Spinach and apple salad with lime dressing

Serves 6 to 8

- 2 10-ounce packages fresh spinach, washed, drained, and patted dry
- 4 tablespoons vegetable oil
- 2 tablespoons lime juice
- 3 red eating apples, chilled, cored, quartered, and chopped into small pieces
- Salt and black pepper

1. Remove any thick spinach stalks; finely shred the leaves.
2. In a small bowl, whisk the oil and lime juice together.
3. In a salad bowl, mix the spinach and the apples, add the dressing and salt and pepper to taste, and toss well.

Stuffed Apple Salad

This is a variation on Waldorf salad, in which the nuts, celery, and raisins are combined and mounded in the center of quartered dessert apples.

Serves 4

4 small red apples, cored and quartered

2 stalks celery, finely chopped

¼ cup coarsely chopped unsalted peanuts

¼ cup coarsely chopped hazelnuts (filberts)

¼ cup golden raisins

½ cup plain low-fat yogurt or mayonnaise, or a combination of both

1 teaspoon lemon juice

1 tablespoon chopped fresh parsley

1. Arrange the apples in small fruit bowls so that the sides are supported and the apples form rosettes. In a small bowl, combine the celery, peanuts, hazelnuts, raisins, yogurt, and lemon juice.

2. Divide the mixture among the four apples and spoon it into the center of each. Garnish with the parsley and serve at once.

AN EASY SOUP

"Leftovers again?" One way to avoid that post-Christmas question is to use some of your leftovers as a base for a hearty soup. First, put the turkey car- *cass and any scraps of the meat in a large soup kettle. Cover them with plenty of cold water, and bring the water to a boil, covered. Skim off the foam, then turn down the heat and simmer, covered, for about 2 hours. About halfway through the cooking period, add fresh onions, peppercorns, celery, and carrots for flavor. If you have some vegetables remaining from the dinner, consider adding them, too. You might even pour in some of the gravy. Strain the broth into containers, and cool it quickly. As it cools, fat will rise to the surface; you may remove this if you wish. Refrigerate or freeze the broth, tightly covered. Use it within a week if stored in the refrigerator, and within four months if frozen. A very simple and delicious soup can be made by cooking sliced vegetables until tender crisp in a steamer or a microwave and adding them to the reheated broth along with herbs and other seasonings.*

MIXED VEGETABLE SLAW

This clean, crisp, confetti-like medley of bright vegetables in a light sweet-sour dressing is a colorful alternative to cole slaw.

Serves 6

¾ pound cabbage, thinly sliced

¼ cup tarragon vinegar

2 teaspoons sugar

2 teaspoons salt

2¼ teaspoons black pepper

½ cup corn oil

3 small carrots, peeled and grated (2½ cups)

1 sweet red pepper or green pepper, seeded, deribbed, and cut into thin strips

2 tomatoes, each cut into 6 wedges

1. If necessary, soak the sliced cabbage briefly in ice water to crisp it, drain well, wrap in a dish towel to soak up excess moisture, and refrigerate.
2. In a small bowl, whisk together the vinegar, sugar, salt, and pepper. Whisk in the oil.
3. In a large salad bowl, combine the cabbage, carrots, and peppers and toss with the dressing. Garnish with the tomato wedges and serve.

SALAD OF THE GOOD NIGHT

Served only once a year, this fruit and vegetable salad is the traditional centerpiece of the Mexican Christmas Eve dinner. The *jícama* called for is a crisp white root vegetable becoming increasingly available at produce counters in this country.

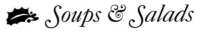

Serves 6 to 10

- 2 beets, cooked, peeled, and sliced
- 2 apples, cored and sliced
- 2 oranges, peeled and sectioned or sliced
- 2 bananas, sliced

Optional (any or all of the following):

- 1 *jícama*, peeled, cut in half, and sliced
- 2 limes, thinly sliced
- 1 cup fresh pineapple cubes
- 2 carrots, thinly sliced
- ½ cup radishes, thinly sliced
- 1 tablespoon sugar
- ½ cup peanuts, salted or unsalted
- Seeds from 1 pomegranate

1. Arrange the fruits and vegetables attractively on a platter or in a large glass bowl, sprinkling the sugar on them as you go.
2. Scatter the peanuts and the pomegranate seeds on top.

NOTE: If you like, make a dressing of mayonnaise mixed with a little raspberry vinegar *(page 195)* and spoon the dressing over the salad.

WATERCRESS AND BIBB SALAD WITH PARSLEY DRESSING

Serves 10 to 12

- 2 bunches watercress, trimmed, washed, and dried (about 9 cups)
- 4 heads Bibb lettuce, washed, dried, and torn into bite-size pieces (about 9 cups)
- 1 large sweet red pepper, seeded, deribbed, and cut into julienne strips (1½ cups)
- 1¾ cups lightly packed fresh parsley leaves
- ¾ cup olive oil, preferably virgin
- 3 tablespoons red wine vinegar
- Salt and freshly ground black pepper

1. In a large bowl, combine the watercress, the lettuce, and the sweet red pepper.
2. In a food processor or blender, purée the parsley with the oil, vinegar, and salt and pepper to taste.
3. Pour the dressing over the watercress mixture, and toss the salad until it is well combined. Serve immediately.

WATERCRESS-ORANGE SALAD

Serves 6 to 8

- 2 bunches watercress, trimmed, washed, dried, and cut into small pieces
- 3 heads Belgian endive, trimmed and cut into ¼-inch slices
- 2 oranges, peeled, sectioned (leaving membranes behind), and seeded
- ⅓ cup olive oil, preferably virgin
- 2 tablespoons lemon juice
- 2 shallots, finely chopped
- Salt and black pepper

1. Place the watercress in a large bowl.
2. Add the endive and orange sections to the watercress.
3. In a small bowl, whisk the oil and lemon juice together, add the shallots, and season with the salt and black pepper. Pour the dressing over the salad. Toss gently before serving.

A WEATHER FORECAST FOR THE NEW YEAR

An old Swiss Christmas Eve custom forecasts the weather for the year ahead. The grandmother of the house selects a perfect onion, which she cuts in half lengthwise. She then arranges twelve cup-shaped layers, designates each as one of the twelve months of the coming year, and sprinkles each with a bit of salt. On Christmas morning, those peels that have dry salt represent the fair months to come, and those with damp salt, the rainy.

BING CHERRY SALAD MOLD

Serves 16 to 18

3 16-ounce cans Bing cherries

3 3-ounce packages black cherry gelatin

2¼ cups hot water

1½ cups dry sherry

2¼ cups reserved cherry syrup

1½ cups sour cream

1½ cups thinly sliced almonds, crumbled

Red leaf lettuce

1. Drain the cherries and reserve 2¼ cups of the syrup.
2. In a large bowl, dissolve the gelatin in the hot water. Add the sherry and reserved cherry syrup to the gelatin. Chill the mixture until it is slightly thickened.

3. Add the cherries, sour cream, and almonds and stir until well blended.
4. Pour the mixture into a 2½-quart mold and chill until firm.
5. Unmold the salad onto a bed of lettuce.

TURKEY SALAD WITH CURRY DRESSING

Salad entrées can be as welcome in winter as in summer. For this curried salad, use leftover turkey from your holiday roast, or if you are multiplying the recipe for the Cookie Swap Luncheon menu *(see page 219)*, roast a turkey breast for the purpose. This adaptable recipe can also be made with chicken instead of turkey, macadamia nuts or almonds instead of cashews or walnuts, and fresh pineapple instead of apples. Put individual servings in small covered containers and garnish with a sprig of watercress, if you wish.

Serves 6

3½ cups cubed cooked turkey

1¼ cups chopped celery

2 cups cubed unpeeled apple

½ cup dried currants

⅔ cup salted roasted cashews, or coarsely chopped walnuts

Greens

Dressing

1¼ cups mayonnaise, preferably homemade

1 teaspoon finely chopped garlic

½ teaspoon nutmeg

¼ teaspoon cinnamon

2 teaspoons curry powder, or to taste

1. To make the dressing, combine the mayonnaise with the garlic, sugar, nutmeg, cinnamon, and curry powder, and blend well.
2. In a large bowl, place the turkey, celery, apple, currants, and nuts. Add the dressing and gently toss the salad until

it is well coated. Serve the salad on a bed of greens.

Estonian vinaigrette with herring and beets

Serves 6 to 8

- 2 hard-cooked eggs, finely chopped
- 2 large or 4 small boiled and peeled fresh beets, or 4 canned beets, cut into ¼-inch cubes
- 1 pound (about 3 medium) potatoes, boiled, peeled, and cut into ¼-inch cubes
- 1 pound (about 2) sour dill pickles, cut lengthwise into narrow strips, then crosswise into ⅛-inch-wide bits
- 1 fillet of pickled or *matjes* herring, drained and cut into ¼-inch cubes
- 1 pound boiled beef, or cooked ham, veal, or lamb, trimmed of fat and cut into ½-inch cubes
- 1 large, tart red apple, peeled, cored, and cut into ¼-inch cubes
- 3 hard-cooked eggs, quartered, for garnish

Dressing

- 3 teaspoons dry mustard
- 1¼ teaspoons sugar
- 1 to 2 tablespoons warm water
- 1 cup sour cream

1. To make the dressing, in a small bowl, combine the dry mustard with ¼ teaspoon of the sugar and stir in 1 to 2 tablespoons of warm water, or enough to make a thick paste. Set the mixture aside for 15 minutes. Then stir in the sour cream and the remaining teaspoon of sugar.
2. To make the salad, in a large mixing bowl, combine the chopped eggs, beets, potatoes, pickles, herring, meat, and apple. Add the sour cream dressing and toss together lightly but thoroughly until all the ingredients are well moistened with the dressing.
3. To serve, mound the salad high on a serving plate, garnish it with hard-

cooked eggs, and chill. Serve as a first course or as part of a buffet table.

Cranberry mold

The red and green of this salad make it especially pretty for holiday entertaining.

Serves 8

- 1 3-ounce package cherry gelatin
- 1 cup boiling water
- ¾ cup sugar
- 1 tablespoon lemon juice
- 1 tablespoon unflavored powdered gelatin
- 1 cup canned pineapple juice
- 1 cup coarsely chopped raw cranberries
- 1 orange, coarsely chopped with its peel
- 1 cup canned crushed pineapple, drained
- 2 stalks celery, chopped
- ½ cup chopped pecans
- Lettuce

1. Place the cherry gelatin in a medium-size bowl and pour the water over it. Stir to dissolve the gelatin and add the sugar and lemon juice.
2. Add the unflavored gelatin to the pineapple juice, and heat the mixture in the top of a double boiler over hot water or in a small bowl in a microwave oven to dissolve the gelatin. Add the pineapple mixture to the cherry mixture and stir until they are well blended. Chill the gelatin mixture until it is partially set, about 45 minutes.
3. Combine the cranberries, orange, pineapple, celery, and pecans in a large bowl, and stir until well mixed. Add the partially set gelatin and continue mixing.
4. Pour the mixture into a 1½- to 2-quart ring mold and chill it until firm, about 2 hours.
5. Unmold the salad on a bed of lettuce and serve.

Vegetables & Relishes

BY DECEMBER, SUMMER GARDENS HAVE long since been put to bed, yet summer's sunshine lingers on in such hearty vegetables as winter squashes, beets, onions, and carrots. In generations past these were stored away in root cellars for winter use, and thus became the staples of traditional holiday meals. To this day they add their special flashes of color and strong, sweet flavors to the Christmas table along with such hearty vegetables as Brussels sprouts, spinach, broccoli, and cauliflower now available throughout the year in supermarkets everywhere. Many vegetables have special associations with the holidays. Christmas would not be Christmas in Sweden or Denmark without Braised Red Cabbage. For many Americans Christmas turkey dinner "with all the trimmings" would be an empty affair indeed without Creamed Onions and Candied Sweet Potatoes. Hearty and colorful, cranberry relish claims a place of equal honor, and, like many other chutneys and relishes, improves as its flavors mingle over days or weeks. Prepare chutneys and relishes early in the season and enjoy the zest they add to your holiday meals. They also make ideal gifts for neighbors and friends.

Glazed Carrots with Red Grapes, Cranberry Orange Relish, and Brussels Sprouts Tossed with Pecans

GLAZED CARROTS WITH RED GRAPES

Serves 6 to 8

> 2 pounds whole baby carrots (frozen)
>
> 3 tablespoons butter
>
> 2 tablespoons sugar
>
> ½ pound seedless red grapes, washed and cut in half lengthwise
>
> 2 tablespoons chopped fresh parsley

1. In a medium-size saucepan, simmer the frozen carrots in ½ cup water for 7 minutes. Drain the carrots and set them aside.

2. In the saucepan, melt the butter and add the sugar and carrots. Sauté for 4 minutes and add the grapes. Sauté 2 more minutes, sprinkle with the parsley, and serve.

SHERRY-GLAZED TURNIPS

Serves 6

> 2 pounds small white turnips, peeled
>
> 4 cups chicken stock
>
> ¼ teaspoon salt
>
> Freshly ground black pepper
>
> ¼ cup cream sherry
>
> 1 tablespoon chopped parsley

1. Put the turnips in a heavy skillet large enough to hold them in one layer. Pour in 2 cups of the stock; add the salt and pepper. Bring the liquid to a boil, then reduce the heat to medium and cook the mixture until almost all of the stock has evaporated, about 15 minutes.

2. Pour in the remaining stock, bring it to a boil, and cook as before until almost none remains. Add the sherry and cook until just enough remains to form a sauce, about 3 minutes more. Transfer the turnips to a dish and sprinkle them with the parsley.

PEAS BRAISED WITH LETTUCE

Here is a modern rendition of a classic French preparation. In December, frozen peas will give fine results, and the pimiento adds a touch of seasonal color.

Serves 6

> ¼ cup finely chopped green onions
>
> 2 tablespoons butter
>
> 2 tablespoons water
>
> 3 cups cooked fresh or frozen peas
>
> ½ cup shredded leaf lettuce
>
> ½ teaspoon salt
>
> 1 tablespoon chopped pimiento (optional)

1. In a large skillet, sauté the onion in the butter over medium heat until it is soft but not brown, about 5 minutes. Add the water, peas, and lettuce and cook over medium heat, stirring constantly, until the lettuce is wilted, about 3 minutes.

2. Add the salt and pimiento, if you are using it, toss lightly, and serve.

BROCCOLI SOUFFLÉ

Serves 6

> 1 10-ounce package frozen broccoli, or 2 cups fresh broccoli florets
>
> 3 tablespoons butter
>
> 3 tablespoons flour
>
> 1 teaspoon salt
>
> 1 cup milk
>
> ⅛ teaspoon nutmeg
>
> 1 teaspoon lemon juice
>
> 4 eggs, separated

Sauce (optional)

> ½ cup sour cream
>
> ½ cup mayonnaise
>
> Dash of curry powder

1. Preheat the oven to 325°F.
2. Cook frozen broccoli according to package directions, or steam fresh broccoli for 8 to 10 minutes. Drain and chop fine, or process briefly in a food processor or blender.
3. In a medium-size saucepan, melt the butter, add the flour and salt, and cook until bubbly. Add the milk and cook until the mixture thickens, stirring frequently. Stir in the nutmeg, lemon juice, and broccoli and set aside to cool.

4. Beat the egg yolks and add them to the cooled broccoli mixture, stirring well.
5. In the large bowl of an electric mixer, beat the egg whites until stiff. Fold them into the broccoli mixture.
6. Pour the soufflé mixture into a buttered 1½-quart casserole; place in the oven in a hot-water bath and bake until firm, about 1 hour. Serve plain or with a sauce made by mixing together the sour cream, mayonnaise, and curry powder and heating until hot but not boiling.

THE RUBY POMEGRANATE

In Christian art, the juicy, seed-filled pomegranate symbolizes fertility and immortality. It is thus often used in paintings of the Virgin Mary and the Nativity, and is especially appropriate for Christmas tables. The tart, ruby-red seeds make an ideal garnish for a variety of holiday foods, from vegetables, soups, meats, and poultry, to fruit desserts and ice cream.

BRUSSELS SPROUTS TOSSED WITH PECANS

Serves 4 to 6

> 4 cups Brussels sprouts
>
> 2 tablespoons butter
>
> ¼ cup finely chopped pecans
>
> ½ teaspoon dried rosemary, crumbled
>
> Salt and freshly ground black pepper

1. Pour enough water into a large saucepan to fill it about 1 inch deep. Set a vegetable steamer in the pan and put the Brussels sprouts into it. Cover the pan and bring the water to a boil. Steam the Brussels sprouts until they are tender crisp, about 5 minutes.
2. In a large skillet, melt the butter. Sauté the pecans and rosemary over medium heat until the pecans are toasted, about 5 minutes. Turn off the heat.
3. Add the Brussels sprouts, season to taste with salt and pepper, and toss to coat them with the buttered pecans. Serve immediately.

BRAISED RED CABBAGE

Red currant jelly and grated apple add piquancy to the cabbage in this traditional Scandinavian dish.

Serves 6

> 1 medium head red cabbage (2 to 2½ pounds)
>
> 4 tablespoons butter, cut into small pieces
>
> 1 tablespoon sugar
>
> 1 teaspoon salt
>
> ⅓ cup water
>
> ⅓ cup white vinegar
>
> ¼ cup red currant jelly
>
> 2 tablespoons grated peeled apple

1. Wash the cabbage under cold running water, remove the tough outer leaves, and cut the cabbage in half from top to bottom. Cut away the core, lay the flat sides down on the chopping board, and slice the cabbage very finely. There should be approximately 9 cups of shredded cabbage when you finish.
2. Preheat the oven to 325°F.
3. In a heavy enameled or nonreactive 4- to 5-quart casserole, combine the butter, sugar, salt, water, and vinegar. When the mixture comes to a boil and the butter has melted, add the cabbage and toss thoroughly. Bring to a boil again, cover tightly, and place in the center of the oven to braise for 2 hours. There is little danger that the cabbage will dry out during the cooking, but it is a good idea to check on the liquid level occasionally. Add a little water if it seems necessary.
4. About 10 minutes before the cabbage is finished, stir in the jelly and grated apple, replace the cover, and complete the cooking. Serve the cabbage hot.

NOTE: The taste of the red cabbage will improve if, after it has cooled, the cabbage is allowed to rest for a day in the refrigerator and is then reheated either on top of the stove or in a 325°F. oven.

CREAMED ONIONS

Serves 8

2½ pounds small white onions

4 tablespoons butter

4 tablespoons flour

1½ cups milk

½ cup heavy cream

¼ teaspoon ground nutmeg, preferably freshly grated

1 teaspoon salt

White pepper, preferably freshly ground

1. To peel the onions, drop them into boiling water and let them boil briskly for about 30 seconds. Drain the onions in a sieve or colander under cold running water and cut off the root ends with a small, sharp knife. Slip off the papery outer skin of each onion and trim the top neatly.

2. Drop the onions into enough lightly salted boiling water to barely cover them. Reduce the heat to its lowest setting, partially cover the pan, and simmer the onions for about 20 minutes, or until they show only slight resistance when pierced with the tip of a sharp knife. Drain the onions in a sieve set over a bowl and set them aside. Measure and reserve 1 cup of the cooking liquid.

3. In a heavy 3- to 4-quart saucepan, melt the butter over moderate heat. When the foam begins to subside, add the flour and mix well. Stirring constantly with a wire whisk, pour in the reserved cup of cooking liquid, the milk, and cream and cook over high heat until the sauce comes to a boil, thickens slightly, and is smooth.

4. Reduce the heat to low and simmer the sauce for 3 to 4 minutes. Then stir in the nutmeg, salt, and white pepper and taste for further seasoning. Add the onions and, turning them about gently with a spoon from time to time, simmer for a few minutes longer until they are heated through. Serve at once from a heated bowl.

RUTABAGA CASSEROLE

Serves 8

2½ pounds (about 2) rutabagas, peeled and cut into ¼-inch dice (8 cups), or substitute 2½ pounds white or yellow turnips, peeled and diced

3 teaspoons salt

¼ cup dry bread crumbs

¼ cup heavy cream

½ teaspoon nutmeg

2 eggs, lightly beaten

2 tablespoons plus 2 teaspoons butter, softened

2 tablespoons butter, cut into small pieces

1. Preheat the oven to 350°F.

2. Place the diced rutabagas (or diced turnips) in a 4- to 6-quart stainless-steel or enameled saucepan. Pour in enough cold water just to cover the vegetables, add 1 teaspoon of salt, and bring to a boil. Lower the heat and simmer, partially covered, until the rutabagas offer no resistance when pierced with the tip of a sharp knife, 15 to 20 minutes.

3. Drain the rutabagas and place them in a sieve set over a small bowl. Force them through the sieve by rubbing them with the back of a wooden spoon.

4. In another bowl, soak the bread crumbs in the heavy cream for a few minutes. Stir in the nutmeg, 2 teaspoons of the salt, and the eggs, then add the puréed rutabagas and mix together thoroughly. Stir in 2 tablespoons of the soft butter.

5. Spread a 2- to 2½-quart casserole with the remaining 2 teaspoons of soft butter and put the rutabaga mixture in the casserole. Dot with the butter and bake, uncovered, for 1 hour, or until the top is lightly browned.

HUBBARD SQUASH AND CHESTNUTS IN MAPLE SYRUP

Serves 10

> 1 small Hubbard squash (about 6 pounds)
>
> 1½ pounds whole chestnuts
>
> 2 tablespoons unsalted butter
>
> 2 shallots, finely chopped
>
> 3 tablespoons chopped fresh sage, or 1 tablespoon dried sage
>
> ½ teaspoon salt
>
> Freshly ground black pepper
>
> 3 tablespoons pure maple syrup

1. To split the squash, steady the blade of a large knife or cleaver lengthwise along the shell. Then use a mallet to strike the spine of the knife or cleaver near its handle, forcing the blade into the squash. Continue striking near the handle until the squash splits in half. Scrape out and discard the seeds and fibers. With a melon baller, scoop out the flesh, dropping the balls into a bowl as you work; there should be about 4 cups.

2. Lay a chestnut with its flat side down on a cutting board. With a small, sharp knife, make a cross in the rounded side of the chestnut, cutting through both the shell and the inner skin. Repeat the process with the other chestnuts. Pour 2 quarts of water into a saucepan and bring the water to a boil. Boil the chestnuts for 10 minutes (5 minutes if they are small).

3. Remove the pan from the heat but do not drain the chestnuts. While the chestnuts are still warm, peel off their outer shells and brown inner skins. (Waiting until the chestnuts cool would make them difficult to peel.) Slice the chestnuts in half and set them aside.

4. Pour enough water into a large pot to fill it about 1 inch deep. Set a vegetable steamer in the pot and bring the water to a boil. Put the squash in the steamer, cover the pan, and steam the squash until it is tender but not mushy, about 5 minutes.

5. Heat the butter in a large, heavy skillet or casserole over medium-high heat.

Sauté the chopped shallots until soft, about 1 minute. Add the squash, sage, salt, and pepper, and cook until the squash is heated through, about 2 minutes more. Add the chestnuts and maple syrup, stir to mix, and cook for a final 3 minutes.

BUTTERNUT SQUASH WITH CANDIED GINGER

Serves 6

1 large butternut squash (about 3 pounds)

4 tablespoons butter

2 tablespoons pure maple syrup

2 tablespoons finely chopped crystallized ginger

½ teaspoon salt

¼ teaspoon freshly ground black pepper

¼ teaspoon ground nutmeg

½ cup heavy cream

Freshly grated nutmeg

1. Preheat the oven to 350°F.
2. Scrub the squash. Split it lengthwise and remove the seeds. Place the squash cut side down on a foil-lined baking sheet, and bake until tender, about 45 minutes.
3. Remove the squash from the oven and allow it to cool until easy to handle. Remove the skin and purée the squash in a food processor, blender, or food mill. Add the butter, syrup, ginger, salt, pepper, and nutmeg, and beat until smooth. Gradually beat in the cream.
4. Keep the squash warm in a 200°F. oven until ready to serve or refrigerate it and then reheat at serving time. Just before serving, sprinkle with a little nutmeg.

HOPPING JOHN

Hopping John is a traditional New Year's Day dish in the South. Legend holds that it must be eaten before noon on New Year's Day to ensure good luck.

Serves 8 to 10

2 cups (1 pound) dried black-eyed peas, picked over

6 cups cold water

1 pound salt pork (rind removed), cut into strips about 2 inches long and ½ inch wide

1 cup finely chopped onion

2½ cups uncooked long-grain white rice (not the converted variety)

1. Place the black-eyed peas in a sieve or colander and run cold water over them until the draining water is clear. Transfer the peas to a 3- to 4-quart casserole, add 6 cups of cold water, and bring to a boil over high heat. Reduce the heat to low and simmer, partially covered, for 30 minutes.
2. Meanwhile, to reduce their salt content, drop the salt pork strips into a pot of boiling water and bring the water back to a boil. Immediately drain the strips, pat them dry with paper towels, then place them in a 10- to 12-inch skillet. Fry them, uncovered, over medium-high heat for 10 to 12 minutes, turning the strips frequently with a large spoon and adjusting the heat, if necessary, to prevent the pork from burning. When the strips are brown and crisp and have rendered all their fat, transfer them with tongs to paper towels to drain, and set them aside.
3. Add the chopped onion to the fat remaining in the skillet and cook over medium heat, stirring frequently, until the onion is soft but not brown, 3 to 5 minutes. Remove the skillet from the heat and set it aside.
4. In a fine sieve, wash the rice under cold running water until the draining water is clear.
5. After the peas have cooked their allotted time, stir in the salt pork, onion, and rice and bring the mixture back to a boil. Cover the casserole tightly, reduce the heat to low, and simmer until the peas are tender and the rice is dry and fluffy, 20 to 30 minutes. Taste for seasoning and serve at once.

THE PLEASURES OF WARM CHESTNUTS

Small wonder that roasting chestnuts by an open fire is a favorite Christmas pastime: the rich, soft meat is well worth the small effort involved. Begin by scoring a criss cross on the flat side of the chestnut shells with a sharp knife, both to keep the nuts from exploding and to make them easy to peel after roasting. Arrange the chestnuts in a single layer in a long-handled skillet and place them over the heat, either on a glowing fire or woodstove, until the shells begin to pop open. Shake them or stir them occasionally to keep them from burning. Alternatively, spread them on a pan in a 425°F. oven. In either case, you will enjoy their uniquely sweet flavor in about 15 to 20 minutes. Some people serve them with sweet butter and coarsely ground salt as an accompaniment to Glögg, a Swedish Christmas beverage (page 24).

PURÉE OF CELERY ROOT AND POTATOES

Serves 8 to 10

> 1½ to 2 pounds celery root, peeled and cut into ¼-inch-thick slices
>
> 1 to 1½ pounds boiling potatoes, peeled and sliced in half
>
> 6 tablespoons unsalted butter, softened
>
> ¾ cup hot milk
>
> 1 teaspoon salt
>
> ¼ teaspoon freshly ground pepper

1. In a large saucepan, boil the celery root in lightly salted water for 30 minutes. Add the potatoes and continue to boil, partially covered, until both vegetables are cooked through, about 20 minutes. Test them for doneness with the tip of a sharp knife. Drain the vegetables in a colander.
2. In a small saucepan or in a small bowl in a microwave oven, melt the butter in the milk, and keep the mixture warm.
3. Put the vegetables through a ricer or food mill. Beat in the butter and milk mixture and season with the salt and pepper. Serve immediately.

CARAMELIZED POTATOES

These golden potatoes are a favorite at Danish Christmas dinners and are particularly good with roast goose, duck, or pork.

Serves 8

> 24 small new potatoes
>
> ½ cup sugar
>
> ½ cup butter, melted

1. Drop the potatoes into a large pot of boiling water and cook until they offer no resistance when pierced with the tip of a sharp knife, 15 to 20 minutes. Let them cool slightly, then peel them.
2. In a heavy 10- to 12-inch skillet, melt the sugar over low heat. Cook slowly until the sugar turns to a light-brown caramel, 3 to 5 minutes. Stir constantly with a wooden spoon and watch the sugar closely; the syrup changes color very rapidly and burns easily. It must not become too dark or it will be bitter.
3. Stir the melted butter into the sugar, and add as many potatoes as possible without crowding the pan. Shake the pan almost constantly to roll the potatoes and coat them on all sides with the caramel. Remove the hot, caramelized potatoes to a heated serving bowl and repeat the procedure until all the potatoes are coated.

MASHED POTATOES

Here common mashed potatoes undergo a holiday transformation.

Serves 8

 4 quarts water

 1 tablespoon salt

 4 pounds baking potatoes

 1 cup butter, softened

 ½ to 1 cup heavy cream

 1 teaspoon salt

 ½ teaspoon white pepper

 2 to 4 tablespoons butter, melted (optional)

 1 tablespoon finely chopped parsley, chives, or dill (optional)

1. In a 6- to 8-quart pot, bring the water to a boil and add the salt. Meanwhile, peel the potatoes, cut them into halves or quarters, and drop them into the boiling water. Boil them briskly, uncovered, until they are tender. Test for doneness by piercing them periodically with the tip of a sharp knife. They should show no resistance in the center but should not fall apart. Drain them at once in a colander.

2. Return the potatoes to the pan in which they were cooked, or transfer them to a large, heavy skillet and shake them over moderate heat until they are as dry as possible, 2 to 3 minutes. Then purée them in a heated mixing bowl either by mashing them with a potato masher, or by forcing them through a ricer or through a large, coarse sieve with the back of a wooden spoon.

3. Beat the softened butter into the purée, 2 or 3 tablespoons at a time, either by hand or with an electric mixer.

4. In a small saucepan, heat the cream and beat it into the potatoes a few tablespoons at a time, using as much as you need to give the purée the consistency that you like. Ideally the mashed potatoes should be neither too wet nor too dry, and they should hold their shape lightly in a spoon.

5. Beat in the salt and the white pepper, and taste for seasoning. Add more salt if you think it is necessary. Serve at once in a heated vegetable dish. If you are using it, float the melted butter in a well in the center of the potatoes and sprinkle them with the parsley, chives, or dill, if desired.

CANDIED SWEET POTATOES

Serves 8

 6 large sweet potatoes, scrubbed

 4 tablespoons butter, melted

 Ground cinnamon

 1 cup firmly packed dark brown sugar

 1 teaspoon grated orange zest

 ½ cup orange juice

1. Preheat the oven to 350°F.

2. In a large pot, place the potatoes in boiling water to cover and cook them until they are tender when pierced with the tip of a sharp knife, 25 to 30 minutes.

3. Drain the potatoes. When they are cool enough to handle, peel and thinly slice them.

4. In a 1- to 2-quart buttered casserole, layer about one-third of the potatoes, drizzle them with about one-third of the butter, and sprinkle them with some cinnamon and one-third of the sugar. Repeat this procedure twice. Sprinkle the top with the orange zest, and pour the orange juice over all.

5. Bake the casserole until the potatoes are well candied and the juices are bubbling, about 30 minutes.

WILD RICE AND APPLES

Serves 8

1½ cups wild rice, washed thoroughly

3 cups hot beef or chicken consommé

1½ cups dry white wine

⅓ cup butter

3 red Delicious apples, cored and sliced thin

2 tablespoons brandy, warmed and lighted

1. Preheat the oven to 400°F.
2. Put the rice, consommé, and wine in a buttered 1½-quart casserole. Cover and bake for 1 hour or until the rice is tender, adding more liquid if necessary.
3. In a medium-size skillet, melt the butter and sauté the apples until they are soft but not mushy. Fork-stir the apples into the rice; add the brandy and serve immediately.

NOTE: You may substitute grapes, toasted almonds, mushrooms, cooked peas—anything your heart and stomach desire—for the apples.

SWEET POTATO AND PEAR MOUSSE

Serves 8

2 pounds sweet potatoes or yams

2 large ripe pears, peeled, cored, and cut into 1-inch cubes

3 tablespoons lemon juice

½ teaspoon curry powder

½ teaspoon ground cinnamon

1 tablespoon unsalted butter

1½ cups chopped onion

1 cup apple juice

Freshly ground black pepper

1 egg yolk

2 egg whites

1. Preheat the oven to 450°F.
2. Prick the sweet potatoes and bake them until they have begun to soften, about 30 minutes. Remove the sweet potatoes from the oven and set them aside to cool. Reduce the oven temperature to 350°F.
3. In a large bowl, combine the pears, lemon juice, curry powder, and cinnamon. When the sweet potatoes are cool enough to handle, cut them in half lengthwise. Peel the sweet potatoes, cut them into 1-inch cubes, and add them to the bowl.
4. Heat the butter in a large, heavy skillet over medium heat. Add the onion and cook it for 5 minutes, then stir in the apple juice, the sweet potato mixture, and the pepper. Cover the skillet, leaving the lid slightly ajar, and cook the mixture for 15 minutes, stirring occasionally.
5. Transfer the contents of the skillet to a food processor or blender. Purée the mixture, stopping two or three times to scrape down the sides. Transfer the purée to a bowl and stir in the egg yolk.
6. In a separate metal bowl, beat the egg whites until soft peaks form.
7. Fold the beaten whites into the purée and pour the mixture into a lightly buttered 2-quart gratin dish. Bake the mousse for 30 minutes. Serve immediately.

SPOON BREAD

In spite of its name, spoon bread is similar to Yorkshire pudding and makes a good substitute for potatoes, rice, and other starchy vegetables. It is a popular southern dish, often served with ham or poultry.

Serves 12

2 cups boiling water

1 teaspoon salt

2 teaspoons baking powder

1 cup cornmeal, preferably white

6 tablespoons butter, melted

1 cup milk

3 eggs, beaten

1. Preheat the oven to 375°F.
2. In a large saucepan, bring the water, salt, and baking powder to a boil. Slowly add the cornmeal, stirring constantly. Continuing to stir, cook over low heat until small bubbles form around the edges, about 5 minutes. Remove the pan from the heat.
3. Add 4 tablespoons of the butter to the cornmeal and mix well. In a small bowl, whisk the milk and eggs together and add them to the cornmeal.
4. Spread the remaining butter in a hot 8-inch square baking dish or a soufflé dish. Pour in the batter and bake until well browned, about 35 minutes. Serve the spoon bread with a spoon from the dish in which it was baked.

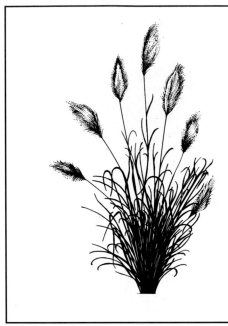

SPIRIT OF THE GRAIN

Many Christmas traditions spring from pre-Christian celebrations of the harvest and the Winter Solstice. Throughout northern Europe, grain long served as a powerful symbol of new life, and intricately woven decorations made from the golden sheaves were believed to contain the "spirit of the grain," which, if honored and protected, would come to life in the spring. In Poland, grain symbolized not only the seed of life but also the straw of the manger, and a few pieces of straw tucked under the Christmas tablecloth were said to guarantee good luck and good harvest the following year.

REFRIGERATED CRANBERRY CHUTNEY

Here is a quick-to-prepare chutney, requiring no cooking.

Makes about 3 pints

- 4 cups cranberries, rinsed and picked over
- 2 small oranges, with peel, cut into eighths and seeded
- 1 lemon, with peel, quartered and seeded
- 2 tart apples, cored
- 1 cup dark raisins
- 1 cup firmly packed light brown sugar
- ½ teaspoon ground ginger
- 2 tablespoons finely chopped candied ginger
- 2 tablespoons grated onion
- 6 tablespoons chopped green pepper

1. In a food processor or food chopper, chop the cranberries, oranges, lemon, apples, and raisins. Put the mixture into a large bowl and add the sugar, ginger, candied ginger, onion, and green pepper. Mix well.

2. Tightly cover the mixture and store in the refrigerator. The chutney will keep for a month.

CRANBERRY ORANGE RELISH

The fresh, tart flavor of the relish comes from using the fruit raw.

Makes about 2½ cups

- 1 12-ounce package fresh cranberries, rinsed and picked over
- 1 orange, with its peel, cut into eighths and seeded
- ¾ cup sugar
- 1 to 2 tablespoons Grand Marnier or other orange-flavored liqueur (optional)

1. Put half the cranberries and half the orange pieces in a food processor or food chopper and process or chop until the fruit is evenly chopped. Place the mixture in a bowl and repeat the procedure with the remaining cranberries and orange pieces.
2. Stir in the sugar and liqueur, chill, and store in the refrigerator or freezer until ready to serve.

Mulled cranberries in red wine

Makes 3 cups

1 12-ounce package cranberries, rinsed and picked over

1½ cups sugar

1 cup full-bodied red wine, such as Cabernet Sauvignon or Zinfandel

1 cinnamon stick (about 3 inches long)

1 piece orange peel (about 7 inches long)

¼ teaspoon ground mace

1. In a medium-size heavy enameled or nonreactive saucepan, combine the sugar and the wine. Bring to a boil over medium-high heat, stirring constantly. Stir in the cranberries, cinnamon stick, orange peel, and mace. Bring the mixture to a boil. Lower the heat to medium and simmer, partially covered, stirring occasionally, until the cranberries burst, 10 to 15 minutes. Remove from the heat.
2. Discard the cinnamon stick. Remove the orange peel and cut it into very thin strips. Stir it back into the cranberry mixture. Cool.

NOTE: Prepare the relish days or even weeks ahead and store it, tightly covered, in the refrigerator. Or spoon it into sterilized ½-pint canning jars, seal the jars, and process them in a boiling water bath for 10 minutes. Cool and test the seals. Stored in a cool, dark place, the cranberries may be kept for up to 6 months.

Apple-tomato chutney

Makes about 10 pints

12 large apples, washed, quartered, and cored

12 large onions, quartered

12 large ripe tomatoes, peeled and cut into eighths

3 cups sugar

4 cups cider vinegar

1 teaspoon ground cinnamon

1 teaspoon dry mustard

½ teaspoon ground cloves

¼ teaspoon black pepper

½ cup firmly packed light brown sugar

1 cup golden raisins

1½ teaspoons salt

2 tablespoons finely chopped candied ginger

2 garlic cloves, mashed

½ teaspoon cayenne pepper

1. In a food processor or food chopper, coarsely chop the apples and onions.
2. Put all the ingredients into a large enameled or nonreactive pot. Bring the mixture to a boil and turn down the heat to simmer the mixture until it is thickened, about an hour. Stir occasionally.
3. Ladle the chutney into sterilized jars and seal at once. Process in a boiling water bath for 5 minutes. Let cool and test the seals.

NOTE: Stored in a cool, dark place, the chutney may be kept for up to 6 months.

Meat

HE BOAR'S HEAD IN HAND BEAR I, BEDECKED in bays and rosemary," begins the ancient English carol, conjuring images of the great halls of the manor houses of England. Here Yule logs blazed in massive fireplaces as traditional boars' heads were triumphantly brought forward, decorated with holly, apples in their mouths, and sprigs of rosemary in their ears. Today, in places as widespread as Italy, Argentina, South Africa, Hawaii, and Puerto Rico a whole suckling pig, garnished in much the same manner as the medieval boar's head, remains a favorite Christmas dinner. More modest, but much more practical for most American tables, is an elegantly served Roast Beef with Yorkshire Pudding and Horseradish Sauce, a colorful Country Ham Stuffed with Greens, a Crown Roast of Lamb with Peas and New Potatoes, or a Pork Loin Stuffed with Prunes and Apples. Presented on your best platter and set off by glazed fruits, vegetables, and Christmas greens or fresh herbs, any one of these can form the same spectacular centerpiece of your Christmas dinner as did the boar's head of old.

Country Ham Stuffed with Greens

MUSHROOM-STUFFED
BEEF FILET

Although any mushrooms can be used, fresh shiitake provide an interesting, slightly chewy texture.

Serves 4

> 4 1¼-inch-thick pieces of beef filet (approximately 5 ounces each)
>
> 6 ounces shiitake or other mushrooms
>
> 1 tablespoon olive oil
>
> 1 tablespoon butter
>
> 2 shallots, finely chopped
>
> 1 garlic clove, finely chopped
>
> ⅓ cup cognac or brandy
>
> Salt and black pepper
>
> 2 tablespoons chopped parsley

1. Remove the stems from the mushrooms and discard or save for another use. Chop the mushroom caps.
2. Heat the oil and butter in a large skillet over medium-high heat. Add the shallots and garlic and cook, stirring, until soft, 2 to 3 minutes. Add the mushrooms and cook, stirring, until soft, about 4 minutes. Add the cognac or brandy and cook until it is absorbed. Season to taste with salt and pepper, add the parsley, and remove from the heat.
3. Make a pocket in each filet by cutting horizontally into one side. Stuff the pockets with the mushroom filling. These steps can be performed a few hours ahead of the actual cooking of the meat.
4. When ready to serve the meat, heat the grill or broiler. Cook the filets, turning once, 10 to 12 minutes total for medium-rare. Serve immediately.

BEEF WELLINGTON

Also known as Steig Wellington, Beef Wellington is an Irish recipe, a favorite of the Duke of Wellington, who was born in Ireland. It makes a splendid old-fashioned dish for a Christmas celebration.

Serves 4 to 6

Pastry

> 4 cups flour
>
> 1 teaspoon salt
>
> ½ cup vegetable shortening
>
> 1 egg, lightly beaten
>
> ½ cup ice water, approximately

Filling

> 1 filet of beef (2½ to 3 pounds), at room temperature
>
> 2 tablespoons brandy
>
> Salt and freshly ground black pepper
>
> 6 slices of bacon
>
> 8 ounces pâté de foie gras or chicken liver pâté
>
> 3 or 4 truffles (optional)
>
> 1 egg, lightly beaten

1. To make the pastry, place the flour, salt, butter, and shortening in a large bowl and blend with the tips of the fingers or with a pastry blender until the mixture resembles coarse cornmeal. Add the egg and some ice water and mix lightly with a fork until it forms a ball. If the mixture is too dry, add more of the water. Wrap the dough in wax paper and chill.
2. To make the pastry with a food processor, place the flour, salt, butter, and shortening in the bowl and process with the steel blade attachment until the mixture resembles coarse cornmeal. Add the egg and, with the motor running, gradually add the ice water until the dough forms a ball. Wrap the dough in wax paper and chill.
3. Preheat the oven to 450°F.

4. Rub the filet all over with the brandy and season with salt and pepper. Lay the bacon over the top, securing with string if necessary.

5. Place the meat on a rack in a roasting pan and roast for 15 minutes for rare, or 20 to 25 minutes for medium. Remove the meat from the oven; remove the bacon. Cool the meat to room temperature before proceeding.

6. With a spatula, spread the pâté all over the top and sides of the beef. If you are using them, cut the truffles into halves and sink the pieces in a line along the top.

7. Reduce the oven to 425°F.

8. Roll out the pastry into a rectangle (about 18 by 12 inches) ¼ inch thick. Place the filet, top down, in the middle. Draw the long sides up to overlap on the bottom of the filet; brush with the beaten egg to seal.

9. Trim the ends of the pastry and make an envelope fold, brushing again with egg to seal the closure. Transfer the pastry-wrapped meat to a baking sheet, seam side down.

10. Brush the pastry all over with the egg. Cut out decorative shapes from the pastry trimmings and arrange the pieces down the center of the pastry. Brush the decorations with the rest of the egg. Bake until the pastry is cooked and lightly browned, about 30 minutes. Serve the dish hot, or serve it cold on a buffet table.

NOTE: Puff pastry may be used to wrap the beef, but care should be taken to roll it very thin. Brioche dough may also be used.

ROAST BEEF WITH YORKSHIRE PUDDING AND HORSERADISH SAUCE

Serves 8 to 10

1 5-pound beef standing rib or sirloin tip roast

Freshly ground black pepper

Yorkshire Pudding

1 cup flour

½ teaspoon salt

2 eggs

1¼ cups milk

1 tablespoon cold water

Horseradish Sauce

1 horseradish root, 4 inches long, or about 3 tablespoons prepared horseradish, drained

¾ cup heavy cream

1 teaspoon sugar

½ teaspoon dry mustard

½ teaspoon salt

½ teaspoon white pepper

2 teaspoons white vinegar

1. Preheat the oven to 425°F. Put the beef into a roasting pan. Sprinkle the beef with pepper. Roast in the oven for 15 minutes. Lower the heat to 375°F. for the rest of the cooking time, allowing 15 minutes to the pound, about 2¼ hours.

2. Baste the meat frequently with the pan juices. The beef should be underdone (150°F. on a meat thermometer is medium-rare), and should be transferred to a heated platter and left to rest for 15 minutes before carving.

3. While the beef is roasting, make the Yorkshire pudding. Sift the flour and salt together into a large bowl. Add the eggs and stir. Add half the milk slowly and stir until the mixture is smooth. Add the remaining milk slowly and beat the batter well, then beat in the cold water.

4. About 20 minutes before the beef comes out of the oven, pour 2 tablespoons of its fat into a baking pan 10 inches square, and put the pan into the oven. When the fat is sizzling hot, pour in the pudding batter.

5. Bake the batter on the top shelf of the oven for 30 minutes. The pudding should be well risen, puffy, crisp and brown on the bottom, and should be served, cut in squares, straight from the pan in which it baked.

6. The spiced horseradish sauce should be made in the morning so it has time to chill. If you are using it, soak the horseradish root in cold water for an hour, scrub it well, and then scrape the root into very thin strips with a sharp knife.

7. In a small bowl, beat the cream until stiff peaks form. Fold in the horseradish, sugar, mustard, salt, pepper, and vinegar. Cover the bowl with plastic wrap and chill the sauce until ready to serve it.

STEAK AND KIDNEY PIE

Don't attempt to improve on this recipe by upgrading the quality of the meat. Bottom round is the right texture and has a rich, full flavor.

Makes one 10-inch pie

2½ pounds bottom round, trimmed of fat and cut into 1-inch cubes

3 veal kidneys (1 pound), trimmed of fat and cut into ½-inch cubes

½ cup flour

6 tablespoons vegetable oil

2 onions, thinly sliced

½ pound mushrooms, sliced

1 teaspoon salt

Freshly ground black pepper

½ teaspoon dried rosemary

½ teaspoon dried tarragon

1 tablespoon tomato paste

2 teaspoons Worcestershire sauce

1 cup beef stock

1 cup dry red wine

Chilled pastry for an 8-inch double-crust pie

1. Put the flour into a large bowl, add the beef and the kidneys, and toss until all the pieces are well coated with the flour.

2. Heat the oil in a Dutch oven over medium-high heat. Add the meat and sear it quickly on all sides. Do this in several stages so as not to crowd the meat and lower the temperature of the oil. Remove the meat as it is browned and set it aside.

3. When all the meat has been browned, add the onions and mushrooms to the drippings, with an additional tablespoon of oil if necessary. Sauté them over medium heat, stirring frequently, until the mushrooms are lightly browned, about 5 minutes.

4. Return the meat to the pot. Add the salt, pepper, rosemary, tarragon, tomato paste, Worcestershire sauce, stock, and wine.

5. Cover the pot and simmer, stirring from time to time, until the meat is tender, about 2 hours. Remove the pot from the heat and let the stew cool.

6. Refrigerate the stew overnight. Remove solidified fat from the surface.

7. Preheat the oven to 400°F.

8. Put the stew into a shallow 2-quart casserole, at least 10 inches in diameter. It is best if the casserole has an edge for the pastry to adhere to.

9. On a lightly floured board or pastry cloth, roll out the chilled pastry until it is about 2 inches larger all around than the top of the casserole. Do not try to roll it too thin. The pastry should be thicker than it would be for a dessert pie.

10. Place the dough on top of the casserole, turning it under to form a double thickness at the edges. Press the dough over and around the edges of the casserole. Cut four gashes for steam in the center of the pastry.

11. Bake the pie for 30 minutes; lower the heat to 350°F. and continue baking until the pastry is golden and the stew bubbles, 15 to 20 minutes more.

NOTE: Cook the dish in two stages: make the stew the day before, to let the flavors blend and to make it easy to remove any fat; add the crust and bake the pie just before serving.

CHRISTMAS IS COME

Christmas is come, hang on the pot
Let spits turn round, and ovens be hot;
Beef, pork, and poltry, now provide
To feast thy neighbours at this tide;
Then wash all down with good wine and beer
And so with mirth conclude the YEAR.

VIRGINIA ALMANACK, EIGHTEENTH CENTURY

GREEK STEW

Serves 6

    3 pounds beef chuck, trimmed of fat
      and cut into 1½-inch cubes

    Salt and freshly ground black pepper

    ½ cup butter

    2½ pounds small white onions, peeled

    1 6-ounce can tomato paste

    ⅓ cup red wine

    2 tablespoons red wine vinegar

    1 rounded tablespoon light brown sugar

    1 garlic clove, finely chopped

    1 bay leaf

    1 small cinnamon stick

    ½ teaspoon whole cloves

    ¼ teaspoon ground cumin

    2 tablespoons dried currants or raisins
      (optional)

1. Season the meat with salt and pepper. In a Dutch oven or heavy kettle, melt the butter over low heat. Add the meat and turn it to coat it with the butter, but do not let it brown. Arrange the onions over the meat. In a small bowl, blend the tomato paste, wine, vinegar, sugar, and garlic; pour the mixture over the meat and onions. Add the bay leaf, cinnamon, cloves, cumin, and currants or raisins, if you are using them.
2. Cover the stew with a plate to keep the onions in place. Then cover the kettle, in turn, with a lid and simmer the stew on low heat until the meat is very tender, about 3 hours. Do not stir.

CHRISTMAS SPICED BEEF

With the beef, serve a fruit salad. The Mexican Salad of the Good Night *(page 42),* traditionally served on Christmas Eve, would be a good choice. This recipe should be started 3 to 6 days before serving.

Serves 8

1 4- to 5-pound beef round or chuck roast

½ cup salt

1 teaspoon ground cinnamon

1 teaspoon ground allspice

1 teaspoon ground cloves

Few grindings of black pepper

1 rounded tablespoon light brown sugar

3 cups hard cider

1 cup cider vinegar

1 bay leaf

6 onions

4 carrots

1 to 2 stalks celery

1 cup stout or dark beer (optional)

1. Rub the salt into the meat. Place it in a bowl, cover it, and let it sit, refrigerated, for 24 hours. Rinse the meat and pat it dry.

2. Rub the cinnamon, allspice, cloves, pepper, and sugar into the meat. Place it in a bowl, and add the cider, vinegar, bay leaf, and 2 onions, sliced. Cover and refrigerate for 2 to 3 days—a week is even better. Turn the meat occasionally.

3. Place the meat in a large enameled or nonreactive pot with the marinade and enough water to barely cover. Slice the remaining onions, the carrots, and celery, and add them to the marinade. Cover the pot, bring the marinade to a boil, reduce the heat, and simmer until the meat is tender and fully cooked, about 3 hours. If you are using it, add the stout or dark beer in the last hour of cooking. Serve hot or cold.

CHILI FOR A CROWD

If you're a busy cook who likes to freeze food for future meals, this chili is the answer. Offer bowls of sour cream, chopped white onion, and grated Cheddar cheese, and let your guests garnish their servings as they please.

Serves 36

2 pounds sweet Italian sausage meat, removed from casings

8 pounds beef chuck, ground

½ cup olive oil

1¾ pounds yellow onions, coarsely chopped

1½ tablespoons freshly ground black pepper

2 12-ounce cans tomato paste

3 tablespoons finely chopped garlic

6 tablespoons ground cumin

½ cup chili powder

½ cup Dijon mustard

4 tablespoons salt

4 tablespoons dried basil

4 tablespoons dried oregano

5 2-pound, 3-ounce cans Italian plum tomatoes, drained

½ cup Burgundy wine

¼ cup lemon juice

½ cup finely cut fresh dill

½ cup chopped Italian parsley

3 16-ounce cans dark red kidney beans, drained

4 5½-ounce cans pitted black olives, drained

1. Heat the olive oil in a very large soup kettle. Add the onions and cook over low heat, covered, until they are tender and translucent, about 10 minutes.

2. Crumble the sausage meat and ground chuck into the kettle and cook over medium-high heat, stirring often, until the meats are well browned. Spoon out as much excess fat as possible.

3. Over low heat, stir in the black pepper, tomato paste, garlic, cumin, chili powder, mustard, salt, basil, and oregano.

4. Add the drained tomatoes, Burgundy, lemon juice, dill, parsley, and drained kidney beans. Stir well and simmer, uncovered, for another 15 minutes.

5. Taste and correct seasoning. Add the olives, simmer for another 5 minutes to heat through, and serve immediately.

BEEF BURGUNDY

Serves 12

> 5 pounds beef chuck, cut into 1½-inch cubes
>
> Flour for dredging
>
> 9 tablespoons butter
>
> 6 tablespoons olive oil
>
> Salt and pepper
>
> ¼ cup brandy, warmed
>
> ½ pound bacon, diced
>
> 3 garlic cloves, coarsely chopped
>
> 2 carrots, coarsely chopped
>
> 2 leeks, coarsely chopped
>
> 3 cups coarsely chopped onions
>
> 4 tablespoons chopped parsley
>
> 1 bay leaf
>
> 1 teaspoon dried thyme
>
> 1 bottle Burgundy wine
>
> Water
>
> 1 tablespoon flour
>
> 36 whole small white onions
>
> Sugar
>
> 36 mushroom caps
>
> Juice of half a lemon

1. Dredge the beef cubes in flour and brown them on all sides in a skillet over high heat in 4 tablespoons each of the butter and olive oil.
2. Sprinkle the meat with salt and pepper, pour the brandy over it, and ignite. When the flame dies, transfer the meat to a 3-quart casserole.
3. Preheat the oven to 350°F.
4. To the skillet add the bacon, garlic, carrots, leeks, chopped onions, and 2 tablespoons of the chopped parsley. Cook, stirring, until the bacon is crisp and the vegetables are lightly browned. Transfer the mixture to the casserole with the meat and add the bay leaf, thyme, Burgundy, and enough water to barely cover the meat. Cover and bake for 1½ hours.
5. Blend 1 tablespoon each of butter and flour and stir into the casserole bit by bit. Return the casserole to the oven and continue cooking until the meat is fork tender, 2 to 3 hours longer.
6. Brown the white onions in the skillet in 2 tablespoons of the butter with a dash of sugar. Add a little water, cover, cook until the onions are almost tender, and remove them from the skillet.
7. In the same skillet, sauté the mushrooms in 2 tablespoons each of the butter and oil until lightly browned on one side. Sprinkle them with lemon juice and turn to brown the other side.
8. To serve, add the onions to the casserole and garnish with the mushrooms and parsley.

DANISH MEATBALLS

Makes 80 meatballs

> 1 pound lean ground beef
>
> ½ pound ground veal or pork
>
> 1 teaspoon salt
>
> ⅛ teaspoon black pepper
>
> 1 egg, slightly beaten
>
> 1 tablespoon grated onion
>
> ¼ cup half-and-half
>
> ½ cup soft bread crumbs
>
> ⅛ teaspoon ground allspice

Dill Sauce

> ¼ cup butter
>
> ¼ cup flour
>
> 2 cups chicken stock or canned chicken broth
>
> ¼ teaspoon salt
>
> 2 tablespoons finely cut fresh dill or 2 teaspoons dried dill
>
> 1 cup sour cream

1. Preheat the oven to 375°F.
2. In a large bowl, combine the beef, veal, or pork, salt, pepper, egg, onion, half-and-half, bread crumbs, and allspice. Using your hands, mix the ingredients thoroughly and shape the mixture into 1-inch balls.

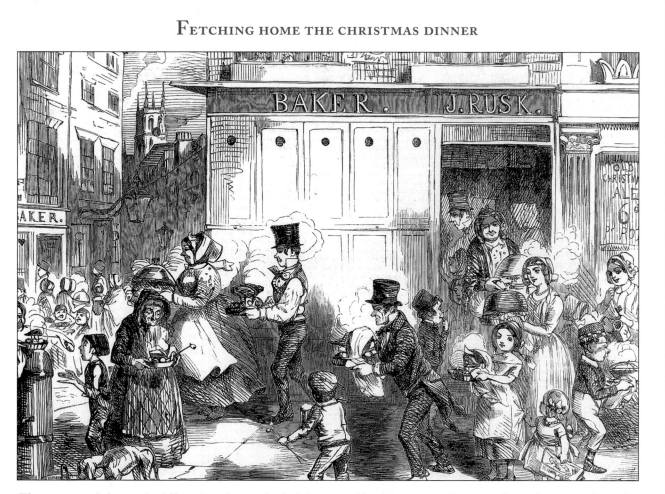

FETCHING HOME THE CHRISTMAS DINNER

The poorer of Scrooge's fellow Londoners had their Christmas dinners made for them at nearby bake-shops. In his famous travels with the Spirit of Christmas Present, the old miser watched as "the steeples called good people all to church and chapel, and away they came, flocking through the streets in their best clothes and with their gayest faces. And at the same time there emerged, from scores of by-streets, lanes, and nameless turnings, innumerable people, carrying their dinners to the bakers' shops." Here, with obvious satisfaction, they steer their steaming roasts homeward.

3. Arrange the meatballs on a rack in a broiler pan and bake until they are browned, 20 to 30 minutes.
4. While the meatballs are baking, make the dill sauce. In a medium saucepan, melt the butter. Add the flour and cook over low heat for 1 minute, stirring constantly. Add the broth, salt, and dill and cook over medium heat, stirring frequently, until the sauce thickens. Remove the pan from the heat and stir in the sour cream.
5. When the meatballs are done, remove them from the pan and place them on paper towels to absorb excess fat. Place the meatballs in a heated chafing dish and pour the dill sauce over them. Serve immediately, with buttered noodles or rice.

Baked ham with brown-sugar glaze

A southern Christmas buffet is incomplete without country ham. Leftovers may be stored, tightly wrapped, in the refrigerator for at least a month.

Serves 20 to 30

1 12- to 16-pound Smithfield ham or a 12- to 16-pound Virginia, Kentucky, Tennessee, or Georgia country ham

½ to ¾ cup fine dry bread crumbs

1 cup firmly packed dark brown sugar

¼ cup whole cloves (optional)

1. Starting a day or two ahead, place the ham in a pot large enough to hold it comfortably and pour in enough water to cover the ham by at least 1 inch. Let the ham soak at room temperature for at least 24 hours, changing the water two or three times. Remove the ham from the pot and discard the soaking water. Then, under lukewarm running water, scrub the ham vigorously with a stiff brush to remove any traces of pepper or mold.
2. With a dampened kitchen towel, wipe the ham and return it to the pot. Pour in enough water to cover the ham by at least 1 inch and bring it to a boil over high heat. Reduce the heat to low and simmer, partially covered, for 3 to 4 hours, allowing 15 to 20 minutes to the pound. When the ham is fully cooked, you should be able to move and easily pull out the small bone near the shank.
3. Transfer the ham to a platter and, if you wish, set the cooking water aside to be used for cooking greens. When the ham is cool enough to handle, remove the rind with a small sharp knife, leaving only a ⅛-inch-thick layer of fat. If you intend to stud the ham with cloves, make crisscrossing cuts about 1 inch apart on the fatty side, slicing down through the fat to the meat.
4. Preheat the oven to 400°F.
5. With your fingers, press enough of the bread crumbs into the fatty side of the ham to coat it thoroughly. Then sift the brown sugar evenly over the crumbs. If you are using cloves, insert them where the scoring lines intersect. Place the ham on a rack set in a shallow roasting pan and bake it, uncovered, in the middle of the oven for about 20 minutes, or until the glaze is richly browned.
6. Set the ham on a large platter and let it cool to room temperature. Carve it into paper-thin slices. Country ham is traditionally served with Beaten Biscuits *(page 119)*.

Toad-in-the-hole

This traditional English recipe consists of small sausages baked in a light batter that puffs as it cooks in much the same way as a Yorkshire pudding.

Serves 4

1 pound small fresh pork sausages

2 eggs

½ teaspoon salt

Freshly ground black pepper

1 cup flour

1 cup milk

1. Beat the eggs, salt, and pepper with a whisk or a rotary or an electric beater until frothy. Slowly add the flour, beating constantly. Then pour in the milk in a thin stream and beat until the mixture is smooth and creamy. (The batter can also be made in a blender or food processor.) Refrigerate for at least 1 hour.
2. Preheat the oven to 400°F.
3. Place the sausages side by side in a heavy 10- to 12-inch skillet, and prick them once or twice with the tines of a fork. Sprinkle them with 2 tablespoons of water, cover the pan tightly, and cook over low heat for 3 minutes. Remove the cover, increase the heat to medium, and continue to cook, turning the sausages frequently with tongs or a spatula, until the water has completely

evaporated and the sausages have begun to brown in their own fat, about 10 minutes.

4. Arrange the sausages at least an inch apart in a single layer in a greased 8-by-10-inch baking dish, and sprinkle them with 2 tablespoons of their drippings. Pour the batter over them and bake in the middle of the oven for 30 minutes, or until the pudding has risen over the top of the pan and is crisp and brown. Serve at once.

COUNTRY HAM STUFFED WITH GREENS

A long-time favorite in Virginia and Maryland, this variation on country ham has a delicious stuffing of fresh greens. Kale may be substituted for the mustard greens.

Serves 20 to 30

    1 12- to 16-pound country ham

    3 tablespoons butter

    ¼ cup finely chopped green onions, including 2 inches of the green tops

    1 stalk celery, finely chopped

    ½ pound fresh mustard greens, trimmed, washed, and coarsely chopped (about 4 cups)

    ½ pound fresh spinach, trimmed, washed, and coarsely chopped (about 4 cups)

    1 teaspoon crushed dried hot red pepper

    ½ teaspoon salt

    Freshly ground black pepper

    Cheesecloth for wrapping ham

1. Starting a day or two ahead, place the ham in a pot large enough to hold it comfortably and pour in enough cold water to cover the ham by at least 1 inch. Let the ham soak at room temperature for at least 24 hours, changing the water two or three times.

2. When you are ready to cook the ham, drain off the soaking water and replace it with fresh cold water to cover the ham by 1 inch. Bring to a boil over high heat,

then reduce the heat to low and simmer the ham, partially covered, for 1 hour. Transfer the ham to cool on a large platter or cutting board. Discard the cooking liquid, wash the pot, and set it aside.

3. With a large sharp knife, cut the rind off the ham and discard it. Remove the excess fat from the entire outside surface of the ham, leaving a layer no more than ⅛ inch thick all around. Set the ham aside.

4. In a heavy 4- to 5-quart saucepan, melt the butter over medium heat. When the foam begins to subside, add the onions and celery and, stirring frequently, cook for about 5 minutes until they are soft and transparent but not brown. Stir in the mustard greens, spinach, red pepper, salt, and a few grindings of black pepper. Reduce the heat to the lowest possible setting, cover the pan tightly, and cook for 15 minutes, or until all the vegetables are tender.

5. Cut 6 to 8 incisions about 2 inches long and spaced 2 inches apart in the ham and stuff them with the mustard-green-and-spinach mixture. Wrap the ham in a double thickness of cheesecloth. Sew up the ends with kitchen cord.

6. Return the ham to the original pot and add enough water to cover by at least 1 inch. Bring to a boil over high heat, reduce the heat to low, and partially cover the pot. Simmer for 3 to 4 hours, allowing about 15 minutes to the pound, or until the ham is tender and shows no resistance when pierced deeply with the point of a small skewer or sharp knife. (The ham should be kept constantly immersed in water. Check the pot from time to time and add more boiling water if necessary.)

7. Transfer the ham to a large platter and, without removing the cheesecloth, cool to room temperature and refrigerate for at least 12 hours. Just before serving, unwrap the ham and with a large sharp knife, carve it into paper-thin slices.

PORK LOIN STUFFED WITH PRUNES AND APPLES

Danes often serve this pork dish at Christmas dinner, which is always eaten on Christmas Eve.

Serves 6 to 8

- 1 4½- to 5-pound boned loin of pork, center cut
- 12 pitted prunes
- 1 large tart apple, peeled, cored, and cut into 1-inch dice
- 1 teaspoon lemon juice
- Salt and freshly ground black pepper
- 3 tablespoons butter
- 3 tablespoons vegetable oil
- ¾ cup dry white wine
- ¾ cup heavy cream
- 1 tablespoon red currant jelly

1. Place the prunes in a saucepan, cover with cold water, and bring to a boil. Remove from the heat and let the prunes soak in the water for 30 minutes. Then drain the prunes, pat dry with paper towels, and set them aside.
2. Sprinkle the apple with the lemon juice to prevent discoloring.
3. With a strong, sharp knife, make a pocket in the pork by cutting a deep slit down the length of the loin, going to within ½ inch of the two ends and to within 1 inch of the other side. Season the pocket lightly with salt and pepper and stuff it with the prunes and apples, sewing up the opening with strong kitchen cord. Tie the loin at 1-inch intervals so it retains its shape while cooking.

4. Preheat the oven to 350°F.
5. In a casserole equipped with a cover and just large enough to hold the loin of pork comfortably, melt the butter and oil over medium heat. When the foam subsides, add the loin, turning it from time to time with two wooden spoons. It should take about 20 minutes to brown the loin evenly on all sides. With a bulb baster or large spoon, remove all the fat from the pan. Pour in the wine, stir in the cream, whisking briskly, and bring to a simmer on top of the stove. Cover the pan and cook in the center of the oven for 2 hours, or until the meat shows no resistance and the liquid runs clear when pierced with the tip of a sharp knife.
6. Remove the loin from the pan and let it rest on a heated platter while you finish the sauce. Skim the fat from the liquid in the pan and bring the liquid to a boil. When it has reduced to about 1 cup, stir in the red currant jelly, reduce the heat, and, stirring constantly, simmer briefly until the sauce is smooth. Taste for seasoning and pour into a heated sauceboat.
7. Cut away the strings from the loin and carve the meat into 1-inch slices. Each slice of meat will surround a portion of the stuffing. Pass the sauce separately.

NOTE: An alternative method of stuffing the loin is somewhat more demanding but presents a more symmetrical appearance when the meat is sliced. Ask your butcher to tie the loin securely at 1-inch intervals. With a sharp knife, make a hole in each end of the loin. Force a long skewer or steel knife sharpener through the length of the loin, turning it to make a tunnel at least ½ inch in diameter. Then, with your fingers, insert the apples and the prunes alternately into the tunnel. Push them through from both sides using a round instrument; the long handle of a wooden spoon would be ideal. Complete the preparation of the meat as above.

ROAST PORK BOULANGER

When surrounded by browned, roasted potato slices and served with a silky gravy, this herb-seasoned pork roast makes a festive centerpiece for a Christmas menu.

Serves 8

1 5-pound pork rib roast

1 garlic clove, slivered

1½ teaspoons salt

1 teaspoon dried thyme

1 bay leaf, crumbled

¼ teaspoon black pepper

1 small onion, chopped

1 carrot, chopped

2 parsley sprigs

2 tablespoons flour

1¾ cups chicken stock

Chopped fresh parsley

Roasted Potatoes and Onions

3 pounds potatoes, peeled and thinly sliced

1 large onion, chopped

1 tablespoon chopped fresh parsley

1 teaspoon salt

⅛ teaspoon black pepper

¾ cup chicken stock

¼ cup butter, melted

1. Preheat the oven to 425°F.

2. Rub the pork with the cut sides of the garlic. With a small paring knife, make slashes in the roast. Insert the garlic slivers.

3. Combine the salt with the thyme, bay leaf, and pepper and rub into the pork.

4. Place the pork with the fat side up on a rack in a large shallow roasting pan. Insert a meat thermometer into the center of the meaty part of the roast.

5. Place the onion, carrot, and parsley in the pan under the roast. Roast, uncovered, for 1 hour.

6. Remove the pork and rack from the pan. Pour off all but 1 tablespoon of the fat. Add the flour to the pan. Over low heat, stir until the flour is lightly browned, 1 to 2 minutes.

7. Gradually whisk the stock into the flour. Bring the mixture to a boil, reduce the heat, and simmer until the gravy is smooth and thickened, about 2 minutes. Strain the sauce through a sieve into a medium saucepan. Discard the vegetables. Set the sauce aside to reheat later. Return the pork to the roasting pan.

8. To prepare the roasted potatoes and onions, gently toss the sliced potatoes with the chopped onion, parsley, salt, and pepper and mix well. Arrange the vegetables around the pork. In a small saucepan, bring the ¾ cup of stock to a boil and pour it over the potatoes. Brush the potatoes with the melted butter.

9. Lower the oven to 400°F. and roast the pork with the potatoes until the meat thermometer registers 170°F. and the potatoes are fork tender and browned, 45 minutes to 1 hour.

10. Remove the pan from the oven. Place the pork on a platter and surround it with the potatoes, garnished with the chopped parsley. Reheat the sauce and serve it with the roast.

LEEK AND SAUSAGE PIE

A hearty dish for a brisk winter night, this pie has a pastry flavored with mustard and a filling both savory and sweet.

Serves 6

Pastry

1½ cups flour

Pinch of salt

2 teaspoons dry mustard

2 teaspoons caraway seeds

½ cup unsalted butter, chilled

3 to 4 tablespoons ice water

Filling

2 tablespoons dry bread crumbs

2 tablespoons freshly grated Parmesan cheese

12 ounces bulk sausage

Dried thyme and sage, to taste (optional)

2 tablespoons unsalted butter

6 leeks, trimmed, split, washed thoroughly to remove all grit, and sliced crosswise into ¼-inch slices

3 large eggs

2 egg yolks

1½ teaspoons Dijon mustard

1 teaspoon salt

¼ teaspoon cayenne pepper

⅓ cup butter, melted

½ cup freshly grated imported Swiss cheese

2½ cups milk, scalded

¼ cup freshly grated Parmesan cheese

1. In a large bowl, combine the flour, salt, mustard, and caraway seeds. Cut in the butter, working the mixture with your fingers, two knives, or a pastry blender until it resembles coarse cornmeal. With a fork, quickly stir in the ice water.

2. To make the pastry with a food processor, place the flour, salt, dry mustard, and butter in the bowl and process with the steel blade attachment until the mixture resembles coarse cornmeal. With the motor running, gradually add the ice water until the dough forms a ball. Quickly knead in the caraway seeds.

3. Gather the dough into a flattened disc, wrap it in plastic wrap, and refrigerate it for 30 minutes.

4. Preheat the oven to 400°F.

5. On a floured surface, roll out the dough until it is slightly larger than a 9- to 11-inch-deep pie pan. Fit the dough into the pan, flute the edges, prick the bottom with a fork, and bake it for 15 minutes. Remove it from the oven and reduce the heat to 350°F. Place the pie pan on a baking sheet.

6. Combine the bread crumbs and the 2 tablespoons of Parmesan cheese and sprinkle the mixture in the pastry shell.

7. To make the filling, place the sausage in a large, cold skillet. Cook it over medium-low heat, breaking it up as it cooks. Drain it thoroughly on paper towels. Taste the sausage and season it with thyme and sage if it seems bland. Sprinkle the sausage over the bread crumbs and cheese in the pastry shell.

8. Melt the 2 tablespoons butter in the skillet over medium heat and cook the leeks until they are soft but not brown, about 7 minutes.

9. In a medium-size bowl, whisk together the whole eggs and egg yolks. Whisk in the mustard, salt, cayenne, melted butter, Swiss cheese, scalded milk, and the cooked leeks. Spoon the mixture into the pastry shell, top with the ¼ cup Parmesan cheese, and bake the pie until the custard is puffed and golden and a knife inserted in the center comes out clean, about 25 minutes. Serve the pie warm or at room temperature.

Un noël français

In France, Christmas Eve has long been a day of fasting (or, at least, light eating) until after midnight Mass, when the celebration, known as the Reveillon, begins. Singing and dancing until dawn are combined with feasting on fresh game, fish, sugar pies, doughnuts, and a Bûche de Noël (page 154). Meat pies are a specialty of this occasion, and among the many French customs imported to North America is the French-Canadian version, the Tourtière.

Tourtière

Makes 2 pies (serves 12)

> 2 pounds ground pork
>
> 2 onions, finely chopped
>
> 1 garlic clove, finely chopped
>
> 1 tablespoon finely chopped celery leaves
>
> 1 teaspoon dried savory or marjoram
>
> ½ teaspoon dried sage
>
> ⅛ teaspoon ground cloves
>
> 2 bay leaves
>
> 1 teaspoon salt
>
> Freshly ground black pepper to taste
>
> 1 cup boiling water
>
> Pie dough for two 9-inch double-crust pies
>
> 3 to 4 tablespoons dry bread crumbs
>
> 2 tablespoons heavy cream (optional)

1. In a large skillet, mix the pork, onions, garlic, celery leaves, savory or marjoram, sage, cloves, bay leaves, salt, and a few grindings of pepper. Add the boiling water. Simmer for about ½ hour, stirring frequently; when ready, the pork should be brown (not pink), and the mixture fairly dry. Drain off any excess fat. Taste for seasoning. Remove the bay leaves.

2. Preheat the oven to 350°F.

3. Divide the pie dough into four pieces and roll out two pieces for the bottom crusts. Fit the rolled-out dough into two 9-inch pie pans.

4. Sprinkle the bread crumbs in the uncooked pie shells. Place half of the meat mixture in each shell. Roll out the other two pieces of dough and cover the pies with crust. Seal and flute the edges, and make some incisions in the crust. (You might make a cross with the tines of a fork or some other symbolic shape or initial.) Brush the crusts with cream, if you like.

5. Bake the pies for 45 minutes, or until the top crusts are golden.

CROWN ROAST OF LAMB WITH PEAS AND NEW POTATOES

Serves 8

    1 crown roast of lamb, consisting of
    16 to 18 chops and weighing about
    4½ pounds

    1 garlic clove, cut into tiny slivers
    (optional)

    2 teaspoons salt

    1 teaspoon freshly ground black pepper

    1 teaspoon crushed dried rosemary

    16 to 18 peeled new potatoes, all about
    1½ inches in diameter

    3 cups cooked fresh or frozen peas

    2 tablespoons melted butter

    6 to 8 sprigs of fresh mint or parsley

1. Preheat the oven to 475°F.
2. If you are using the garlic, with the point of a small, sharp knife make small incisions a few inches apart in the meaty portions of the lamb and insert the slivers of garlic.
3. Combine the salt, pepper, and rosemary, and with your fingers pat the mixture all over the bottom and sides of the crown.
4. To help keep its shape, stuff the crown with a crumpled sheet of aluminum foil and wrap the ends of the chop bones in strips of foil to prevent them from charring and snapping off. Place the crown of lamb on a small rack set in a shallow roasting pan just large enough to hold it comfortably and roast it in the center of the oven for about 20 minutes.
5. Turn down the heat to 400°F. and surround the crown with the new potatoes. Baste them with the pan drippings and sprinkle them lightly with salt. Continue to roast the lamb (basting the lamb is unnecessary, but baste the potatoes every 15 minutes or so) for about an hour to an hour and 15 minutes, depending upon how well done you like your lamb. Ideally, it should be served when it is still somewhat pink, 140° to 150°F. on a meat thermometer.

6. When the crown is done, carefully transfer it to a large circular platter, remove the foil, and let the lamb rest about 10 minutes to make carving easier. Meanwhile, combine the peas with the melted butter and season them with as much salt as is necessary. Fill the hollow of the crown with as many of the peas as it will hold and serve any remaining peas separately. Put a paper frill on the end of each chop bone and surround the crown with the roasted potatoes. Garnish with mint or parsley and serve at once.
7. To carve the lamb, insert a large fork in the side of the crown to steady it and with a large, sharp knife cut down through each rib to detach the chops. Two rib chops per person is a customary portion.

BRAISED SHOULDER OF LAMB

Serves 6 to 8

    1 shoulder of lamb, 4 to 4½ pounds,
    boned and tied, with most of the fat
    removed

    2 tablespoons olive oil

    Salt and freshly ground black pepper
    to taste

    3 garlic cloves

    2 onions, chopped

    1 rutabaga, peeled and cut into ½-inch
    cubes

    2 carrots, peeled and quartered

    ½ cup water

    4 sprigs fresh dill or 2 teaspoons
    dried dill

    1 tablespoon finely cut fresh dill

    1 tablespoon chopped fresh parsley

1. Heat the oil in a heavy Dutch oven over medium-high heat and brown the lamb on all sides. Pour off the fat.
2. Add the salt, pepper, garlic, onions, rutabaga, and carrots to the pot. Pour in the water and place the dill sprigs or dried dill on top of the lamb.
3. Cover and simmer the lamb over low heat until it is tender but not dry, 1½ to

2 hours. Transfer the meat to a warm platter, remove the strings, and spoon the vegetables around it. Sprinkle the lamb with the fresh dill and parsley, and serve.

VEAL SCALLOPINI WITH CREAM, CALVADOS, AND APPLES

Serves 6

12 veal scallops, about 4 inches in diameter and ½ inch thick, not pounded

3 golden or red Delicious apples, peeled, cored, and cut into ½-inch cubes

5 to 6 tablespoons lemon juice

1 teaspoon salt

1 teaspoon freshly ground black pepper

½ cup flour

4 tablespoons butter

2 tablespoons vegetable oil

⅓ cup calvados (French applejack) or applejack

1½ cups heavy cream

1. Place the apples in a medium-size bowl, add the lemon juice, and mix thoroughly so the apples are well coated. Set aside.
2. Sprinkle the veal with salt and pepper, then with the flour, shaking off any excess.
3. Heat the butter and oil in a large skillet about 15 inches in diameter (or use two skillets). When hot, add the veal, a few pieces at a time, and sauté over medium heat until it is lightly browned on both sides, about 4 minutes on each side.
4. Preheat the oven to 180°F.
5. When the scallops are cooked, arrange them on a platter and set it in the oven.
6. Add the apples, lemon juice, and the calvados or applejack to the skillet. Stir and scrape up all the brown bits in the bottom and cook over medium heat, stirring frequently, for about 3 minutes.
7. Add the cream and continue cooking

OUR JOYFULST FEAST!

Lo! now is come our joyfulst feast!
Let every man be jolly;
Each room with ivy leaves is dressed,
And every post with holly.
Now all our neighbours' chimneys smoke,
And Christmas logs are burning;
Their ovens they with baked meats choke,
And all their spits are turning.

GEORGE WITHER, SEVENTEENTH CENTURY, "A CHRISTMAS CAROL"

until the mixture has turned a rich ivory color. Reduce the heat and cook, uncovered, stirring frequently, until the cream has reduced by about half and the sauce coats a spoon, about 10 minutes. Taste for seasoning; you will probably need to add about ½ teaspoon of salt. Spoon the sauce over the scallops and serve.

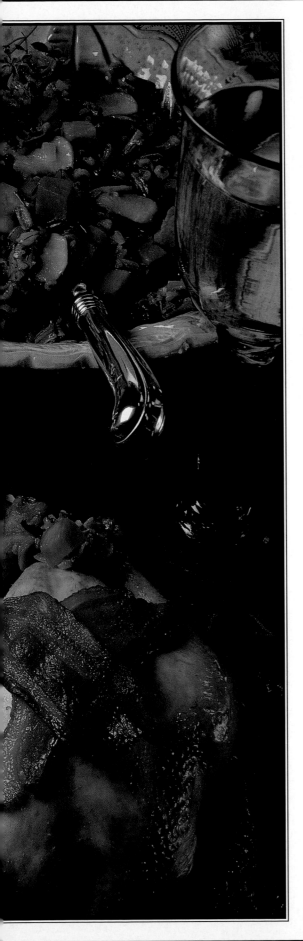

Poultry, Stuffing, & Sauces

URKEY AND GOOSE STAND ALMOST EQUALLY as the birds of the season. Benjamin Franklin called turkey "the true and original native," and who can forget Bob Cratchit's Christmas goose, which, when it was pierced in the breast by Mrs. Cratchit and the "long-expected gush of stuffing issued forth," elicited "one murmur of delight all round the board, and even Tiny Tim beat on the table with the handle of his knife, and feebly cried, Hurrah!" Hurrah indeed for all of those succulent, golden brown birds, whether goose, turkey, duck, or even chicken, and their savory stuffings of bread, corn bread, oyster, or chestnut. Stuffings both enhance the flavor of the bird and provide another delicious side dish for the meal. You will find stuffing recipes included with directions for roasting various birds as well as additional stuffings at the end of the chapter. It is very important to cool the dressing before stuffing the bird and then immediately to begin roasting it. Do not let a stuffed bird stand uncooked, even in the refrigerator—an invitation for bacteria to grow.

Cornish Hens with Wild Rice Stuffing

CHICKEN MARBELLA

This dish keeps and even improves over several days of refrigeration. Conveniently versatile, it can be served hot, at room temperature, or cold. Marinating the chicken overnight is essential to the moistness of the finished product.

Serves 10

> 4 chickens, 2½ pounds each, quartered
>
> 1 whole garlic bulb, peeled and finely puréed
>
> ¼ cup dried oregano
>
> Coarse salt and freshly ground black pepper
>
> ½ cup red wine vinegar
>
> ½ cup olive oil
>
> 1 cup pitted prunes
>
> ½ cup pitted Spanish green olives
>
> ½ cup capers with a bit of juice
>
> 6 bay leaves
>
> 1 cup firmly packed dark brown sugar
>
> 1 cup dry white wine
>
> ¼ cup finely chopped fresh Italian parsley or cilantro (fresh coriander)

1. In a large bowl, combine the chicken, garlic, oregano, coarse salt and pepper to taste, vinegar, oil, prunes, olives, capers and juice, and bay leaves. Cover and let the chicken marinate, refrigerated, overnight.
2. Preheat the oven to 350°F.
3. Arrange the chicken in a single layer in one or two large, shallow baking pans and spoon the marinade over it evenly. Sprinkle the chicken pieces with the brown sugar and pour the white wine around them.
4. Bake for 50 minutes to 1 hour, basting frequently with the pan juices. The chicken is done when the thigh pieces, pricked with a fork at their thickest point, yield clear yellow (rather than pink) juices.

5. With a slotted spoon, transfer the chicken, prunes, olives, and capers to a serving platter. Moisten them with a few spoonfuls of pan juices and sprinkle generously with parsley or cilantro. Pass the remaining pan juices in a sauceboat.

CHICKEN BREASTS AND HAM WITH SHERRIED CREAM SAUCE

Serves 6

> 3 1-pound chicken breasts, halved, skinned, and boned
>
> 9 tablespoons butter
>
> 2 tablespoons finely chopped shallots
>
> 1½ cups chicken stock, fresh or canned
>
> ¼ cup flour
>
> ½ cup heavy cream
>
> 2 tablespoons pale dry sherry
>
> 1 tablespoon finely chopped parsley
>
> ½ teaspoon salt
>
> Pinch of white pepper
>
> 6 thin slices cooked country ham, plus 1 thin slice country ham cut into julienne strips

1. In a heavy 12-inch skillet, melt 2 tablespoons of the butter over medium heat. When the foam begins to subside, add the shallots and, stirring frequently, cook until they are soft and translucent but not brown, 2 to 3 minutes. Add the chicken breasts and stock, and bring to a boil over high heat, skimming off the foam as it rises to the surface. Reduce the heat to low and simmer, partially covered, until the chicken feels firm to the touch, about 10 minutes. With a slotted spoon, transfer the chicken to a plate and drape it with foil to keep it warm. Set the stock aside.
2. Melt 3 tablespoons of the remaining butter in a 1- to 2-quart saucepan over medium heat. Add the flour and mix to a paste. Then, stirring the mixture constantly with a wire whisk, pour in the reserved chicken stock and shallots,

and cook over high heat until the sauce comes to a boil, thickens heavily, and is smooth.

3. Whisking constantly, add the cream, sherry, parsley, salt, and white pepper. Reduce the heat to low and simmer, uncovered, for 3 minutes to remove any taste of raw flour. Taste for seasoning.

4. While the sauce is simmering, melt the remaining 4 tablespoons of butter in a heavy 12-inch skillet over high heat. Add the ham slices and, turning them over frequently with kitchen tongs, cook them for a few minutes to heat the ham through.

5. To serve, place the ham slices on six individual serving plates and set a chicken breast half on each slice. Pour the sauce over the chicken and ham, dividing it evenly among the portions. Garnish the top with the strips of ham and serve immediately.

SHAKER CHICKEN PUDDING

The Shakers' distinctive fare, like the functional and attractive furniture for which they are also famous, expressed their belief in the rich rewards of simple living.

Serves 4 to 6

 2 to 3 cups diced cooked chicken or turkey

 6 tablespoons butter

 1 apple, diced

 1 onion, chopped

 1 stalk celery, chopped

 ½ cup apple cider

 ½ teaspoon salt

 ¼ teaspoon black pepper

 Pinch of ground nutmeg

 1 cup bread crumbs

Sauce

 2 tablespoons flour

 2 tablespoons butter

 1 cup heavy cream

1. In a large skillet, melt 4 tablespoons of butter and gently sauté the apple, onion, and celery until they are soft. Add the cider, salt, pepper, and nutmeg. Simmer the mixture, covered, until the vegetables are very soft, about 30 minutes. Uncover the pan and continue to cook the mixture until it has thickened.
2. Preheat the oven to 350°F.
3. To make the sauce, cook the flour and 2 tablespoons of butter in a saucepan over medium-low heat for a few minutes, stirring until the mixture just begins to change color. Add the cream and cook, stirring, until the sauce thickens.
4. Combine the chicken and vegetables with the sauce. Pour the mixture into a buttered baking dish. Sprinkle with the bread crumbs. Melt 2 tablespoons butter in a small skillet or in a small bowl in a microwave oven and drizzle it over the top of the casserole. Bake until the top is browned, about 20 minutes.

CHICKEN STEW IN WHOLE GREEN AND RED PEPPERS

Serves 4

 4 chicken thighs, skinned and boned, the meat cut into 1-inch chunks

 1½ tablespoons olive oil

 2 large garlic cloves, finely chopped

 1 onion, cut in half, the halves cut into pieces about 1 inch square

 1 tablespoon dried oregano

 Freshly ground black pepper

 ½ teaspoon salt

 1½ pounds ripe tomatoes, peeled, seeded, and coarsely chopped, with their juice, or 16 ounces canned whole tomatoes, with their juice

 3 green peppers, 1 seeded, deribbed, and cut into 1-inch squares, 2 left whole

 3 sweet red peppers, 1 seeded, deribbed, and cut into 1-inch squares, 2 left whole

1. Pour the oil into a large, heavy skillet over medium-high heat. When the oil is hot, add the garlic and onion and sauté them, stirring often, for 2 minutes. Add the chicken, oregano, pepper, and salt, and sauté the chicken until the pieces are golden brown, about 5 minutes.
2. Reduce the heat and add the tomatoes with their juice to the skillet; if you are using canned whole tomatoes, coarsely chop the tomatoes in the skillet. Then add the squares of green and red pepper. Cover the skillet and simmer the stew until the chicken is tender and the peppers are soft, about 20 minutes. If the stew absorbs all the liquid, pour in ½ cup of water.
3. While the stew is simmering, carefully cut the top off each of the remaining peppers. Seed and derib the peppers. If necessary, shave a thin slice from the bottom of each pepper so it

will stand upright. Set a steamer in a saucepan and pour in enough water to barely reach the bottom of the steamer. Bring the water to a boil, put the peppers in the steamer, and tightly cover the pan. Steam the peppers until they are tender, 5 to 10 minutes.

4. Stand each steamed pepper in a small bowl. Spoon the stew into the peppers; distribute any remaining stew around the peppers and serve immediately.

CHICKEN CHILI

A spicy dash of cinnamon and a handful of grated chocolate give this dish a flavor reminiscent of Mexican *mole*.

Serves 6

- 6 whole chicken breasts (12 halves), skinned, boned, and cut into 1-inch cubes
- 6 tablespoons olive oil
- 1 very large yellow onion, chopped
- 5 garlic cloves, finely chopped
- 2 sweet red peppers, seeded, deribbed, and diced
- 1 to 4 jalapeño peppers (depending on your tolerance for hot foods), seeded, deribbed, and finely chopped
- 3 tablespoons chili powder
- 1½ teaspoons cumin seeds
- 1 teaspoon ground coriander
- Pinch of ground cinnamon
- 2 16-ounce cans tomatoes in purée, chopped
- 8 ounces pitted black olives, sliced
- 1 cup beer
- ¼ cup grated unsweetened chocolate
- Salt

Garnish

- Sour cream
- Grated Cheddar cheese
- Sliced green onions
- Diced avocado

CHRISTMAS IS COMING

Christmas is coming, the geese are getting fat,
Please to put a penny in the old man's hat.
If you haven't a penny a ha'penny will do.
If you haven't got a ha'penny, God bless you.

ENGLISH NURSERY RHYME

1. Heat half the olive oil in a Dutch oven over high heat. Add the onion and garlic and sauté for 5 minutes.
2. Add the red and jalapeño peppers and sauté over medium heat for 10 minutes.
3. Stir in the chili powder, cumin, coriander, and cinnamon and cook for 5 minutes more. Remove from the heat and set aside.
4. In a large skillet, brown the chicken, a few pieces at a time, in the remaining 3 tablespoons of oil over medium-high heat, until cooked through.
5. Add the chicken, tomatoes with their purée, olives, and beer to the Dutch oven and stir to combine. Simmer over medium heat for 15 minutes.
6. Stir in the chocolate and season to taste with salt. Serve immediately. Pass sour cream, Cheddar cheese, green onions, and avocado in separate small bowls.

GREEN CHILI AND CHICKEN ENCHILADA CASSEROLE

Serves 6

- 1 3- to 4½-pound roasting chicken
- 4 cups water, or more
- 1 Spanish onion, cut into thick slices
- 1 carrot, chopped
- 2 garlic cloves, chopped
- 1 teaspoon salt
- 4 cups corn oil
- 12 corn tortillas
- 1 cup heavy cream
- ½ cup sour cream
- 1 cup chopped green onions, including the tender part of the green tops
- 1½ cups each coarsely grated Monterey Jack and sharp Cheddar cheese, mixed
- 6 romaine lettuce leaves

6 radish roses, prepared in advance

Green Salsa

- 1 13-ounce can tomatillos (available in specialty foods stores)
- ½ cup chopped hot green New Mexico chilies or canned chopped green chilies
- ½ teaspoon salt (optional)
- 1 large garlic clove, finely chopped

1. Place the chicken in a 5- to 6-quart heavy stewing pot. Add the water, onion, carrot, garlic, and salt, cover, and cook until very tender, about 1½ hours. Allow to cool in the cooking liquid for another hour. Remove the skin and debone the chicken. With your fingers, tear the meat into pieces about ½ inch wide and not over 2 inches long.
2. Meanwhile, heat the oil to 375°F. in a deep-fat fryer or deep skillet. Quickly slip the tortillas in and out of the hot oil—two or three at a time—holding them with tongs. Drain well on

absorbent paper toweling.

3. Prepare the green salsa by puréeing the tomatillos, chilies, salt, and garlic in a food processor or blender.

4. In a small bowl, combine the cream and sour cream.

5. Preheat the oven to 375°F.

6. Lightly oil your most Christmasy-looking casserole. Then begin layering the ingredients. On the bottom of the casserole, place some salsa, then cover with 3 or 4 tortillas, depending on the size of the casserole. Add more salsa, then a layer of chicken. Sprinkle some of the green onions, cheeses, and the combined creams on the chicken. Repeat the procedure. When you get to the final layer, dribble the green salsa around the edges, and add the last of the cream mixture, cheeses, and green onions on top. No chicken should be showing.

7. Place the casserole in the oven and bake until the cheeses melt and the dish is hot, about 30 minutes.

8. To serve, place on heated plates with a garnish of lettuce leaf and a radish rose.

NOTE: You may prepare the enchilada casserole as much as 3 days ahead, cover it with plastic wrap, and store it in the refrigerator. Bring it to room temperature before baking.

ROAST GINGERED TURKEY BREAST

If you want to serve turkey and prefer not to prepare a large stuffed bird, turkey breast is a welcome alternative. The marinade in this recipe combines popular oriental flavors and helps to keep the turkey moist. Preparation should be started in the morning of the day you plan to serve the dish, or the day before.

Serves 6

   1 turkey breast half (about 1½ pounds)

   2 teaspoons vegetable oil

Ginger Marinade

   3 garlic cloves, finely chopped

   ¾ teaspoon ground cinnamon

   2 tablespoons peeled and grated fresh ginger

   ¼ cup chicken or turkey stock

   1 teaspoon Oriental sesame oil

   1 tablespoon soy sauce

1. To make the marinade, in a shallow bowl just large enough to hold the turkey breast, combine the garlic, cinnamon, ginger, stock, sesame oil, and soy sauce.

2. Using a knife with a sharp point, poke several ½-inch-deep slits in the thick part of the turkey breast, to allow the marinade to penetrate. Put the turkey into the bowl with the marinade and turn to coat it. Cover the bowl and refrigerate the turkey for 8 to 24 hours, turning occasionally.

3. Remove the turkey from the marinade, scraping any clinging garlic and ginger back into the bowl. Reserve the marinade and allow the turkey to come to room temperature.

4. Preheat the oven to 350°F.

5. In a heavy, ovenproof skillet, heat the vegetable oil over medium-high heat. Sauté the turkey until it is golden on one side—about 4 minutes—and turn. Use a pastry brush to baste with the accumulated juices and continue cooking for 1 minute.

6. Put the skillet in the oven and roast the turkey until it feels firm but springy to the touch—15 to 20 minutes—basting once with the reserved marinade. Let the turkey rest for at least 5 minutes before slicing. Serve hot or cold.

NOTE: Oriental sesame oil is a spicy flavoring available with oriental products at most supermarkets. It should not be confused with cold-pressed sesame oil, which is a cooking oil.

ROAST TURKEY WITH CORN BREAD, SAUSAGE, AND PECAN STUFFING

Serves 8 to 12

1 12- to 14-pound oven-ready turkey, thoroughly defrosted in the refrigerator if frozen, and the turkey liver, finely chopped

1½ teaspoons salt

Freshly ground black pepper

1 pound breakfast-type sausage, in bulk form or with casings removed

1 large onion, finely chopped

1 stalk celery, finely chopped

5 cups coarsely crumbled, cooled corn bread *(see below)*

1½ cups coarsely chopped pecans (about ½ pound)

¼ cup pale dry sherry

¼ cup milk

¼ cup finely chopped fresh parsley

½ teaspoon dried thyme

¼ teaspoon ground or freshly grated nutmeg

12 tablespoons butter, melted

1 small onion, coarsely chopped

3 tablespoons flour

1½ cups turkey stock *(see Note)*, or fresh or canned chicken stock

1. Preheat the oven to 400°F.

2. Pat the turkey completely dry inside and out with paper towels. Rub the cavity with 1 teaspoon of the salt and a few grindings of pepper, and set the bird aside.

3. In a heavy 10- to 12-inch ungreased skillet, fry the sausage meat over medium heat, stirring frequently and mashing the meat with the back of a fork to break up any lumps as they form. When no trace of pink remains, scoop up the sausage meat with a slotted spoon and transfer it to a fine sieve to drain.

4. Pour off all but a few tablespoonfuls of the sausage fat remaining in the skillet and add the finely chopped onions and celery. Stirring frequently, cook the mixture over medium heat until the vegetables are soft but not brown, about 5 minutes. With a slotted spoon, transfer them to a deep bowl. Add the drained sausage meat, the corn bread, pecans, sherry, milk, turkey liver, parsley, thyme, nutmeg, the remaining ½ teaspoon of salt, and a few grindings of pepper, and toss together gently but thoroughly. Taste for seasoning and let the stuffing cool to room temperature.

5. Fill both the breast and the neck cavities of the turkey with the stuffing and close the openings by lacing them with small skewers and kitchen cord or sewing them with heavy white thread. Truss the bird securely.

6. With a pastry brush, spread the melted butter evenly over the entire surface of the turkey. Place the bird on its side on a rack set in a large shallow roasting pan and roast in the middle of the oven for 15 minutes. Turn the turkey on its other side, and roast for 15 minutes more.

7. Reduce the oven temperature to 325°F., turn the turkey breast side down, and roast for 1 hour, basting it every 15 minutes or so with the juices that have accumulated in the pan. Turn the bird breast side up and scatter the coarsely chopped onion around it. Roast for about 1 hour longer, basting the turkey every 15 minutes with the pan juices.

8. To test for doneness, pierce the thigh of the turkey with the tip of a small sharp knife. The juice that trickles out should be a clear yellow; if it is slightly pink, return the bird to the oven and roast for another 5 to 10 minutes. Transfer the turkey to a heated platter and let it rest for at least 15 minutes for easier carving.

9. Meanwhile, skim off and discard all but a thin film of fat from the roasting pan. Stir the flour into the fat and cook over medium heat for 2 to 3 minutes, scraping up the brown particles clinging to the bottom and sides of the pan.

10. Pour in the turkey or chicken stock and, stirring constantly with a wire whisk, cook over high heat until the

sauce comes to a boil, thickens, and is smooth. Reduce the heat to low and simmer, uncovered, for about 5 minutes, then strain the gravy through a fine sieve into a serving bowl or sauceboat. Taste for seasoning. Carve the turkey at the table and present the gravy separately.

NOTE: If you would like to make your own turkey stock, start about 2 hours before you prepare the stuffing. Combine the turkey neck, gizzard, and heart, 1 scraped chopped carrot, 1 peeled and quartered onion, 4 fresh parsley sprigs, 1 small bay leaf, 1 teaspoon of salt, and 4 cups of water in a saucepan. Bring to a boil over high heat, reduce the heat to low, and simmer, partially covered, for 1½ hours. Strain the liquid through a fine sieve into a bowl and skim as much fat as possible from the surface. There should be about 2 cups of stock.

Corn Bread

- ½ cup flour
- 1 cup white cornmeal
- 1 teaspoon baking powder
- ½ teaspoon baking soda
- 1 teaspoon salt
- 1 cup buttermilk
- 1 egg
- 2 tablespoons butter, melted

1. Preheat the oven to 400°F.
2. Put the flour, cornmeal, baking powder, soda, and salt into a sifter and sift together into a bowl. Add the buttermilk and stir well. Add the egg and butter and beat well.
3. Pour the mixture into a hot, greased 9-inch iron skillet or a 9-inch square baking pan. Bake until brown, about 20 minutes. Remove the corn bread from the skillet or pan, let it cool, and crumble it.

HONEY-GLAZED ROAST TURKEY WITH ORANGE AND SWEET POTATO STUFFING

Serves 12

1 12-pound fresh or thawed turkey, the neck, gizzard, and heart reserved for gravy

¾ teaspoon salt

Freshly ground black pepper

2 tablespoons honey

Orange and Sweet Potato Stuffing

Zest of 1 lemon, cut into fine strips

4 navel oranges, the zest of 2 cut into fine strips

6 sweet potatoes, peeled and cut into ½-inch cubes

6 tablespoons unsalted butter

3 large onions, chopped

¼ cup lemon juice

½ cup chicken or turkey stock *(see page 89)*

⅛ teaspoon salt

Freshly ground black pepper

½ teaspoon ground cloves

¾ teaspoon dry mustard

6 slices cracked-wheat bread, cut into cubes and lightly toasted

2 tablespoons brandy

Port and Orange Gravy

The turkey neck, gizzard, and heart, the neck chopped into 1-inch pieces

1 tablespoon vegetable oil

1 carrot, chopped

1 celery stalk, coarsely chopped

2 onions, coarsely chopped

1 garlic clove, coarsely chopped

1 cup dry white wine

1 bay leaf

1 teaspoon fresh thyme, or ¼ teaspoon dried thyme

The roasting juices from the turkey (about 1 cup), degreased

The juice and grated zest of 1 orange

1 tablespoon red wine vinegar

2 tablespoons cornstarch

⅓ cup port wine

½ teaspoon salt

Freshly ground black pepper

1. To prepare the stuffing, blanch the lemon and orange zest in 1 cup of boiling water for 1 minute. Drain and set aside. Using a sharp knife, peel the oranges and divide them into sections, cutting away the inner membranes. Cut each section in half and reserve.

2. In a large saucepan, bring 2 quarts of water to a boil. Drop in the sweet potato cubes and blanch them for 3 minutes. Drain them and set them aside.

3. In a large, heavy casserole, melt 4 tablespoons of the butter over medium-low heat. Add the onion and cook it until translucent, stirring occasionally, about 10 minutes. Add the lemon and orange zest, oranges, sweet potatoes, lemon juice, stock, salt, and pepper. Cook until the sweet potato cubes are tender, 7 to 10 minutes. Remove from the heat and add the cloves, mustard, the remaining 2 tablespoons of butter, the bread cubes, and the brandy. Mix thoroughly. Allow the stuffing to cool before using it.

4. To make a stock for the gravy, heat the oil in a heavy saucepan over medium-high heat. Add the neck, gizzard, heart, carrot, celery, onions, and garlic. Sauté, stirring, until the vegetables begin to brown, about 5 minutes. Add the white wine, bay leaf, thyme, and 3 cups of water. Reduce the heat to low and simmer for 1 hour, skimming off impurities as necessary. Strain the stock, pushing down on the contents to extract all the liquid; there should be 2 to 2½ cups. Set it aside.

5. Preheat the oven to 350°F.

6. Rinse the turkey inside and out under cold running water and dry it thoroughly with paper towels. Rub the salt and pepper inside the body and

PROUD AS A PEACOCK

To the Victorian gourmet, presentation was as important as taste. In an imaginative and idealized description of a fictional banquet at an old English manor, an American visitor recalled, "I could not but notice a pie, magnificently decorated with peacock's feathers, in imitation of the tail of that bird, which overshadowed a considerable tract of the table." This, his host confessed, "with some little hesitation, was a pheasant-pie, though a peacock-pie was certainly the most authentical; but there had been such a mortality among the peacocks that he could not prevail upon himself to have one killed."

WASHINGTON IRVING / THE SKETCH BOOK OF GEOFFREY CRAYON, GENT.

neck cavities and outside the bird.

7. To stuff the turkey, loosely fill both cavities. Tie the drumsticks together with butcher's twine and tuck the wing tips under the bird. Put the turkey on a rack in a shallow roasting pan. Add 1 cup of water to the pan.

8. To keep the turkey moist and prevent it from over-browning, make a tent of aluminum foil. Use an extra-wide sheet of foil (or two sheets of regular foil crimped together) that measures 1½ feet longer than the pan. Lay the foil shiny side down over the turkey, and tuck it loosely around the inside edges of the pan. Roast the turkey in the oven for 2½ hours.

9. Take the turkey from the oven and carefully remove the foil tent. Brush the turkey all over with the honey. Turn the heat down to 325°F., then return the turkey to the oven, and roast it, uncovered, for 1 hour. The bird is done when a meat thermometer inserted in the thickest part of the thigh reads 180°F. There should be about 1 cup of roasting juices in the pan.

10. Let the turkey stand for at least 15 minutes before carving it. In the meantime, remove the stuffing from the cavities and set it aside in a bowl loosely covered with foil to keep it warm.

11. To make the gravy, combine the stock, reserved roasting juices, orange juice and zest, and vinegar in a saucepan. Bring the mixture to a boil. Mix the cornstarch and the port and whisk them into the saucepan; return the gravy to a boil. Reduce the heat to low and simmer for 5 minutes. Add the salt and pepper and serve piping hot with the carved bird and the stuffing.

NOTE: If you wish to cook the stuffing separately as a dressing, put it in a baking dish with an additional ¼ cup of stock. Cover the dish with aluminum foil and bake the dressing in a preheated 325°F. oven for 45 minutes. Uncover the dish and return it to the oven for another 45 minutes.

TURKEY TURNOVERS

Here's an excellent use for leftover turkey.

Serves 4

 1½ cups chopped leftover cooked turkey meat

 1 tablespoon finely chopped fresh parsley

 1 tablespoon finely cut fresh chives or green onion tops

 1 tablespoon finely chopped white boiling onion

 1 tablespoon chopped green pepper

 ½ cup leftover turkey gravy

 2 tablespoons dry sherry

 Salt and black pepper

 1 egg yolk

 2 tablespoons heavy cream

Pastry

 1 cup flour

 ¼ teaspoon salt

 6 tablespoons unsalted butter

 ⅓ to ½ cup ice water

1. In a medium-size bowl, mix the turkey, parsley, chives or green onion tops, onion, and green pepper with the turkey gravy. Add the sherry, season to taste with salt and pepper, and place in the refrigerator until ready to use.
2. Preheat the oven to 375°F.
3. For the pastry, sift the flour and salt into a bowl. Cut the butter into the flour and rub the mixture with your fingertips until it resembles coarse cornmeal. Add just enough ice water (the least possible amount) to work the ingredients quickly into a firm dough.
4. To make the pastry with a food processor, put the flour, salt, and butter in the bowl and process with the steel blade attachment until the mixture resembles coarse cornmeal. With the motor running, gradually add ice water until the dough forms a ball.
5. On a lightly floured board, roll out the dough very thin, about ⅛ inch thick, and cut it into 4-inch squares. Put 1 tablespoon of the turkey filling on each square. Fold the dough over the filling into a triangle. Brush the edges with a little water and seal them securely.
6. Beat the egg yolk with the cream and use it to brush the tops of the turnovers. Bake them on an ungreased baking sheet for about 15 minutes or until they are golden brown.
7. Pile the freshly baked turnovers on a hot folded napkin on a warmed serving plate and serve immediately.

CURRIED TURKEY

The water chestnuts in this mild curry add a nice crunch.

Serves 6 to 8

 3 cups cooked turkey or chicken, cut in large dice
 6 tablespoons butter
 1 onion, finely chopped
 2 tablespoons diced green pepper
 4 tablespoons flour
 1½ cups chicken or turkey stock *(page 89)*
 1¼ cups sliced mushrooms
 1 large tart apple, cored and diced
 1 5-ounce can water chestnuts, drained and sliced
 3 tablespoons chopped pimiento
 1 tablespoon finely chopped parsley
 Salt and black pepper
 1½ teaspoons curry powder, or to taste

1. In a large casserole, melt the butter and sauté the onion and green pepper over medium heat until they are soft. Stir in the flour, cook a moment, and gently whisk in the stock and the mushrooms. Simmer the mixture, stirring occasionally, until it thickens, 15 to 20 minutes.
2. In a large bowl, combine the turkey, apple, water chestnuts, pimiento, parsley, salt and pepper to taste, and curry powder.
3. Stir the turkey mixture into the sauce, heat slowly, and simmer 10 to 15 minutes over low heat. Serve the curry with plenty of fresh hot rice and such accompaniments as chutney, fresh grated coconut, chopped salted peanuts, preserved or candied ginger, poppadums (large thin wafers from India), and Bombay duck (a dried Indian fish, for which shredded salt cod serves about as well).

NOTE: Curry always improves with time. Make this in the morning or the day before and refrigerate, then bring to room temperature, and reheat at serving time.

CORNISH HENS WITH WILD RICE STUFFING

Serves 6

 6 Cornish game hens
 1 teaspoon salt
 6 slices bacon, cut in half lengthwise
 2 tablespoons butter

Stuffing

 1 cup wild rice
 4 cups water
 1 teaspoon salt
 6 tablespoons butter
 1 small onion, chopped
 ½ pound mushrooms, sliced
 1½ cups diced or chopped cooked ham
 ½ teaspoon salt
 ½ teaspoon marjoram
 ½ teaspoon thyme

1. To make the stuffing, rinse the rice and place it in a medium-size heavy saucepan with the water and salt. Bring to a boil and simmer, covered, until tender, about 45 minutes. Fluff the rice with a fork and simmer, uncovered, for another 5 minutes. Drain off any excess liquid.
2. Melt the 6 tablespoons of butter in a large skillet over medium heat, and sauté the onion, mushrooms, and ham for about 5 minutes. Add the rice and mix well. Season with salt, marjoram, and thyme. This makes about 3½ cups of stuffing, which is ample for 6 game hens.
3. Preheat the oven to 350°F.
4. Sprinkle the cavities of the hens with salt. Loosely stuff the birds with the wild rice and truss them. Lay 2 half-slices of bacon over each bird, and roast, uncovered, until tender, 1 to 1½ hours, basting now and then with pan drippings to which you have added the 2 tablespoons of butter.
5. Transfer the Cornish hens to individual plates, spoon over the pan drippings, and serve immediately.

ROAST DUCK WITH CRANBERRY COMPOTE

Here the ducks are steamed before being roasted, a process that helps to de-fat them considerably. The results are a crisp skin and fewer calories.

Serves 6

> 2 4½-pound ducks, rinsed and patted dry, necks chopped in 4 pieces and reserved
>
> ½ teaspoon salt
>
> 2 onions, quartered
>
> 4 bay leaves, crumbled

Balsamic-Vinegar Sauce

> 4 cups chicken stock
>
> 1 onion, quartered
>
> 1 carrot, sliced into ¼-inch rounds
>
> 4 garlic cloves, crushed
>
> ½ teaspoon dried thyme
>
> ½ cup dry white wine
>
> 2 tomatoes, peeled, seeded, and diced
>
> 2 tablespoons balsamic vinegar (available at some supermarkets and in specialty foods stores)
>
> ⅛ teaspoon salt
>
> Freshly ground black pepper
>
> 1 tablespoon grainy mustard

Cranberry Compote

> Juice of 3 oranges (1¼ to 1½ cups)
>
> 1 cup dark raisins
>
> 1 12-ounce package cranberries
>
> 1 tablespoon sugar

1. Trim any excess skin and fat from around the necks of the ducks. Remove any fat from the cavities. Pour enough water into a turkey roaster to fill it 1 inch deep, and set a metal rack or steamer in the water. Bring the water to a boil on top of the stove. To release fat from the ducks without rendering their juices, lightly prick both legs with a wooden pick or a skewer, taking care not to pierce the flesh below the layer of fat. Place one duck breast side down in the pan. Cover and steam it for 15 minutes. Remove the duck from the roaster; steam the other duck.

2. Preheat the oven to 375°F.

3. Lightly prick the legs of both ducks again and pour off the juices from their cavities. Sprinkle the ducks inside and out with the ½ teaspoon of salt. Place half of the onions and bay leaves in the cavity of each duck. Put the ducks breast side down on a rack in a large roasting pan, and roast them for 30 minutes. Remove the ducks from the oven and reduce the temperature to 325°F.

4. Turn the ducks breast side up and prick the entire skin. Return them to the oven and roast until the skin turns a deep golden brown, 1 hour and 15 minutes to 1 hour and 30 minutes.

5. While the ducks are roasting, begin preparing the sauce. In a large saucepan, place the duck necks, stock, onion, carrot, garlic, and thyme. Bring the liquid to a simmer over medium heat and cook it until it is reduced to 2 cups, about 45 minutes. Pour the enriched stock through a fine sieve and reserve it.

6. While the stock is simmering, make the cranberry compote. Put the orange juice and raisins in a saucepan and bring the liquid to a boil. Reduce the heat to low, cover, and cook for 5 minutes. Remove the pan from the heat and let it stand, still covered, for 5 minutes more. Purée the raisins and juice in a food processor or blender. Return the purée to the saucepan and add the cranberries and sugar. Bring the mixture to a boil, then reduce the heat to low, cover, and simmer until the cranberries have burst and almost all the liquid has been absorbed, about 15 minutes. Pour the compote into a serving bowl.

7. When the ducks are done, place them on a carving board while you finish making the sauce. Pour off the fat from the roasting pan and then deglaze the pan with the wine over medium-low heat. Add the enriched stock, the tomatoes, and vinegar to the pan, and bring the liquid to a simmer. Stir in the salt, some pepper, and the mustard. Raise the heat to medium high and cook rapidly until the sauce is reduced to about 1¾ cups.

8. Carve the ducks, arranging the pieces on a serving platter. Pour the sauce over the pieces and serve the cranberry compote on the side.

ROAST DUCK STUFFED WITH PEARS AND GARLIC

In this recipe, as in the preceding one, the duck is steamed, then roasted, to eliminate as much fat as possible.

Serves 4

> 1 5-pound duck, rinsed and patted dry
>
> 1 tablespoon unsalted butter
>
> 15 to 20 garlic cloves, peeled, the large ones cut in half
>
> 1 pound Seckel or Bosc pears, slightly underripe, cut into ¾-inch cubes and tossed with 1 tablespoon lime juice
>
> 1 tablespoon fresh rosemary, or 1 teaspoon dried rosemary
>
> 1 teaspoon sugar
>
> ¼ teaspoon salt
>
> 1 bunch watercress for garnish

1. Trim any excess skin and fat from around the neck of the duck. Remove any fat from the cavity. Cover the bottom of a large pot with 1 inch of water and set a metal rack or steamer in the pot. Bring the water to a boil on top of the stove. To help release fat while steaming, lightly prick the duck around the legs with a wooden pick or a skewer, taking care not to pierce the flesh below the layer of fat. Place the duck breast side down in the pot. Cover it tightly and steam the duck for 30 minutes.

2. Preheat the oven to 350°F.

3. While the duck is steaming, make the stuffing. Melt the butter in a heavy skillet over medium heat. Cook the

THE GOOSE CLUB

The secret to Bob Cratchit's ability to buy even a small Christmas goose for his large family may have been his membership in a goose club. Forerunner of this century's Christmas Clubs, English goose clubs collected a small weekly sum year round from subscribers, usually working-class folk. Thus, like their wealthier neighbors, they, too, might relish a goose on Christmas Day—most likely purchased at London's overflowing Leadenhall or Newgate markets.

garlic cloves in the butter, stirring frequently, until they begin to soften and brown, about 12 minutes. Stir in the pears, rosemary, and sugar, and cook until the pears are soft, about 8 minutes more. Set the stuffing aside.

4. When the duck has finished steaming, sprinkle it inside and out with the salt. Place the duck on a rack in a roasting pan, breast side down, and roast it for 15 minutes. Remove the duck and reduce the oven temperature to 325°F.

5. Turn the duck breast side up on the rack. Prick the breast and legs of the duck. Fill the cavity with the pear-garlic mixture. Return the bird to the oven and roast it until the skin turns a deep golden brown, about 1 hour and 30 minutes. Cut the duck into quarters and garnish with the watercress.

ROAST GOOSE STUFFED WITH APPLES AND PRUNES

━━━━━◆◆◆◆◆━━━━━

Serves 8 to 10

1 8- to 10-pound young goose

½ lemon

Salt and freshly ground black pepper

2 cups peeled, cored, and coarsely chopped apples

2 cups presoaked dried prunes, pitted and chopped

1 large onion, peeled and quartered

1. Preheat the oven to 325°F.
2. Wash the goose under cold running water. Pat it thoroughly dry with paper towels, then rub the bird inside and out with the cut side of half a lemon. Lightly salt and pepper the inside, and stuff the cavity with the apples, prunes, and onion. Close the opening by lacing it with skewers or by sewing it with heavy white thread. Fasten the neck skin to the back of the goose with a skewer and truss the bird securely so that it will keep its shape while cooking.
3. Roast the goose on a rack set in a shallow open pan for 3 to 3½ hours (about 20 to 25 minutes to the pound). As the goose fat accumulates in the pan, draw it off with a bulb baster or large kitchen spoon. Basting the goose is unnecessary.
4. To test whether the bird is done, pierce the thigh with the tip of a small, sharp knife. If the juice is a pale yellow, set the finished bird in the turned-off oven with the door ajar for about 15 minutes to make it easier to carve.
5. Transfer the goose to a large heated platter and remove the string and skewers. Scoop out the stuffing and discard it. The fruits and onion will have imparted their flavor to the goose but will be far too fatty to serve.

NOTE: If you like, additional chopped apples and prunes may be cooked separately and served with the goose.

OYSTER STUFFING FOR TURKEY

Makes enough for a 10-pound turkey

   1 pint shucked oysters, drained (about 18 oysters)

   2 cups unsalted soda-cracker crumbs or crumbled water biscuits

   1 cup light cream

   4 tablespoons butter, melted

   Salt and pepper

1. Place the oysters and the cracker crumbs in a large bowl. Pour in the cream and butter, season with salt and pepper, and mix all the ingredients gently together.
2. Set the mixture aside for about 1 hour to allow the flavors to mingle.

NEW ENGLAND DRESSING

Makes enough for a 10-pound turkey

   8 cups cubed stale bread, crusts removed

   1 cup finely chopped onion

   ½ cup butter

   ¾ teaspoon dried thyme

   ¾ teaspoon dried sage

   1 tablespoon salt

   1½ teaspoons white pepper

   ¼ teaspoon powdered bay leaf

   1 stalk celery, diced

   ½ cup coarsely chopped celery leaves

   1 small apple, peeled, cored, and diced

1. Preheat the oven to 300°F.
2. Place the bread cubes in a shallow pan and bake them until dry but not brown, 10 to 15 minutes. Place the dried cubes in a large bowl.
3. In a medium-size skillet over medium heat, cook the onion in the butter, stirring often, until it is transparent, about 5 minutes. Add the thyme, sage, salt, pepper, and bay leaf, and blend.
4. Add the celery, celery leaves, and the apple to the skillet. Cook 3 to 5 minutes more.

5. Add the cooked vegetables and herbs to the bread cubes and toss to mix thoroughly.

LOUISIANA YAM AND APPLE STUFFING

Makes enough for 2 ducklings, 2 capons, or a 12-pound turkey

   4 cups peeled, cored, and diced apples

   1 cup chopped celery

   1 cup water

   6 large yams (about 3 pounds)

   2 tablespoons lemon juice

   1 teaspoon ground cinnamon

   8 tablespoons butter

   1 cup firmly packed dark brown sugar

   Salt

   1 cup chopped pecans

   Grated zest of 1 lemon

1. In a large saucepan, simmer the apples and celery in the water until just tender. Drain, reserving the liquid.
2. Meanwhile, in another large saucepan, boil the yams in water to cover, about 25 minutes until they are tender when pierced with a fork.
3. Peel the yams into a bowl and mash them together with the lemon juice, cinnamon, butter, brown sugar, and salt. Moisten the mixture with the apple and celery liquid. Stir in the apples, celery, pecans, and lemon zest. Taste and correct the seasoning.

Seafood

ANY ITALIAN-AMERICANS HONOR THE custom of the feast of the Seven Fishes on Christmas Eve, a tradition that symbolizes the seven sacraments of the Roman Catholic Church. Though seven seafood dishes in one meal may stagger the imagination of some of us, seafood in its many forms offers a multitude of ideas for both holiday entertaining and quick family meals, and a nice change from the somewhat heavier holiday meals involving roasts and hams. Rich, steamy chowders or stews, hot, spicy curries or chilies, elegant stuffed fillets or a seafood risotto are appropriate for almost every taste and occasion. Fish offers delectable results in the shortest amount of time of almost any food. Since fish requires very little cooking, and indeed is often ruined by overcooking, many seafood dishes are quick to prepare, a particularly appealing feature for busy holiday cooks. Dishes such as Lobster and Pasta with Marsala-Tomato Sauce and the traditional Spanish specialty, Paella, would be especially colorful features of any holiday buffet table.

Lobster and Pasta with Marsala-Tomato Sauce

BRAISED SALMON IN RED WINE

Serves 6 to 8

  6 to 8 pounds whole salmon

  2 onions, thinly sliced

  2 stalks celery, cut into strips

  1 carrot, cut into thin strips

  3 sprigs parsley

  1 leek, cleaned and cut into strips

  10 tablespoons butter

  Salt

  4 cups (or more) red wine

  1 teaspoon dried thyme

  1 bay leaf

  18 small white onions, peeled

  1 pound mushrooms

1. Place the sliced onions, celery, carrot, parsley, and leek in the bottom of a large fish cooker or braising pan with 5 tablespoons of the butter. Cover and let cook over medium heat until the vegetables are soft, about 10 minutes. Salt the salmon inside and out, and place it on the bed of vegetables. Add red wine to half the depth of the fish in the pan, and put in the thyme and bay leaf.
2. Bring just to a boil. Cover the fish with a piece of parchment paper, and simmer it for 30 to 40 minutes or until the salmon is cooked through.
3. Meanwhile, brown the small onions in 3 tablespoons of butter in a large skillet. Cover the pan and let them cook until tender, about 10 to 15 minutes. In another skillet, sauté the mushrooms lightly in the remaining butter and season to taste.
4. Baste the fish from time to time.

When it is cooked, arrange the salmon on a hot platter and surround it with the onions and mushrooms. Strain the pan juices and serve in a separate sauce dish.

ROLLED STUFFED FISH FILLETS

Serves 4 to 6

  8 fillets firm-fleshed white fish, such as pike, perch, or sole

  6 tablespoons unsalted butter, plus 1 tablespoon butter, softened, and 1 tablespoon butter, cut into ¼-inch bits

  4 to 6 slices white bread, trimmed and cut into ¼-inch dice (2½ cups)

  3 tablespoons finely cut chives or green onion tops

  ¼ teaspoon dried thyme

  ½ teaspoon dried tarragon

  ½ teaspoon salt

  ¼ teaspoon white pepper

Sauce

  ½ cup sour cream

  1 tablespoon flour

  1 teaspoon strained lemon juice

  ½ teaspoon salt

  1 tablespoon tomato purée

1. Wash the fish fillets under cold running water and pat them thoroughly dry with paper towels. Place the fillets side by side on a flat surface and trim them evenly to 8- or 9-inch lengths. Place the fillets in the refrigerator while you prepare the stuffing. Gather all the fish you have trimmed from the fillets and chop it fine.
2. In a 10- to 12-inch skillet, melt 2 tablespoons of the butter over medium heat. Stir in the chopped fish and, stirring it constantly, cook it over medium heat until the flesh becomes opaque, about 4 to 5 minutes. Transfer it to a large bowl and set it aside.
3. Add 4 tablespoons of butter to the

skillet and drop in the bread cubes. Toss them with a wooden spoon until they are a light gold, then add them to the bowl of fish. Sprinkle the fish and bread cubes with the chives or green onion tops, thyme, tarragon, salt, and pepper, and toss them together lightly but thoroughly.

4. Preheat the oven to 400°F.

5. With a pastry brush, lightly coat the bottom and sides of a 9-by-12-inch flameproof baking dish with the table-spoon of softened butter. Place 2 table-spoons of the herbed stuffing on the narrow end of each fillet and gently roll up the fillets. Arrange them seam side down in the baking dish and dot with the tablespoon of butter bits. Bake in

the center of the oven until the fish feels firm when prodded gently with a finger, 12 to 15 minutes. Turn off the oven. With a spatula, transfer the fish rolls to a heated platter and keep them warm in the turned-off oven while you make the sauce.

6. To make the sauce, in a small bowl combine the sour cream with the flour. Place the flameproof baking dish over moderate heat and gradually whisk in the sour cream and flour mixture, the lemon juice, and salt. Stir in the tomato purée and taste for seasoning.

7. Spoon the sauce over the fish rolls. Or, if you prefer, present the sauce sep-arately in a heated sauceboat.

CHRISTMAS IN JAMESTOWN

Hospitality began early in the history of American Christmases. In 1607, Chief Powhatan's friendly Indians offered a Christmas feast to the discouraged, stranded, and chilled Jamestown settlers. And what did they eat? "Good oysters, fish, flesh, wild foule, and good bread," recorded a grateful Captain John Smith, noting that "we were never more merrie nor fedd on more plentie."

CODFISH CAKES WITH GINGER

These spicy codfish cakes bear little resemblance to the traditional New England ones that were made with salted dried cod and served with baked beans for Sunday breakfast.

Serves 4

- 2 pounds cod fillets
- 2 eggs, slightly beaten
- ⅔ cup fresh white bread crumbs (about 5 slices of bread)
- 2 tablespoons chopped cilantro (fresh coriander) or parsley
- 1 tablespoon grated fresh ginger root
- ¼ cup mayonnaise
- 1 teaspoon hot pepper oil (available with Oriental products at some supermarkets and in specialty foods stores)
- Salt
- ½ cup butter

1. Pour enough water into a large saucepan or steamer to fill it about 1 inch deep. Set a steaming rack into the pan and place the cod fillets on it. Cover the pan and bring the water to a boil. Reduce the heat to medium and steam the cod for 7 minutes.
2. Drain the cod. Place it in a large bowl and gently separate it into flakes. Add the eggs, bread crumbs, cilantro or parsley, ginger, mayonnaise, hot pepper oil, and salt to taste. Mix well.
3. Shape the codfish mixture into 7 or 8 patties.
4. Melt the butter in a large skillet. Sauté the patties over medium heat until brown, about 3 minutes on each side.

BLACK-EYED PEAS, SAUSAGE, AND MONKFISH

Serves 6

- 1 pound hot Italian sausages, cut into 12 pieces
- 1 pound monkfish, cut crosswise into ½-inch slices
- 1½ cups dried black-eyed peas, picked over, soaked overnight, and drained
- Chicken stock
- 1 large garlic clove, finely chopped
- ¼ cup red wine
- Soy sauce
- Lemon juice
- 3 tablespoons unsalted butter
- 2 tablespoons finely chopped fresh parsley
- 1 large sweet red pepper, seeded, deribbed, and cut into strips
- 1 large green pepper, seeded, deribbed, and cut into strips

1. Preheat the oven to 450°F.
2. Put the black-eyed peas in a medium-size saucepan and pour in enough chicken stock to come about an inch above the peas. Simmer until they are tender, about 30 minutes. Set them aside.
3. Put the sausages in a large cold skillet, turn the heat to medium-low, and

cook them for 5 minutes. Add the garlic and cook until the sausages begin to brown, about 10 minutes more. Add the wine and simmer, covered, for 15 minutes.

4. While the sausages are cooking, rub the monkfish slices on all sides with soy sauce and place them in a single layer in a foil-lined baking pan. Squeeze lemon juice over the fish. Bake in the oven for 7 minutes. Then set them aside in the pan.

5. Add the butter to the sausages and wine. When it melts, add the parsley and peppers. Toss to coat them with butter. Cook over low heat, covered, until the peppers are tender, about 4 minutes.

6. To assemble, drain the cooked black-eyed peas (reserving the liquid) and add them to the sausage-pepper mixture. Then stir in 2 tablespoons of liquid from the fish pan and ¼ cup of the reserved black-eyed pea liquid. Simmer for 5 minutes, covered. Cut each slice of fish in half and toss very carefully with the other ingredients. Cover and simmer only until the fish is heated through, 2 to 3 minutes. Correct the seasoning, if necessary.

LINGUINE WITH MUSSELS IN SAFFRON SAUCE

Serves 4

- 2 pounds large mussels, scrubbed and debearded
- 1 tablespoon vegetable oil
- 1 shallot, finely chopped
- 2 tablespoons flour
- ½ cup dry vermouth
- ½ teaspoon saffron threads, steeped for 10 minutes in ¾ cup hot water
- 12 ounces linguine
- 1½ teaspoons plus ¼ teaspoon salt
- ¼ cup freshly grated Romano cheese
  Freshly ground black pepper
- 1 tablespoon finely cut chives or green onion tops

1. Put the mussels and ½ cup of water in a large pan; cover the pan and steam the mussels over high heat until they open, about 5 minutes. Remove the mussels from the pan with a slotted spoon and set them aside. Discard any mussels that do not open.

2. When the mussels are cool enough to handle, remove the meat from the shells, working over the pan to catch any liquid; set the meat aside and discard the shells. Strain the liquid left in the bottom of the pan through a very fine sieve to remove any sand. Set the liquid aside.

3. Heat the oil in a heavy skillet over medium-high heat. Add the shallot and sauté it for 30 seconds. Remove the pan from the heat. Whisk in the flour, then the vermouth and the saffron liquid (whisking prevents lumps from forming). Return the skillet to the heat and simmer the sauce over medium-low heat until it thickens, 2 to 3 minutes.

4. Meanwhile, cook the linguine in 3 quarts of boiling water with 1½ teaspoons of salt. Start testing the pasta after 10 minutes and cook it until it is al dente.

5. While the linguine cooks, finish the sauce. Stir in ¼ cup of the strained mussel-cooking liquid along with the cheese, the ¼ teaspoon salt, pepper, chives or green onion tops, and mussels. Simmer the sauce to heat the mussels through, 3 to 4 minutes more.

6. Drain the linguine, transfer it to a bowl, and toss it with the sauce. Serve immediately.

SCALLOPS IN WHITE WINE

Serves 6

    2 pounds bay or sea scallops

    1½ cups cracker meal

    6 slices bread, crusts removed

    ¾ cup butter

    ½ teaspoon salt

    ¼ teaspoon white pepper

    ⅛ teaspoon paprika

    ⅓ cup dry white wine

    Pinch of dried tarragon

    Parsley sprigs for garnish

1. If sea scallops are used, cut them into small pieces. Place the cracker meal in a paper bag, add the scallops, and shake until they are evenly coated with the cracker meal. Put the scallops on a plate and let them sit, uncovered, for 20 minutes, to set the coating.

2. Preheat the oven to 200°F.

3. Toast the bread until it is lightly browned and place it on a serving platter in the oven to keep it warm.

4. In a large skillet, melt the butter and add the salt, pepper, and paprika. Add the scallops and sauté them over medium-high heat, tossing and turning them until they are opaque and golden brown, about 5 minutes.

5. Remove the scallops from the skillet and heap them on the toast slices. Return the platter to the oven to keep it warm.

6. Add the wine to the pan juices and simmer for 1 minute, stirring constantly, to dissolve the browned particles on the bottom of the pan. Add the tarragon, crumbled. Pour the sauce over the scallops, garnish with parsley, and serve immediately.

PAELLA

In Spain, a paella can be deliciously simple or splendidly elaborate. Vary the combination of chicken, meats, and shellfish to your taste. Cubed pork, smoked ham, beef, or veal can be added. Rabbit could replace the chicken legs. Squid and even snails are appropriate additions. Green beans can replace the peas, and artichoke hearts add a touch of elegance.

Serves 6 to 8

    4 cups chicken stock

    ½ teaspoon crumbled saffron threads

    ½ cup olive oil

    6 to 8 chicken legs

    1 large onion, chopped

    2 garlic cloves, finely chopped

    2 cups uncooked long-grain white rice

    1 teaspoon salt

    Freshly ground black pepper

    3 1-pound lobsters, cut into serving pieces *(see Note)*

    1½ pounds shrimp, peeled with tails left on, deveined, rinsed, and patted dry

    2 dozen mussels, scrubbed and debearded

    2 dozen hard-shell clams, scrubbed

    1 pound chorizo or other garlic-seasoned smoked pork sausage, sliced

    4 tomatoes, peeled, seeded, and quartered

    1½ cups green peas

    4 ounces pimientos, sliced

1. Preheat the oven to 325°F.
2. Bring the chicken stock to a boil in a stainless-steel pan, and in it dissolve the saffron. Set the pan aside. In a heavy 10- to 12-inch skillet, heat the olive oil over medium heat until it is very hot but not smoking. Add the chicken legs and brown them evenly. With tongs or a perforated spoon, transfer the legs to a bowl and cover it to keep them warm. Add the onion and garlic to the oil in the skillet and cook, stirring frequently with a wooden spoon, until the onion is soft but not brown, about 5 minutes.
3. Add the rice to the pan and cook it until it is translucent and faintly golden, about 2 minutes. Pour in the chicken stock, add the salt and a generous grinding of pepper, cover the skillet, and cook over low heat for 10 minutes so the rice absorbs some stock.
4. With a pastry brush, spread a generous coating of olive oil inside one 10- to 12-quart or two 6- to 8-quart casseroles or paella pans. Place half of the lobsters, shrimp, mussels, clams, chorizo slices, tomatoes, peas, and pimiento in the casserole. Top this with about three-quarters of the rice mixture. Arrange the chicken legs and the rest of the shellfish, chorizo, tomatoes, peas, and pimiento on top, and spoon the remaining rice and broth around them.
5. Cover the casserole and bake for 30 minutes. Check once or twice and, if it seems too dry, add boiling liquid—either stock or water. Remove the cover from the casserole and bake until the rice is fluffy, about 10 minutes more. Serve from the casserole.

NOTE: Before cutting the lobsters into serving pieces, kill them by turning them on their backs and making a slit down the center with a sharp knife.

LOBSTER AND PASTA WITH MARSALA-TOMATO SAUCE

Serves 4

- 2 live lobsters (about 1¼ pounds each)
- 1 tablespoon vegetable oil
- 1 small onion, finely chopped
- 2 garlic cloves, finely chopped
- 1 cup Marsala wine
- 2½ pounds ripe tomatoes, peeled, seeded, and chopped, the juice reserved, or 28 ounces canned tomatoes, chopped, the juice reserved
- 2 tablespoons tomato paste
- 1 tablespoon chopped fresh oregano, or ½ tablespoon dried oregano
- Freshly ground black pepper
- ¼ teaspoon salt
- 6 ounces penne or ditalini (macaroni-shaped pastas), about 2 cups
- 4 or 5 oregano sprigs for garnish (optional)

1. To cook the lobsters, pour enough water into a large pot to fill it about 1 inch deep. Bring the water to a boil, place the lobsters in the water, and tightly cover the pot. Cook the lobsters until they turn red, about 10 minutes. Remove the lobsters from the pot and set them aside until they are cool enough to handle.

2. Scoop out and reserve the tomalley, the greenish liver of the lobster, and extract the meat from the shells, reserving the larger pieces of shell. Cut the meat into 1-inch chunks and set it aside.

3. To make the sauce, heat the oil in a large casserole over medium heat. Add the onion and cook it, stirring occasionally, until it is translucent, about 2 minutes. Add the garlic and cook it for 30 seconds, then pour in the Marsala and add the reserved lobster shells. Cook the mixture until the wine is reduced by half, about 2 minutes. Add the tomatoes and their juice, the tomato paste, the tomalley, the oregano, some pepper, and the salt. Partially cover the pot, and cook the sauce at a brisk simmer until the liquid is reduced by three quarters, about 20 minutes.

4. While the sauce is simmering, add the penne or ditalini to 2½ quarts of boiling water with 1 teaspoon of salt. Start testing the pasta after 10 minutes and cook it until it is al dente.

5. Remove the lobster shells from the sauce and discard them. Drain the penne and add it to the sauce, then add the lobster meat and cook the mixture over medium heat until it is heated through, about 3 minutes. Garnish the dish with oregano sprigs, if you wish, and serve immediately.

SHRIMP CURRY

Serve the curry with one or more chutneys and, if you wish to be traditional, pass small bowls of chopped peanuts, minced green onions, flaked coconut, and sliced bananas.

Serves 6 to 8

- 3½ pounds raw shrimp, peeled and deveined
- ¼ cup butter
- 4 large onions, chopped
- 3 garlic cloves, chopped
- 3 cups unsweetened coconut milk or water
- 3 large tomatoes, peeled, seeded, and chopped
- 2 large apples, peeled, cored, and chopped
- 2 stalks celery, chopped
- 1 tablespoon unsweetened shredded coconut
- 1 slice fresh ginger root the size of a quarter, finely chopped, or ¾ teaspoon ground ginger
- 1 tablespoon sugar
- 1½ tablespoons (or more) curry powder
- 1½ tablespoons flour
- 1½ teaspoons salt

¼ teaspoon freshly ground black
  pepper

Hot cooked rice

1. In a large skillet, melt the butter over medium heat, add the onions and garlic, and cook until lightly browned, about 5 minutes. Add the coconut milk or water and bring to a boil.
2. Add the tomatoes, apples, celery, coconut, and fresh ginger, if used.
3. In a small bowl, combine the sugar, curry powder, flour, salt and pepper, and ground ginger, if used. Whisk in enough cold water to make a paste. Add the paste gradually to the boiling mixture, stirring constantly. Simmer, partly covered, stirring occasionally, until the vegetables are tender, about 40 minutes.
4. Add the shrimp and cook 5 minutes longer. Serve over rice.

NOTE: Unsweetened coconut milk is available in many supermarkets and in Asian food markets.

LOBSTER IN SHERRIED CREAM

Serves 4 to 6

2 cups cooked lobster meat (frozen, canned, or fresh)

¼ cup butter

1½ tablespoons flour

½ teaspoon curry powder

½ cup dry sherry

2 cups light cream

2 egg yolks

¼ cup heavy cream

¼ cup freshly grated Gruyère or Parmesan cheese

1. Preheat the oven to 300°F.
2. In a large skillet, melt the butter over medium heat. When the foam subsides, add the lobster meat and sauté it, stirring frequently, until it is well coated, about 3 minutes. Remove the lobster from the skillet with a slotted spoon and set it aside.

CHRISTMAS CATS

For true cat fanciers—those whose cats dine on gourmet fare all year through—this may seem superfluous. But French tradition has it that it is unlucky for a cat to meow on Christmas Eve, and thus the felines of France are fed all they can eat on that night of all nights.

3. Add the flour and curry powder to the pan and rub with a wooden spoon to make a paste. Stir in the sherry and the light cream. Simmer for 3 minutes over very low heat, stirring constantly.
4. In a small bowl, mix together the egg yolks and heavy cream. Pour some of the sherry mixture into this mixture, slowly. Stir the egg-cream mixture back into the sauce, add the lobster, and mix well.
5. Transfer the lobster and sauce to a buttered gratin dish and bake until the sauce bubbles, about 10 minutes. Sprinkle the top with the cheese and place it under the broiler until it is lightly browned.

Vermicelli with tomatoes and clams

Before steaming the clams, discard any that fail to close when they are tapped.

Serves 4

    36 small hard-shell clams, scrubbed
    ⅓ cup red wine
    5 parsley sprigs
    6 garlic cloves, finely chopped
    1½ tablespoons olive oil
    1 small carrot, peeled and thinly sliced
    1 onion, finely chopped
    4 pounds ripe tomatoes, peeled, seeded, and chopped, or 48 ounces canned whole tomatoes, drained and chopped
    2 teaspoons finely chopped fresh oregano, or 1 teaspoon dried oregano
    1½ teaspoons finely chopped fresh thyme, or ½ teaspoon dried thyme
    Freshly ground black pepper
    8 ounces vermicelli or thin spaghetti
    1½ teaspoons salt
    1 tablespoon unsalted butter

1. In a large pot, combine the clams, wine, parsley, and half of the garlic. Cover the pot tightly and steam the clams over medium-high heat for 5 minutes. Transfer to a bowl any clams that have opened. Re-cover the pot and steam the remaining clams for about 3 minutes more. Again, transfer the opened clams to the bowl; discard any clams that are still closed. Strain the wine mixture remaining in the pot through a very fine sieve to remove any sand and reserve ⅓ cup of it for the sauce. When the clams are cool enough to handle, remove them from their shells and reserve them along with any liquid remaining in the bowl.
2. To make the sauce, pour the oil into a large heavy saucepan over medium heat. Add the carrot and onion, and sauté them until the onion is translu-

cent, about 5 minutes. Add the remaining garlic and cook the mixture for 3 minutes more. Stir in the tomatoes, oregano, and thyme. Reduce the heat to low and continue cooking, stirring often, until the sauce is quite thick, about 15 minutes. Then add the clams to the sauce, along with their liquid and the reserved wine mixture. Stir in a generous amount of black pepper.
3. About 5 minutes after adding the tomatoes to the sauce, put the vermicelli into 3 quarts of boiling water with the salt. Start testing the vermicelli after 6 minutes and cook it until it is al dente.
4. Drain the vermicelli and return it to the cooking pot; add the butter and toss well to coat the pasta. Pour the clam sauce over the pasta and serve at once.

Sherried crab meat

Serves 8

    2 6½-ounce cans crab meat, picked over
    ¼ cup butter
    3 tablespoons flour
    ½ teaspoon salt
    Dash of black pepper
    Dash of cayenne pepper
    ¾ cup bottled clam juice
    ½ cup heavy cream
    1½ tablespoons dry sherry
    1 egg, hard-cooked, peeled, and finely chopped
    1 tablespoon finely chopped onion
    ½ cup sliced mushrooms
    1 tablespoon finely cut chives or green onion tops
    1 tablespoon finely chopped fresh parsley
    ¼ cup dry bread crumbs
    8 baked puff pastry shells (available frozen at supermarkets)
    Grated Parmesan cheese

1. In a medium-size saucepan, melt 3 tablespoons of the butter. Remove the pan from the heat and whisk in the flour, salt, black pepper, and cayenne. Return it to the heat and cook until the mixture bubbles, about 2 minutes. Gradually stir in the clam juice and cream. Bring the mixture to a boil, stirring constantly, and continue cooking until it is thickened and smooth, about 5 minutes.
2. Add the sherry, egg, and crab meat, reduce the heat, and gently stir as the mixture heats through.
3. Heat the remaining butter in a small skillet over medium heat and sauté the onion, mushrooms, chives or green onion tops, and parsley until the mushrooms are tender, about 5 minutes. Stir in the bread crumbs.
4. Turn on the broiler.
5. Place the puff pastry shells on a baking sheet. Fill the shells with the crab meat mixture and top with the mushroom mixture. Sprinkle each shell with grated Parmesan cheese. Place under the broiler until the cheese is browned, about 3 minutes (watch carefully to be sure the top doesn't burn). Serve immediately.

CRAB MEAT QUICHE

Serves 8

Crust

> 1½ cups flour
>
> ½ teaspoon salt
>
> ½ cup unsalted butter
>
> 1 egg yolk
>
> 2 to 3 tablespoons chilled dry white wine

Filling

> 1 pound crab meat, picked over
>
> 6 tablespoons unsalted butter
>
> 3 tablespoons chopped fresh parsley
>
> 1 teaspoon dried tarragon
>
> Salt and white pepper
>
> 3 eggs

> 3 egg yolks
>
> 2 cups heavy cream
>
> Dash of nutmeg
>
> A few drops of Worcestershire sauce
>
> ¾ pound Swiss cheese, preferably Jarlsberg, grated

1. To make the crust, sift the flour and salt into a large bowl. With a pastry blender or two knives, cut the butter into the flour until the texture resembles coarse cornmeal. Mix the egg yolk and wine and add it to the flour mixture, stirring with a fork until the dough forms a ball.
2. To make the crust in a food processor, place the flour, salt, and butter in the bowl and process with the steel blade attachment until the mixture resembles coarse cornmeal. Add the egg yolk and, with the motor running, gradually add white wine until the dough forms a ball.
3. On a floured surface, roll out the dough to fit a 10- or 11-inch quiche or pie pan. Flute the edges and prick the bottom of the crust with a fork. Chill the crust while making the filling.
4. Preheat the oven to 450°F.
5. To make the filling, melt the butter in a large skillet over medium heat and sauté the crab meat for several minutes to coat with butter. Add the parsley, tarragon, and salt and pepper to taste. Remove the seasoned crab meat from the heat.
6. In a large bowl, beat the eggs and egg yolks together until frothy. Add the cream, nutmeg, Worcestershire sauce, and cheese and stir well.
7. Add the crab meat to the cream mixture and blend thoroughly. Pour the filling into the chilled pie shell and bake for 10 minutes. Reduce the heat to 350°F. and continue baking until the filling is puffed and golden brown, 30 to 35 minutes more.

THE FAVORITE OYSTER

Oysters were once extremely plentiful along American shores. In fact, to the first settlers it must have seemed almost as it did to the Walrus and the Carpenter in Alice in Wonderland that

> *Thick and fast they came at last,*
>
> *And more, and more, and more—*
>
> *All hopping through the frothy waves,*
>
> *And scrambling to the shore.*

Because of their abundance, oysters were a staple food and have thus long been an integral part of many traditional American Christmas foods, including Oyster Stew (page 35), Oyster Stuffing (page 97), and Scalloped Oysters below. Once thought unwholesome to eat in months whose names have an R in them, oysters are now available for eating year round.

SCALLOPED OYSTERS

Serves 4

> 1 pint shucked oysters
> ¼ cup oyster liquor
> 2 tablespoons light cream
> ½ cup day-old bread crumbs
> 1 cup cracker or rusk crumbs
> ½ cup butter, melted
> Salt and freshly ground black pepper
> Paprika

1. Preheat the oven to 425°F.
2. Drain the oysters, reserving ¼ cup of the liquor. In a small bowl, combine the oyster liquor and the cream and set it aside.
3. In another small bowl, mix the bread and cracker crumbs with the melted butter.
4. Sprinkle about one-third of the crumbs on the bottom of a buttered 1-quart casserole. Cover the crumbs with half of the oysters, half of the liquor and cream mixture, and sprinkle with salt and pepper. Add a second layer of crumbs (about one-third), the remaining oysters, the remaining liquor and cream, and more salt and pepper. Top the dish with the last of the crumbs and sprinkle them with paprika.
5. Bake in the oven until bubbly around the edges, about 30 minutes.

NOTE: Never make more than two layers of oysters in a scallop because the middle layer will remain uncooked.

SHRIMP WITH HERBS

Serves 6

> 2 pounds large shrimp, peeled, deveined, rinsed, and patted dry
> 2 tablespoons butter
> 4 green onions, trimmed and chopped
> 2 garlic cloves, crushed
> 1 tablespoon lemon juice
> ¼ cup dry white wine
> 1 tomato, peeled, seeded, and chopped
> 1 teaspoon dried basil
> 3 tablespoons finely chopped fresh parsley
> ½ teaspoon salt
> Freshly ground black pepper

1. Heat the butter in a large skillet and sauté the shrimp over medium-high heat until they are pink, about 5 minutes. Remove the shrimp from the pan and cover with foil to keep warm.
2. Add the green onions and garlic to

the skillet and sauté for 4 minutes. Add the lemon juice, wine, tomato, basil, and half of the parsley. Simmer the mixture for 3 minutes, stirring frequently.

3. Return the shrimp to the skillet and add the salt and pepper. Cook over medium heat, stirring constantly, until the shrimp are hot. Garnish with the remaining parsley and serve with rice.

FETTUCCINE WITH SCALLOP SAUCE

Serves 6 to 8

Pasta

    3 cups flour

    4 eggs

    Pinch of salt

    1 teaspoon olive oil

    (Or you may use 2 pounds packaged fettuccine noodles)

Sauce

    ¾ pound bay or sea scallops

    4 tablespoons unsalted butter

    2 small carrots, finely chopped (about 1 cup)

    ¾ cup finely chopped green onions

    ½ cup finely chopped fresh parsley

    1½ cups dry white wine

    2 tomatoes, peeled, seeded, and finely chopped

    Salt and freshly ground black pepper

    ¾ cup heavy cream

    1 tablespoon fresh tarragon, or 1 teaspoon dried tarragon

    1 tablespoon fresh thyme, or 1 teaspoon dried thyme

1. To make the pasta, mound the flour on a flat work surface and make a well in the center. Place the eggs, salt, and olive oil in the well and, using a fork, mix them with the flour. When the dough becomes stiff enough to form a ball, knead it until it becomes smooth and elastic, at least 10 minutes. Let the dough rest, covered with a paper towel, for 20 minutes.

2. Using a pasta machine, roll the dough to the next-to-narrowest setting, cut fettuccine noodles, and let the pasta dry on a baking sheet for several hours.

3. To make the sauce, melt the butter in a saucepan over medium heat. Add the carrots, green onions, and parsley, and sauté until the vegetables are limp, 3 to 5 minutes. Stir in the wine and tomatoes, reduce the heat to low, and simmer the sauce gently for 10 to 12 minutes. Add salt and pepper to taste. Add the scallops and cook them until they are no longer translucent, about 2 minutes. Remove the scallops from the sauce with a slotted spoon and set them aside.

4. Stir the cream, tarragon, and thyme into the sauce, and cook it over medium heat until it is reduced by half, about 10 minutes.

5. When almost ready to serve the dish, bring a large pan of salted water to a boil and cook the pasta until al dente (2 to 3 minutes for fresh pasta; follow package directions for packaged pasta). Drain the fettuccine well and keep it warm.

6. Return the scallops to the sauce and toss them gently to heat them through. Spoon the sauce over the cooked pasta and serve immediately.

SEAFOOD CHILI

Serves 4

1 cup black beans, picked over

8 ounces bay scallops, rinsed

4 ounces small shrimp, peeled, deveined if necessary

4 ounces tilefish fillet (or haddock or sea bass), rinsed and cut into pieces about 2 inches long and 1 inch wide

1 lime, carefully peeled to remove the white pith, sliced into thin rounds

1¼ teaspoons ground cumin

⅛ teaspoon ground ginger

1 tablespoon plus ¼ teaspoon chili powder

3 tablespoons coarsely chopped cilantro (fresh coriander) or parsley

2 garlic cloves, finely chopped

½ jalapeño pepper, seeded, deribbed, and finely chopped

3 tablespoons vegetable oil

1 onion, cut into chunks the size of scallops

½ teaspoon dried tarragon

¼ teaspoon salt

¼ teaspoon ground cloves

⅛ teaspoon ground cinnamon

⅛ teaspoon cayenne pepper

1½ cups chicken stock

8 ounces canned crushed tomatoes, with their juice

10 tomatillos, husked, cored, and quartered *(see Note)*

1 sweet red pepper, seeded, deribbed, and cut into chunks the size of the tomatillo quarters

1 yellow or green pepper, seeded, deribbed, and cut into chunks the size of the tomatillo quarters

1. Rinse the beans under cold running water, then put them into a large pot and pour in enough cold water to cover them by about 3 inches. Discard any beans that float to the surface. Cover the pot, leaving the lid ajar, and bring the liquid to a boil over medium-low heat. Boil the beans for 2 minutes, then turn off the heat, cover the pot, and soak them for at least 1 hour. (Alternatively, soak the beans overnight in cold water.)

2. Drain the beans in a colander and return them to the pot. Pour in enough water to cover the beans by about 3 inches, and bring the liquid to a boil over medium-low heat. Reduce the heat to maintain a strong simmer and cover the pot. Cook the beans, stirring occasionally and skimming any foam from the surface, until they are tender, 1½ to 2 hours.

3. While the beans are cooking, combine in a large, nonreactive bowl the scallops, shrimp, fish pieces, lime, ¼ teaspoon of the cumin, the ginger, ¼ teaspoon of the chili powder, 1 tablespoon of the cilantro or parsley, half of the garlic, the jalapeño pepper, and 1 tablespoon of the oil. Marinate the seafood in this mixture for 30 minutes at room temperature.

4. While the seafood is marinating, prepare the chili base. Heat 1 tablespoon of the remaining oil in a large, heavy pot over medium heat. Add the onion and the remaining garlic, and cook until the onion is translucent, about 5 minutes. Add the remaining teaspoon of cumin, the remaining tablespoon of chili powder, the tarragon, salt, cloves, cinnamon, and cayenne. Cook the mixture, stirring constantly, for 2 to 3 minutes to meld the flavors.

5. Gradually stir in the stock and tomatoes, and bring the mixture to a boil. Reduce the heat to medium low and cover the pot, leaving the lid slightly ajar. Simmer the liquid until it is slightly thickened, 20 to 25 minutes. Drain the beans and add them to the tomato mixture. Set the chili base aside.

6. Pour the remaining tablespoon of oil into a large, heavy skillet over high heat. Add the tomatillos and pepper chunks, and sauté them for 2 minutes. Using a slotted spoon, carefully spread the cooked vegetables over the chili base; bring the mixture to a simmer over low heat. Arrange the marinated seafood in a layer atop the chili and vegetables, then cover the pot, and steam the chili until the scallops, shrimp, and fish are opaque, 7 to 10 minutes. Sprinkle the remaining 2 tablespoons of cilantro or parsley over the chili and serve immediately.

NOTE: Though they are often called husk tomatoes, tomatillos are actually relatives of the ground cherry or cape gooseberry. They are commonly used in Southwestern American cooking, and fresh and canned tomatillos are fairly widely available in specialty foods stores throughout the country.

SEAFOOD RISOTTO

Serves 6

- ½ pound cooked shrimp, cut into large pieces
- ½ pound cooked lobster (or crab meat), cut into large pieces
- 12 steamed littleneck clams
- 2 tablespoons unsalted butter
- 2 tablespoons margarine
- 3 tablespoons olive oil
- 1 large carrot, peeled and finely chopped
- 1 large stalk celery, finely chopped
- 1 large onion, finely chopped
- 1 teaspoon fennel seed
- 1 garlic clove, crushed
- 1 cup chopped fresh parsley
- Approximately 1 quart fish stock
- 1½ cups Arborio rice (available at specialty foods stores) or regular rice
- ¾ cup dry white wine
- ½ teaspoon saffron threads
- ½ cup hot water
- Salt and freshly ground black pepper
- Butter for sautéing
- Lemon slices
- Parsley sprigs

1. In a large pot, melt the butter and margarine and heat with the olive oil over medium heat. When the mixture bubbles, add the carrot, celery, onion, and fennel seed. Sauté them gently for about 10 minutes. Add the garlic and continue cooking for 1 minute, then add the parsley. Stir and cook for 1 to 2 minutes more.

2. In a 2-quart saucepan, bring the fish stock to a boil over high heat. Turn off the heat and set it aside.

3. Add the rice to the vegetables and stir until it is well coated. Cook over medium heat, stirring constantly, until the rice begins to turn white, 2 to 3 minutes. Add the white wine and cook over medium heat until all the liquid has been absorbed.

4. Begin adding the fish stock in stages, just enough each time to barely cover the rice. Let it simmer, not boil. Stir occasionally to keep the rice from sticking to the bottom of the pot. It is better for it to cook too slowly than too fast. Continue this process until about three quarters of the stock is used. When the rice starts to become al dente, dissolve the saffron in the hot water and add it to the rice mixture, stirring constantly. The rice is done when it is al dente, chewy but not crunchy. Add pepper and salt to taste.

5. In a large skillet over medium-high heat, sauté the cut-up lobster and shrimp in a little additional butter. Using a fork, carefully combine them with the rice.

6. Spoon the rice mixture onto six individual plates and top each with two steamed clams in their opened shells. Garnish with lemon slices and parsley. Serve immediately.

NOTE: Arborio rice, grown in northern Italy, is especially appropriate for risotto, since it remains firm after cooking but releases a fair amount of starch, providing the creaminess that is typical of the dish.

Breads

HEREVER CHRISTMAS IS CELEBRATED, one finds special holiday breads, including German Stollen, Polish Poppy-Seed Roll, Danish Christmas Fruit Loaf, Italian Panettone, Greek Christmas Bread, and Portuguese Sweet Bread. Hot from the oven, these and other holiday yeast breads, quick breads, muffins, biscuits, and fritters will add old-fashioned warmth and comfort to family meals and holiday tables. Yeast bread baking, in particular, is a delight to the senses of touch, smell, and taste from the moment you begin a project until the last crumb of the rich, tender loaf has disappeared. Dough kneading is a delightfully productive way of easing tensions and getting in a bit of daydreaming at this busy time of year, as through the rhythmic pushing and folding you shape the smooth, elastic ball in your hands. Whether for gifts, entertaining, or "just" family, fill your kitchen with the rich aroma of fresh-baked bread. Who knows, producing your own loaves may be something you will want to go on doing once the holidays are over—your year-round gift to those you love.

Stollen and Apricot Ginger Muffins

115

WHEAT BERRY BREAD

Makes 3 loaves

- 1 cup wheat berries (available in natural foods stores)
- 1 envelope fast-rising dry yeast
- 2 teaspoons sugar
- ¼ cup nonfat dry milk
- ¼ cup honey
- ¼ cup molasses
- ½ cup wheat germ
- ¼ teaspoon salt
- 7 to 8 cups flour, preferably bread flour
- 1 egg, beaten
- ½ teaspoon coarse salt

1. Put the wheat berries and 3 cups of water into a saucepan and bring the water to a boil. Reduce the heat and simmer the wheat berries until they are tender, 30 to 45 minutes. Let the wheat berries cool in the cooking liquid, then drain them over a bowl; reserve the liquid.
2. In a large bowl, combine the yeast, sugar, dry milk, honey molasses, wheat germ, salt, and drained wheat berries with 6 cups of the flour.
3. Measure the reserved cooking liquid and add enough water to make 3 cups of liquid. Heat the liquid just until it is hot to the touch (130°F.). Pour the hot liquid into the flour mixture and blend well with a wooden spoon.
4. Gradually blend in up to 2 cups of additional flour, working it in with your hands until the dough becomes stiff but not dry. Turn the dough out onto a floured surface and knead the dough until it is smooth and elastic, 5 to 10 minutes. Place the dough in a clean, oiled bowl; turn the dough over to coat it with the oil, cover the bowl with a damp towel or plastic wrap, and let the dough rise in a warm, draft-free place until it is doubled in bulk, about 45 minutes.
5. Punch the dough down and divide it into three pieces. Knead one piece of the dough and form it into a ball.

Knead and form the remaining two pieces of dough into balls. Put the balls of dough onto a large baking sheet; leave enough space between the loaves for them to expand. Cover the loaves and let them rise until they have doubled in bulk, about 30 minutes.
6. About 10 minutes before the end of the rising time, preheat the oven to 350°F.
7. Bake the loaves for 25 minutes. Remove the baking sheet from the oven, brush each loaf with some of the beaten egg, then sprinkle each with a little of the coarse salt. Return the loaves to the oven and continue to bake them until they are brown and sound hollow when tapped on the bottom, 25 to 30 minutes more. Let the loaves cool to room temperature; each yields 16 slices.

NOTE: This recipe calls for fast-rising yeast, which requires a different procedure from that used with active dry or compressed yeast.

BRAIDED CHEESE BREAD WREATH

Makes 2 loaves

- 2 envelopes active dry yeast
- 2 teaspoons sugar
- ½ cup lukewarm water
- ½ cup cold unsalted butter, cut into ½-inch pieces
- 1¾ teaspoons salt
- 2½ teaspoons freshly grated nutmeg
- ½ teaspoon white pepper, preferably freshly grated, or to taste
- 1 cup milk, scalded
- 6 cups flour
- 3 eggs (at room temperature), lightly beaten
- 8 ounces coarsely grated Gruyère cheese (about 2 cups)
- An egg wash, made by beating 1 egg with 1 tablespoon water
- 1 teaspoon coarse sea salt

1. In a small bowl, sprinkle the yeast and the sugar over ½ cup lukewarm water. Let the mixture stand in the bowl until it is foamy, about 5 minutes. In the bowl of an electric mixer, beat together the butter, salt, nutmeg, pepper, and milk; add 1½ cups of the flour, and beat the mixture until it is combined well.

2. Beat in the yeast mixture and the eggs and, at low speed, beat in 1 cup of the remaining flour. Beat the mixture at high speed for 3 minutes. With a spoon, stir in about 3 cups of the remaining flour, stirring until the mixture is a soft dough.

3. Knead the dough on a surface sprinkled with the remaining flour, incorporating as much as is necessary to prevent the dough from sticking. Knead the dough until it is smooth and elastic, 8 to 10 minutes.

4. Put the dough in a clean, oiled bowl, turn the dough over to coat it with the oil, cover it with plastic wrap, and let it rise in a warm place until it is almost triple in bulk, 50 minutes to 1 hour.

5. Turn the dough out onto a lightly floured surface and knead in the Gruyère, a little at a time. Divide the dough in half, cover it with plastic wrap, and let it rest for 10 minutes.

6. Cover two baking sheets with parchment paper.

7. Divide the dough into six equal pieces and, working with one piece at a time and keeping the remaining pieces covered, roll each piece of the dough between the palms of the hands to form a 32-inch rope.

8. Arrange three ropes side by side and, starting at one end, braid them together. Transfer the braid to a baking sheet and form it into a ring 9 to 10 inches in diameter. Moisten the ends of the braid with water and join them together neatly. In the same manner, braid the remaining three ropes and form the braid into a ring on a second baking sheet.

9. Cover the loaves loosely with plastic wrap and let them rise in a warm place until they are double in bulk, 1½ to 2 hours.

10. About 10 minutes before the end of the rising time, preheat the oven to 350°F.

11. Brush the loaves with the egg wash, being careful not to let it drip onto the baking sheets, and sprinkle the loaves with the sea salt. Bake them in the lower two-thirds of the oven for 25 minutes, switch the positions of the baking sheets, and continue baking the loaves until they are golden, 15 to 20 minutes more. Transfer the loaves to racks to cool slightly and serve them warm.

SKILLET CORN BREAD AND CORN STICKS

Makes one 9-inch round, or 8 corn sticks

1½ cups cornmeal, preferably white, water-ground

½ cup flour

1 tablespoon baking powder

1 teaspoon salt

2 eggs

1½ cups buttermilk

Melted butter

1. Combine the cornmeal, flour, baking powder, and salt, and sift them into a deep bowl. In a separate bowl, beat the eggs lightly with a wire whisk or fork, then add the buttermilk and mix well. Pour the liquid ingredients over the dry ones and, with a wooden spoon, stir them together until the batter is smooth; do not overbeat.
2. Preheat the oven to 350°F.
3. To make the corn bread, place a heavy 9-inch skillet with an ovenproof handle over high heat until the skillet is very hot, about 2 minutes. Remove the skillet from the heat and, with a pastry brush, quickly coat the bottom and sides with melted butter. Immediately pour in the batter, spreading it even and smoothing the top with a rubber spatula. Bake until the corn bread begins to draw away from the edges of the skillet and the top is a rich golden

brown, 30 to 35 minutes.
4. To serve, run a knife around the edges of the skillet to loosen the sides of the bread. Place a warmed platter upside down over the skillet and, grasping platter and skillet together, invert them. Rap the platter sharply on a table, and the bread should slide out of the skillet easily. Cut the bread into wedge-shaped pieces and serve at once.
5. To make corn sticks, brush the inside surfaces of the molds in a cast-iron corn stick pan with melted butter. Spoon the batter into the molds, dividing it evenly among them. Bake until the corn sticks are golden brown, 25 to 30 minutes. Turn the corn sticks out of the pan and serve at once on a warmed platter.

MEXICAN CORN AND CHEESE BREAD

Serves 12

¼ cup olive oil

½ cup finely chopped onion

1 egg, lightly beaten

2 tablespoons honey

1 cup milk

1 cup flour

1 cup yellow cornmeal

3 teaspoons baking powder

½ teaspoon salt

1 cup fresh corn kernels or frozen corn kernels, thawed and drained

½ cup grated Cheddar cheese

1. Preheat the oven to 375°F.
2. Heat the oil in a small skillet. Add the onion and sauté over medium heat until the onion is soft and translucent, 5 to 8 minutes. Set aside to cool.
3. In a small bowl, beat together the egg, honey, and milk.
4. In a large bowl, combine thoroughly the flour, cornmeal, baking powder, and salt.

5. Add the milk mixture to the cornmeal mixture and stir until it is well blended.
6. Add the corn kernels, sautéed onions (be sure to scrape in all the excess olive oil from the pan), and grated cheese. Mix well.
7. Spread the batter in a well-greased 8-inch square pan. Bake 25 to 30 minutes, or until brown and firm on top.

BEATEN BISCUITS

These biscuits are a Southern tradition—the perfect foil for salty country ham. The "beaten" refers to the old custom of pounding the dough with a rolling pin or mallet for 30 minutes or more. The purpose of this hard work was to produce an unusually crumbly texture. In this recipe, putting the dough through a food grinder achieves a similar effect.

Makes about 2 dozen 1½-inch biscuits

      1 teaspoon butter, softened
      2 cups flour
      1½ teaspoons sugar
      1 teaspoon salt
      2 tablespoons lard, cut into ¼-inch bits
      ¼ cup milk combined with ¼ cup water

1. Preheat the oven to 400°F.
2. With a pastry brush, spread the softened butter evenly on a large baking sheet and set aside.
3. Combine the flour, sugar, and salt, and sift them into a deep bowl. Drop in the lard and, with your fingers, rub the flour and fat together until they resemble coarse cornmeal. Add the milk-and-water mixture, about 2 tablespoonfuls at a time, rubbing and kneading after each addition until the liquid is completely absorbed. Knead the dough vigorously in the bowl until it is smooth. Then put it through the coarsest blade of a food grinder four times, or until the dough is pliable and elastic.

A FORTUNE FOR A BISCUIT

How many of us would choose bread over gold? Yet the California Forty-niners would happily have made that choice at Christmas. One miner told how he made a present of two heavy gold nuggets to friends. "It was a poor enough gift," he wrote. "Gold was a common commodity with us. They'd have appreciated a hot biscuit a lot more."

4. To shape beaten biscuits the Maryland way, take a handful of the dough and squeeze your fingers into a fist, forcing the dough up between your thumb and forefinger. When it forms a ball about the size of a walnut, pinch it off and gently pat the dough into a flat round about ½ inch thick. (To shape the biscuits as they do in Virginia, gather the dough into a ball and roll it out to a ½-inch thickness on a lightly floured surface. With a biscuit cutter or the rim of a small glass, cut the dough into 1½-inch rounds. Collect the scraps into a ball again, roll it out as before, and cut as many more biscuits as you can.)
5. Place the biscuits about 1 inch apart on the buttered baking sheet. Prick the top of each one lightly with a three-tined fork to make a pattern of two or three parallel rows. Bake in the middle of the oven until the biscuits are a delicate golden color, about 20 minutes. Serve them at once with butter.

APRICOT GINGER MUFFINS

Makes 12 muffins

- 1½ cups unsalted butter
- 1 cup sugar
- 3 eggs
- 1½ teaspoons ground ginger
- 3 cups flour
- 1 teaspoon salt
- 1 tablespoon baking powder
- ½ cup milk
- 1 14-ounce can apricot halves, drained and chopped
- 3 ounces crystallized ginger, finely chopped

1. Preheat the oven to 350°F.
2. In a large bowl, cream the butter and sugar together well. Add the eggs and beat until the ingredients are thoroughly combined.
3. Sift together the ginger, flour, salt, and baking powder. Add the sifted dry ingredients to the butter mixture alternately with the milk, beginning and ending with the dry ingredients. Work quickly; do not overbeat. Fold the apricots and crystallized ginger into the batter until just combined.
4. Fill greased muffin tins to the top and bake until lightly browned around the edges, about 20 minutes.

CURRANT SCONES

Makes 12 scones

- 3 cups flour
- 2½ teaspoons baking powder
- 1 teaspoon sugar
- Pinch of salt
- Pinch of grated nutmeg
- ½ cup unsalted butter, cut into ¼-inch pieces
- ½ cup dried currants
- 2 eggs
- ½ cup heavy cream
- ½ cup milk
- An egg wash, made by beating 1 egg yolk with 1 tablespoon cream or milk

1. Preheat the oven to 375°F.
2. Sift together the flour, baking powder, sugar, salt, and nutmeg, and place them in a large bowl. Add the butter and cut it in with a pastry blender or two knives until the mixture resembles coarse cornmeal. Add the currants. Set the mixture aside.
3. In a separate bowl, whisk the eggs, cream, and milk together. Add the egg and milk mixture to the flour mixture. Mix lightly. Turn the dough out onto a floured board and roll it to a ½-inch thickness. Using a 2-inch floured biscuit cutter, cut the dough into rounds. Place the rounds on a greased baking sheet and brush the tops with the egg wash. Bake the scones until they are light golden brown, about 15 minutes. Serve them hot with plenty of butter.

CRANBERRY FRITTERS

Makes about 18 fritters

- 2 cups raw cranberries, rinsed, picked over, and coarsely chopped
- 2 eggs
- 6 tablespoons honey
- 2 tablespoons unsalted butter, melted
- 2 teaspoons grated orange zest
- 1¼ cups flour
- ¼ teaspoon salt
- 2 teaspoons baking powder
- Vegetable oil, for deep frying
- Confectioners' sugar (optional)

1. Place the cranberries in a medium-size saucepan and pour in enough water to cover the berries. Bring the water to a boil, reduce the heat to low, and cook the berries until just soft, about 7 minutes. Drain them well in a colander and then on paper towels.
2. In a medium-size bowl, beat the eggs until light and slightly thickened.

Add the honey and continue to beat. Add the melted butter and orange zest and beat to mix. Stir in the cranberries.

3. Sift together the flour, salt, and baking powder. Add the flour mixture to the cranberry mixture and stir just until the ingredients are blended; do not overmix.

4. Preheat the oil to between 350° and 365°F.

5. Drop the batter from a teaspoon into the fat. Keep a candy thermometer in the oil so you can maintain the right temperature. Fry the fritters, a few at a time, until they are golden brown on both sides, 3 to 4 minutes. Remove them with a slotted spoon and drain them on paper towels. Break open one of the first ones to check for proper doneness; the interior should be slightly moist but not runny. Sift confectioners' sugar over the fritters, if desired, and serve them while they are still warm.

NOTE: While you are making new batches, the fritters can be kept warm for a few minutes in a 200°F. oven.

MUFFINS CRÉCY

Makes 12 muffins

    1¾ cups flour

    1 teaspoon baking powder

    ½ teaspoon baking soda

    ½ teaspoon salt, or to taste

    ¼ cup firmly packed light brown sugar

    ½ cup puréed cooked carrots

    3 tablespoons vegetable oil

    1 cup buttermilk

    1 egg

1. Preheat the oven to 425°F.
2. In a medium-size bowl, combine the flour, baking powder, baking soda, and salt.
3. In a large bowl, beat together the brown sugar, carrots, oil, buttermilk, and egg.
4. Add the flour mixture to the carrot mixture. Stir only until the flour mixture is moistened but not smoothly blended.
5. Fill greased muffin cups two-thirds full and bake for 20 to 25 minutes, or until a tester inserted in the center comes out clean. Serve warm.

THE FINISHING TOUCHES

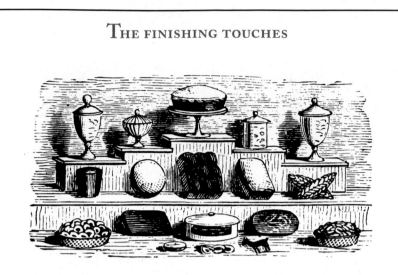

Bread dough can be formed into a variety of appealing and seasonal shapes. Braids, wreaths, and spirals, such as those of Swedish St. Lucia Buns, are surprisingly easy to do and result in impressive creations of which you will be justly proud. Add a professional touch by beating an egg with milk or water and brushing it over the loaf before baking to give a golden sheen to the finished loaf. A thin confectioners' sugar glaze drizzled over still-warm loaves puts the finishing touch on many sweet breads.

1. Preheat the oven to 375°F.

2. In a small baking pan, toast the walnuts in the oven until they are fragrant and slightly darker, about 10 minutes. Set the toasted nuts aside to cool.

3. In a bowl, combine the all-purpose flour, sugar, cinnamon, baking powder, and salt. Using a pastry blender or two knives, cut in the butter and margarine until the mixture resembles coarse cornmeal. Transfer ¼ cup of the mixture to a food processor; add the cardamom or allspice and the toasted walnuts and process to fine crumbs; this will be used as a topping for the muffins. Set the topping aside.

4. Add the whole-wheat flour and the baking soda to the remaining flour mixture and mix them in well. Pour in the buttermilk and vanilla, and stir the ingredients just until they are blended; do not overmix.

5. Spoon the batter into a lightly oiled muffin tin, filling each cup about half full. Sprinkle the muffins with the crumb topping. Bake the muffins until they are well browned and firm to the touch, 20 to 25 minutes.

CARDAMOM MUFFINS

Makes 12 muffins

¼ cup walnuts

1½ cups all-purpose flour

¾ cup sugar

½ teaspoon ground cinnamon

½ teaspoon baking powder

¼ teaspoon salt

2 tablespoons chilled unsalted butter, cut into pieces

2 tablespoons chilled unsalted margarine, preferably corn oil margarine, cut into pieces

1 teaspoon ground cardamom or ground allspice

1 cup whole-wheat flour

½ teaspoon baking soda

1¼ cups buttermilk

1 teaspoon pure vanilla extract

CARAMEL-ORANGE-PECAN STICKY BUNS

Serves 12

2 tablespoons firmly packed dark brown sugar

1½ cups plus 1 tablespoon all-purpose flour

½ teaspoon ground cinnamon

½ cup whole-wheat flour

1 tablespoon granulated sugar

1 tablespoon baking powder

¼ teaspoon salt

¾ cup milk

2 tablespoons vegetable oil

Grated zest of 1 orange

¼ cup dark raisins

Caramel-Pecan Topping

    ½ cup firmly packed dark brown sugar

    2 tablespoons freshly squeezed orange juice

    2 tablespoons honey

    ¼ cup chopped pecans

1. Preheat the oven to 375°F.

2. To make the caramel-pecan topping, combine the ½ cup brown sugar, the orange juice, and the honey in a small saucepan. Bring the mixture to a boil, then reduce the heat and simmer the liquid for 1 minute. Stir in the pecans and pour the topping into a 10-inch ring mold or an 8-inch round cake pan.

3. In a small bowl, combine the 2 tablespoons of brown sugar, 1 tablespoon of the all-purpose flour, and the cinnamon; set the bowl aside.

4. In a larger bowl, combine the remaining 1½ cups all-purpose flour,

the whole-wheat flour, granulated sugar, baking powder, and salt. Add the milk, oil, and orange zest; stir the ingredients together just until they are blended; do not overmix. Turn the dough out onto a floured surface and gently knead it just until it is smooth. Roll the dough into an 8-by-12-inch oblong. Sprinkle the dough evenly with the reserved cinnamon mixture, then with the raisins.

5. Beginning with a long side, roll the dough into a log. Cut the log into 12 slices. Set the slices in the pan, on top of the pecan mixture. Bake the coffee cake until it is brown and the pecan mixture is bubbly, 20 to 25 minutes. Remove the pan from the oven and invert it immediately onto a large serving platter. Serve warm.

When Christmas preparations are about to get you down, pause for a good cup of tea. While it may not solve all your problems, it both stimulates and relaxes. You can also use tea to entertain on a fairly simple scale. Teatime can become a special occasion if you offer some of the traditional accompaniments, such as butter cookies, small cakes, cheese crackers, tarts, fruitcakes, tiny buttered sandwiches, or scones. And make tea the proper English way: Heat a china or ceramic teapot by letting it stand filled with just boiled water while you boil a fresh kettle of water for the tea itself. When the tea water is boiling vigorously, empty the teapot, place 1 heaping teaspoon in the pot for each cup of tea you wish to serve, plus "one for the pot," and pour the boiling water over the tea. Keep the teapot warm in a tea "cozy," brew the tea for 5 minutes, then strain the tea into teacups. Experiment with different kinds of teas, including such old standbys as Earl Grey and jasmine or caffeine-free herbal or spice teas. Spiced teas are especially appropriate at Christmastime.

APPLE FRITTERS

Serves 4 to 6

> 4 to 6 cooking apples, peeled, cored, and cut crosswise into ½-inch slices
>
> White wine
>
> 2 egg yolks, slightly beaten
>
> ⅔ cup milk
>
> 1 tablespoon lemon juice
>
> 1 tablespoon butter, melted
>
> 1 cup flour
>
> ¼ teaspoon salt
>
> 2 tablespoons sugar
>
> 2 egg whites, stiffly beaten
>
> Vegetable oil, for deep frying

1. Put the apples into a large bowl. Pour in enough wine to cover the apples. Soak the slices in the wine for 2 hours.

2. In a medium-size bowl, combine the egg yolks, milk, lemon juice, butter, flour, salt, and sugar and stir with a wooden spoon until the batter is smooth. Fold in the egg whites.

3. Drain the apple slices and dip them one at a time in the fritter batter. Heat the oil in a large skillet. Fry the apple fritters until they are lightly browned all over, about 3 minutes. Drain them on paper towels and serve piping hot.

POLISH POPPY-SEED ROLL

Makes 1 roll

Filling

> ¾ cup black poppy seeds
>
> 1 tablespoon unsalted butter
>
> 3 tablespoons sugar
>
> 3 tablespoons honey
>
> 2 tablespoons dark raisins
>
> ¼ cup blanched almonds, ground in a food processor or blender or with a mortar and pestle
>
> 1 egg white

Dough

> ¾ cup lukewarm milk (110° to 115°F.)
>
> 1 envelope active dry yeast
>
> ¼ cup confectioners' sugar
>
> 2¼ cups flour
>
> 3 egg yolks
>
> 2 tablespoons rum
>
> ½ teaspoon pure vanilla extract
>
> 1½ teaspoons finely grated orange zest
>
> 6 tablespoons unsalted butter, softened

Finishing

> 1 tablespoon unsalted butter, softened
>
> 1 egg white, lightly beaten
>
> 1 egg, lightly beaten

1. To make the filling, place the poppy seeds in a small heatproof bowl, pour in enough boiling water to cover them by at least 1 inch, and let them soak for 3 hours.

2. Drain the poppy seeds in a fine sieve and spread them out on paper towels to dry. Then pulverize them in a food processor or blender or with a mortar and pestle.

3. In a small skillet, melt the butter over medium heat. When the foam begins to subside, stir in the poppy seeds, sugar, and honey. Reduce the heat to low and, stirring frequently, simmer until all the liquid in the pan has evaporated and the mixture is thick enough to hold its shape in a spoon, about 10 minutes. With a rubber spatula, scrape the entire contents of the skillet into a deep bowl. Cool to room temperature, then add the raisins and almonds, and stir until well mixed.

4. Beat the egg white with a wire whisk or a rotary or an electric beater until it forms stiff peaks on the beater when it is lifted from the bowl. Scoop the egg white over the poppy-seed mixture and, with a spatula, fold them together gently but thoroughly. Cover the bowl with foil or plastic wrap and refrigerate for at least 1 hour.

5. To make the dough, pour the milk into a small bowl and sprinkle it with the yeast and ½ teaspoon of the confectioners' sugar. Let the mixture stand for 2 to 3 minutes, then stir to dissolve the yeast completely. Set the bowl aside in a warm, draft-free place (such as an unlighted oven) until the mixture almost doubles in bulk, about 10 minutes.

6. Sift 2 cups of the flour and the remaining confectioners' sugar into a deep bowl and make a well in the center. Pour in the yeast mixture, egg yolks, rum, and vanilla and, with a large spoon, gradually stir the flour into the liquid ingredients. Continue to stir until well mixed, then stir in the orange zest and beat in the softened butter a few tablespoonfuls at a time. The dough should be just firm enough to be gathered into a ball. If necessary, stir in up to ¼ cup more flour, adding it by the tablespoon.

7. On a lightly floured surface, knead

the dough by pushing it down with the heels of your hands, pressing it forward, and folding it back on itself. Repeat—pushing, pressing, and folding—until the dough is smooth and elastic, about 10 minutes. Gather it into a ball, place it in a lightly buttered bowl, and dust the top with flour. Drape the bowl with a towel and set it aside in the draft-free place until the dough doubles in bulk, about 1 hour.

8. To finish the preparation, with a pastry brush, spread 1 tablespoon of softened butter evenly on a 15½-by-10½-inch jelly-roll pan. Punch the dough down with a single blow of your fist and, on a lightly floured surface, roll it out into a rectangle about 15 inches long and 10 inches wide and no more than ¼ inch thick. Brush the dough with the beaten egg white and then, with a metal spatula, spread the poppy-seed filling over the surface to within about ½ inch of the edges. Starting at one of the 15-inch-long sides, roll the dough jelly-roll fashion into a tight cylinder. Carefully transfer the roll, seam side down, to the buttered jelly-roll pan. Let it rise in the draft-free place for about 20 minutes, then brush the top and sides of the roll with the beaten egg.

9. About 10 minutes before the end of the rising time, preheat the oven to 325°F.

10. Bake the poppy-seed roll in the middle of the oven until it is golden brown, about 30 minutes. Transfer the roll to a wire rack and let it cool to room temperature before slicing and serving.

ST. LUCIA'S DAY

In Sweden, December 13th marks the beginning of the holiday season. In honor of the martyred St. Lucia, the prettiest young girl in each Swedish household dons a white dress and a crown with seven lighted candles, and, in the dark hours before dawn, goes through the house serving coffee and cakes, or often a wreath-shaped loaf of sweet yeast bread (St. Lucia's Buns, below). In the past, the day was spent readying the house for Christmas by scrubbing and polishing it from top to bottom and bringing in the winter's supply of wood.

PORTUGUESE SWEET BREAD

Makes 2 loaves

    1 envelope active dry yeast

    ⅓ cup lukewarm water

    5½ cups flour

    ½ teaspoon salt

    1 cup sugar

    4 eggs, well beaten

    ⅔ cup lukewarm milk

    ⅓ cup butter, melted

1. In a small bowl, dissolve the yeast in the water and set it aside.
2. Sift 5 cups of the flour and the salt into a large bowl.
3. In another bowl, mix the sugar and eggs with the milk. Add the yeast mixture and stir to blend. Add the butter and mix well.
4. Add the milk mixture to the flour and stir with a wooden spoon until well combined.
5. Turn the dough out on a lightly floured surface and knead it until the dough is smooth and elastic, about 10 minutes. If the dough becomes sticky, add the remaining ½ cup flour.
6. Place the dough in a lightly oiled bowl, turn it over to coat it with the oil, cover it with plastic wrap, and let it rise in a warm, draft-free place until doubled in bulk, about 1 hour.
7. About 10 minutes before the end of the rising time, preheat the oven to 350°F.
8. Punch the dough down and divide it in half. Shape each half into a round, slightly flattened loaf. Place each loaf in a greased 9-inch pie pan and bake until nicely browned, about 40 minutes.

SWEDISH ST. LUCIA BUNS

St. Lucia buns are made in various shapes—this one is called the Double "S."

Makes 24 buns

    1 cup milk

    ½ teaspoon powdered saffron or saffron threads

    ¾ cup sugar

    1 teaspoon salt

    ½ cup butter, softened

    2 envelopes active dry yeast

    ¾ cup warm water

    6 to 7 cups flour

    2 eggs

    ½ cup golden raisins, scalded, drained, and dried, plus 48 raisins for decorating

    ½ cup ground blanched almonds

    An egg wash, made by beating 1 egg yolk with 1 tablespoon water

1. In a small saucepan, heat the milk until it is just scalded. Remove it from the heat and add the saffron, sugar, salt, and butter, blending well. Let the mixture cool to lukewarm.

2. In a large mixing bowl, combine the yeast and water, stirring until the yeast is dissolved. Blend in the milk mixture. Add 2½ cups of flour and beat until smooth. Add the eggs, the ½ cup of raisins, and the almonds. Gradually add sufficient flour to make a soft, workable dough that pulls away from the sides of the bowl.

3. Turn the dough out onto a lightly floured surface, cover it, and let it rest for 10 minutes. Knead the dough until it is smooth and elastic, about 8 minutes. Form the dough into a ball and place it in a clean, oiled bowl; turn the dough over to coat it with the oil. Cover the bowl loosely with plastic wrap and a towel and let it rise in a warm, draft-free place until it is doubled in bulk, about 1 hour.

4. Grease two baking sheets. Divide the dough into 4 pieces. Divide one piece of the dough into 6 pieces. Cut each in half; you will have 12 pieces in all.

5. Using your hands, roll each piece into a rope 10 to 12 inches long. Cross 2 ropes on a baking sheet and roll each end into a snail or curl. Press a large raisin in the center of each curl and brush the bun with the egg glaze. Repeat the procedure with the remaining portions of the dough. Cover the buns and let them rise until light and puffy, about 50 minutes.

6. About 10 minutes before the end of the rising time, preheat the oven to 400°F.

7. Bake the buns until golden, about 10 minutes. Let the buns cool on wire racks.

One of the most common pitfalls in yeast bread baking is using liquids that are too hot for the yeast. Though warm water is necessary to dissolve the yeast, water that is too hot (over 110°F.) will kill the yeast and the bread will not rise. If the recipe calls for melted butter, or other heated ingredients, be careful that they, too, are not so hot that they will kill the yeast when added to the flour and yeast mixture.

Pᴀɴᴇᴛᴛᴏɴᴇ

Panettone is the traditional Christmas bread of Italy. It is a light bread baked into round loaves with a symbolic cross cut into the top. A glass of sweet wine is a favorite accompaniment.

Makes 2 tall loaves

    2 envelopes active dry yeast

    1 teaspoon sugar

    ¼ cup warm water (110°F.)

    ½ cup butter

    ¾ cup cold milk

    ½ cup sugar

    1 teaspoon salt

    7 egg yolks (at room temperature), lightly beaten

    5 to 5½ cups unsifted flour

    ½ cup dark raisins

    ½ cup citron or mixed candied fruit, cut into thin slivers

    ¼ cup butter, melted

1. In a small bowl, sprinkle the yeast and the 1 teaspoon of sugar over the warm water. Let the mixture stand for about 5 minutes, then stir it until the yeast and sugar are dissolved. Let it stand until quite foamy, 5 to 10 minutes more.

2. In a large saucepan, melt the butter over low heat. Add the cold milk, which will cool the butter to lukewarm. Add the ½ cup of sugar, salt, and beaten egg yolks; then stir in the dissolved yeast. Add enough flour—about 4½ cups—to make a very soft, sticky dough.

3. Turn the dough out onto a lightly floured board and knead it until it is smooth and elastic, kneading in as much of the remaining 1 cup of flour as is needed. (The dough should be soft; kneading will take about 10 minutes.)

4. Shape the dough into a ball and place it in a clean, oiled bowl; turn the dough over to coat it with the oil. Cover the dough with a towel and let it rise in a warm, draft-free place (85°F.) until it is doubled in bulk, about 2 hours.

5. To prepare the pans, use two 8-inch round layer-cake pans. Cut heavy brown paper (grocery sacks) into two strips, each 5 inches wide by 20 inches long. Butter one side of each strip generously and fit it inside (greased side in) the edge of the pan, overlapping the ends. Use paper clips to hold the paper strip in place.

6. Turn the dough out onto a board and knead in the raisins and citron or candied fruit (knead the dough as little as possible to prevent the gluten from developing excessively). Divide the dough in half and shape it into two balls.

7. Place one ball in each of the two prepared pans. Using a sharp knife, cut a deep cross on top of each loaf. Let the dough rise again until almost doubled, about 1 hour.

8. About 10 minutes before the end of the rising time, preheat the oven to 350°F.

9. Brush the tops of the loaves with a

little of the melted butter. Bake them on the middle shelf of the oven for 30 to 40 minutes. When done, the tops should be crisp and dark brown.

10. Remove the loaves from the pans to cooling racks. Brush them again with melted butter (this will soften the crust). Cool them, then strip off the paper. Cut the panettone into wedges for serving.

STOLLEN

Makes 3 loaves

  ½ cup warm water

  2 envelopes active dry yeast

  ¾ cup lukewarm milk

  ½ cup sugar

  1 teaspoon salt

  ⅔ cup butter, melted

  3 eggs

  1 tablespoon grated lemon zest

  6 to 7 cups flour

  ⅔ cup blanched almonds, chopped

  ¾ cup mixed candied fruit, chopped

  ⅔ cup golden raisins, scalded, drained, and dried on paper towels

Icing

  1 cup confectioners' sugar

  ¼ teaspoon pure vanilla extract

  Milk

  Whole blanched almonds (optional)

  Candied cherries, halved (optional)

1. Combine the water and yeast in a small bowl, stirring until dissolved.

2. In a large bowl, combine the milk, sugar, salt, and butter. Stir in the eggs, lemon zest, and yeast mixture. Beat in 2½ cups of flour to make a smooth batter. Gradually add sufficient flour to make a soft, workable dough that pulls away from the sides of the bowl.

3. Turn the dough out on a lightly floured surface and knead the dough until it is smooth and elastic, about 10 minutes. Place the dough in a clean, oiled bowl; turn it over to coat with the oil. Cover the bowl loosely with plastic wrap and a towel and let the dough rise until doubled in bulk, 1 to 1½ hours.

4. In a small bowl, combine the almonds, fruit, and raisins. Punch down the dough, pat it out flat, and place the almond and fruit mixture in the center. Bring the edges together and begin kneading the dough to distribute the mixture. If the fruit mixture tends to stay in one spot, cover the dough, let it rest for 10 minutes, and resume kneading quickly.

5. Grease three baking sheets. Divide the dough into three equal portions. Roll each piece into a 12-by-18-inch oval. Fold the dough in half lengthwise so that the top portion does not quite reach the bottom edge. Place the stollens on the prepared baking sheets, cover them, and let them rise until doubled in bulk, 45 to 60 minutes.

6. About 10 minutes before the end of the rising time, preheat the oven to 375°F.

7. Bake the stollens until golden brown, 25 to 30 minutes.

8. To make the icing, in a small bowl combine the confectioners' sugar, the vanilla, and sufficient milk to make an icing of spreadable consistency. With a spatula, frost the cakes while they are warm. Decorate them, if you wish, with whole blanched almonds and candied cherries.

NOTE: Stollen tastes even better a few days after it is made. Wrap the loaves carefully in plastic wrap or aluminum foil so that the bread does not dry out during storage. When properly wrapped, stollen also freezes well.

GREEK CHRISTMAS BREAD

Fragrant, tender, and rich, this spectacular bread is sumptuous with tea or coffee, either warm or at room temperature. It is a round loaf with ropes of dough laid on top to form a cross. The four ends of the cross are curled into the shape of an anchor.

Makes 1 large loaf

    1 cup milk

    ½ cup unsalted butter

    ½ cup honey

    1½ teaspoons salt

    2 envelopes active dry yeast

    ½ cup warm water

    ½ teaspoon sugar or honey

    4 eggs

    1 teaspoon anise seed, bruised with the back of a spoon (or 1½ teaspoons if you prefer a more pronounced flavor)

    6 to 7 cups flour

    Melted butter

    An egg wash, made by beating 1 egg white with 1 tablespoon of water

    9 perfect walnut or pecan halves

1. In a small saucepan, scald the milk over low heat. Add the butter, honey, and salt; stir and let the mixture sit until it is lukewarm.

2. In a large mixing bowl, combine the yeast, warm water, and ½ teaspoon of sugar or honey. Wait until this mixture is foaming, then add the cooled milk mixture, the eggs, and anise and beat it thoroughly. Add 3 cups of the flour and beat at least 200 strokes by hand or 2 minutes with an electric mixer. Gradually add more flour until the dough clings together in the center of the bowl.

3. Turn the dough out onto a floured board and knead it until it is smooth and elastic, adding a little more flour if necessary. This should be an easy dough to knead and should lose its stickiness early, although it will feel somewhat oily because of the butter.

4. Place the dough in a clean, oiled bowl, turn it over to coat it with the oil, cover it with a towel, and let it rise in a warm, draft-free place until doubled in bulk, about 45 minutes.

5. Punch the dough down, turn it out onto a lightly floured board, knead it a few times to press out air bubbles, and cut off two small pieces of dough, each the size of a small apple. Cover all three pieces of dough with a towel and let them rest for about 10 minutes.

6. Shape the large piece of dough into a smooth ball. Press it out with your hands into a flattened round, tucking all the edges underneath and sealing them together at the center of the bottom. Then coax the dough into a ball, pressing it again to flatten it slightly (it should still swell in the middle). Place the dough on a large, greased baking sheet or jelly-roll pan.

7. Using your palms, roll out each small piece of dough into a thin rope about half again as long as the diameter of the flattened ball. Try to make the ropes even in thickness. Use a sharp knife to split 4 inches of the end of each rope in half lengthwise.

8. Carefully place one of the ropes across the large loaf so that it crosses it in the middle, leaving equal amounts of overhang on either side. Place the second rope at right angles to the first one so that they form a cross on top of the loaf. Curl each half of each split end away from the center to make a small circle; the end of each rope should look like an anchor. Form the anchors high enough up on the loaf so that they don't collapse down over the sides during baking. Tack each curlicue in place with toothpicks or pieces of raw spaghetti. Brush the dough with melted butter and let it rise, covered with a towel, until almost doubled in bulk, about 1 hour.

9. About 10 minutes before the end of the rising time, preheat the oven to 350°F.

10. Brush the loaf with the egg wash. Place a walnut or pecan half in the hollow of each curlicue (two for each "anchor") and at the center of the cross. Press them into the dough gently.

11. Bake the bread for 40 to 50 minutes. With a pancake turner, raise the loaf carefully to tap the bottom for doneness (there should be a hollow sound), or plunge a cake tester into the side. Cool it on a wire rack. Remove the toothpicks or spaghetti and cut the bread in wedges or slices.

BROWN BREAD

Makes 2 loaves

> 1 cup yellow cornmeal
>
> 1 cup all-purpose flour
>
> 1 cup whole-wheat or graham flour
>
> 1 teaspoon salt
>
> 2 teaspoons baking soda
>
> ¼ cup pure maple syrup
>
> ½ cup molasses
>
> 2 cups buttermilk

1. Put the cornmeal, flours, salt, and baking soda into a large bowl. Add the maple syrup, molasses, and buttermilk. Mix together thoroughly.

2. Fill two well-greased 1-quart molds, coffee cans, or bowls half full of the batter. Cover them tightly with a lid or aluminum foil.

3. Place the containers on a rack in a large pot of simmering water (the water should reach halfway up the sides of the containers). Cover the pan and steam the bread over low heat for 3 hours (the water should continue to simmer but not boil).

4. Twenty minutes before the end of the steaming, preheat the oven to 350°F.

5. Remove the containers from the pan and take off the covers. Place the bread molds in the oven for 5 minutes to dry out. Unmold the bread and serve it hot.

NOTE: To reheat, wrap the bread in aluminum foil and place it in a 350°F. oven for a few minutes.

RAPID-RISING YEASTS

Rapid-rising yeast may be substituted in any recipe that calls for compressed or active dry yeast. Instead of proofing the yeast by dissolving it in warm water and letting it stand until it froths, mix the granular rapid-rising yeast directly into all but about 1 cup of the dry ingredients. Heat the liquids to between 125° and 130°F.— slightly hotter than with the traditional methods, as the living yeast is buffered by the dry ingredients. Beat the hot liquid into the flour and proceed as usual with mixing, kneading, rising, and baking.

BISHOP'S BREAD

Here's a holiday loaf from New England, made colorful and delicious with Christmas fruit and tidbits of chocolate.

Makes 1 loaf

        1½ cups sifted flour

        1½ teaspoons baking powder

        ½ teaspoon salt

        6 ounces semisweet chocolate bits

        2 cups walnuts, broken

        1 cup dried apricots, chopped

        1 cup candied cherries, halved

        3 eggs

        1 cup sugar

1. Preheat the oven to 325°F.

2. Sift the flour, baking powder, and salt into a medium-size bowl. Stir in the chocolate bits, walnuts, apricots, and cherries.

3. In a large bowl, beat the eggs. Then gradually beat in the sugar. Fold in the flour mixture.

4. Line the bottom of a 9-by-5-by-3-inch loaf pan with wax paper; grease the paper and the sides of the pan. Turn the batter into the pan and spread it evenly.

5. Bake the loaf until it pulls away from the sides of the pan, about 1 hour and 30 minutes. Let it sit in the pan on a wire rack for several minutes. Remove it from the pan and let it continue to cool on the rack.

BOURBON BREAD

Here's a celebratory loaf for a season of celebrations. It keeps well, is nice to have on hand to serve to drop-in guests, and makes a jolly gift, with its slight taste—and whiff—of bourbon. Bake it in a mold or Bundt pan and place a sprig of holly tied with a plaid bow in the middle.

Makes 1 loaf

        1 cup unsweetened dates, chopped

        ⅓ cup bourbon

        3 eggs

        ½ cup honey

        ¼ cup unsalted butter, melted

        ¼ cup heavy cream, or evaporated milk, half-and-half, or milk

        1 teaspoon pure vanilla extract

        3 tablespoons brandy or cognac

        ½ cup dark raisins

        1 cup chopped pecans

        2 cups flour

        2½ teaspoons baking powder

        ½ teaspoon baking soda

        ½ teaspoon salt

        ½ teaspoon grated nutmeg

        ¼ teaspoon ground cloves

1. In a small bowl, soak the dates in the bourbon for at least an hour, or several hours.

2. Preheat the oven to 325°F.

3. In a large mixing bowl, beat the eggs until light and thick. Add the honey and beat again. Beat in the butter, cream or milk, vanilla, and brandy. Stir in the raisins, pecans, and the date-bourbon mixture (scrape out the bourbon bowl with a rubber spatula so none will go to waste) until well combined.

4. Sift together the flour, baking powder, soda, salt, nutmeg, and cloves. Add the egg mixture and stir the ingredients gently until just blended; do not overmix.

5. Pour the batter into a buttered mold, a small Bundt pan or Kugelhopf pan, or a large loaf pan. Bake it until the top feels springy and the edges are beginning to brown and shrink away from the pan, about 50 minutes. Do not overbake.

6. Let the bread rest in the pan for about 10 minutes before unmolding it onto a rack to cool. Wrap it in plastic wrap and store in a cool dry place (not the refrigerator); it will keep for about 5 days.

DANISH CHRISTMAS FRUIT LOAF

Makes 1 large loaf

> 2 envelopes active dry yeast, or 2 cakes compressed yeast
>
> ¼ cup sugar
>
> ½ cup lukewarm milk
>
> ¼ teaspoon salt
>
> ½ teaspoon pure vanilla extract
>
> ½ teaspoon grated lemon zest
>
> 2 eggs, lightly beaten
>
> ½ teaspoon ground cardamom
>
> 3 to 4 cups sifted flour
>
> 1 cup mixed candied fruits (lemon, orange, cherry, pineapple)
>
> 1 tablespoon flour
>
> ½ cup unsalted butter, softened

1. In a small bowl, sprinkle the yeast and 1 tablespoon of the sugar over the lukewarm milk. Let the mixture stand in the bowl for 2 to 3 minutes, then stir gently to dissolve the yeast and sugar. Set the bowl in a warm place, perhaps in an unlighted oven. When the yeast begins to bubble, in 8 to 10 minutes, stir it gently, and pour it into a large mixing bowl.

2. Stir in the salt, vanilla, lemon zest, eggs, cardamom, and the remaining sugar. Then add 3 cups of flour, a little at a time, stirring at first and then mixing with your hands until the dough becomes firm enough to be formed into a ball.

3. Shake the candied fruits in a small paper bag with 1 tablespoon of flour. (The flour will prevent the fruits from sticking together and enable them to disperse evenly throughout the dough.) Now add the fruits and the softened butter to the dough and knead for about 10 minutes, adding more flour, if necessary, to make the dough medium soft. The finished dough should be shiny and elastic, and its surface blistered. Shape the dough into a ball and place it in a large bowl. Dust the top lightly with flour, cover with a kitchen towel, and set the bowl in a warm, draft-free spot (again, an unlighted oven is ideal). In 45 minutes to 1 hour the dough should double in bulk and leave a deep depression when two fingers are pressed into the center.

4. After removing the rising dough from the oven, preheat the oven to 350°F.

5. Punch the dough down with your fists and knead it again quickly. Shape it into a fat loaf and put it into a lightly buttered 1½-quart loaf pan. Cover again with the towel and let the dough rise in a warm spot for 15 to 20 minutes until it is almost double in bulk.

6. Bake the fruit loaf in the center of the oven for 45 minutes. Remove the loaf from the pan and let it cool on a wire rack. It will keep well for 2 to 3 weeks if tightly wrapped in aluminum foil and refrigerated.

Cookies & Candies

 VERYONE HAS A SWEET TOOTH AT Christmas, and those of us who never find time to make cookies and candy the rest of the year turn into master confectioners at holiday time. Planning the annual cookie baking spree involves endless choices in order to combine family favorites, ethnic specialties, and a variety of flavors, shapes, and sizes. You will want a balanced selection of rolled, drop, and bar cookies, and a variety of featured ingredients, such as nuts, chocolate, and fruit. The baking process fills the house with warmth and heavenly aromas, the results make thoughtful gifts for family and friends, and, best of all, a platter of assorted cookies and candies is an easy dessert for family dinners and buffet tables throughout the season. Candy making may be a less familiar activity than cookie baking in most kitchens, but with careful attention to instructions and a few basic pieces of equipment at hand—a candy thermometer, for example, and a saucepan with a heavy bottom to prevent burning—the mystery quickly fades.

Clockwise from upper left: Cinnamon Stars, Pecan Brandy Balls, Chocolate Truffles, Sugar Cookie Cutouts, Lemon Logs Dipped in Chocolate, Fruitcake Cookies

SUGAR COOKIE CUTOUTS

Sugar cookies may be decorated not only with colored sugars but with pieces of fruit or icing. Press dried fruit into the unbaked surface or bake and cool the cookies and brush them with a thin confectioners' sugar glaze. When the glaze hardens, outline the cookie with a fine line of a slightly thicker icing, and then before the outline dries, dip the cookie in colored sugars. The sugars will stick to the icing. For special holiday effects, dye both the glaze and outline icing with food coloring and use contrasting colored sugars.

Use this basic recipe with your choice of cookie cutters. The yield given is for 5-inch Christmas trees.

Makes 2 dozen

½ cup vegetable shortening *(see Note)*
1 cup sugar
1 egg, lightly beaten
¼ cup milk
1 teaspoon pure vanilla extract
2½ cups flour
2 teaspoons baking powder
Assorted colored sugars for decoration

1. In a large bowl, cream the shortening and sugar until light and fluffy. Beat in the egg, milk, and vanilla until well combined.
2. Combine the flour and baking powder and gradually add to the shortening-sugar mixture, beating until well mixed. Wrap the dough in plastic wrap and refrigerate until firm.
3. Preheat the oven to 350°F.
4. On a lightly floured surface, roll the dough to a ¼-inch thickness. Cut into shapes with floured cookie cutters and sprinkle with colored sugar. Bake them on greased baking sheets for 10 minutes or until lightly browned. Remove the cookies from the baking sheets and cool on wire racks.

NOTE: This recipe calls for vegetable shortening in order to make the dough easy to handle. If you prefer a more buttery flavor, substitute butter for a small part of the shortening.

PFEFFERNÜSSE

The secret of good "peppernuts" is to let the dough ripen for 2 to 3 days before baking and to store the cookies (with a piece of apple to keep them moist) for 1 to 2 weeks before eating.

Makes 3½ dozen

3 cups flour
1 teaspoon ground cinnamon
⅛ teaspoon ground cloves
¼ teaspoon white pepper
3 eggs
1 cup sugar
⅓ cup finely chopped blanched almonds
⅓ cup finely chopped mixed candied orange peel and citron
Confectioners' sugar (optional)

1. In a medium-size bowl, sift the flour with the spices and set aside.
2. In the large bowl of an electric mixer, beat the eggs until frothy, slowly add the sugar, and continue beating until the mixture becomes thick and lemon colored. At low speed, gradually add the flour mixture, then the almonds and candied fruit, and mix until well blended.
3. Wrap dough in foil and refrigerate for 2 to 3 days so the flavors can meld.
4. Preheat the oven to 350°F.
5. Roll about one-third of the dough at a time to a ¼- to ½-inch thickness and cut with a 1¾-inch round cutter. Place the cookies 1 inch apart on greased baking sheets, and bake until lightly browned, 15 to 18 minutes. Remove them from the baking sheets and let them cool on wire racks. Store in an airtight container. If desired, dust with confectioners' sugar before serving.

SPRINGERLE

The flavor of these well-known German cookies is best if they are allowed to age for 2 to 4 weeks before serving. Here anise extract is used in place of the traditional anise seeds. Wooden springerle molds are pressed into or rolled over the dough to produce cameo images, such as animals or flowers, on the white cookie. The word "springerle" refers to the jumping horse, a common motif of the molds.

Makes 3 to 4 dozen

    4 eggs

    2 cups sugar

    1 teaspoon anise extract

    4½ cups flour

    1 teaspoon baking soda

1. In the large bowl of an electric mixer, beat the eggs at high speed, until light and fluffy. Add the sugar and continue beating at high speed for 15 minutes, scraping down the sides of the bowl with a rubber spatula from time to time. Add the anise extract and blend well.

2. Sift the flour and baking soda and gradually add to the egg and sugar mixture and beat until well combined. Chill the dough for 1 hour.

3. On a well-floured surface, roll the dough into a rectangle ¼ to ½ inch thick. Press a springerle mold into the dough, or roll a springerle rolling pin over it, and cut the dough apart between the individual patterns. Place the cookies on greased baking sheets, reroll the scraps, and repeat the procedure. Cover the cookies lightly with wax paper and let them stand at room temperature overnight to dry.

4. Preheat the oven to 300°F.

5. Bake the springerle until they are slightly golden, 25 to 30 minutes. Remove the cookies from the baking sheets and cool them on wire racks. Store the springerle in an airtight container for at least 2 weeks before serving.

A MATTER OF TIMING

Perfectly shaped cookies are more likely to result if you allow them to set on the baking sheet for about one minute after you remove them from the oven. Very hot cookies are soft and pliable and will easily become distorted if you try to slide them off the sheet too soon. If, on the other hand, you wait a bit too long and the cookies become brittle or begin to stick to the pan, simply put the sheet back in the oven for a minute or two. The butter or shortening in the cookies will melt enough to allow you to free them from the pan. Allow the cookies to cool completely in a single layer on a rack before storing them.

CARDAMOM COOKIES

Cardamom is a favorite spice of Scandinavian cooks, especially at Christmastime.

Makes about 6 dozen

3¾ cups flour

2 cups butter, softened

1½ cups confectioners' sugar

1½ teaspoons pure almond extract

1 teaspoon ground cardamom

⅛ teaspoon salt

1 cup chopped walnuts

Confectioners' sugar (optional)

1. Preheat the oven to 350°F.
2. In a large bowl, combine all the ingredients and knead them in the bowl with your hands until the dough is well blended.
3. Shape the dough into 1-inch balls and place them 2 inches apart on ungreased baking sheets. Bake the cookies until they are lightly browned, about 20 minutes. Remove them from the baking sheets and roll the warm cookies in additional confectioners' sugar if desired. Cool the cookies on wire racks.

BROWN SUGAR SPRITZ

Spritz are traditional German butter cookies molded in various decorative shapes by being forced through a cookie press. If you do not have a cookie press, bar spritz can be made by using a pastry bag and forcing the dough through the star tip.

Makes about 5 dozen

1 cup butter, softened

1 cup firmly packed light brown sugar

3 egg yolks

¼ cup heavy cream

1 teaspoon pure vanilla extract

3 cups flour

½ teaspoon baking powder

1. In a large bowl, cream the butter and sugar until light and fluffy. Add the egg yolks, cream, and vanilla and beat until smooth. Combine the flour and baking powder and add to the butter mixture, blending well. The dough must be fairly stiff in order to hold its shape while being pressed. If it seems too soft, chill it for an hour or so.
2. Preheat the oven to 375°F.
3. Place the dough in a cookie press fitted with your choice of form and press out the cookies onto ungreased baking sheets. Bake until the cookies are golden around the edges, 8 to 10 minutes.

Remove the cookies from the baking sheets and cool on wire racks.

NOTE: Be sure to let the baking sheets cool between batches. A warm sheet will quickly melt the butter in the dough, and the cookies will pull away from the sheet rather than sticking to it properly as the dough is released from the press. Still-warm baking sheets are also likely to produce misshapen spritz.

FRUITCAKE COOKIES

Makes 4 dozen

4 cups flour

3 teaspoons baking soda

½ teaspoon ground ginger

1 teaspoon ground nutmeg

1 teaspoon ground allspice

2 cups chopped walnuts

1 cup chopped dark raisins

½ cup chopped citron

1 cup butter, softened

2 cups firmly packed light brown sugar

4 eggs

1 cup light rum

2 tablespoons buttermilk

1. Preheat the oven to 350°F.
2. Sift the flour, baking soda, and spices onto wax paper. In a medium-size bowl, combine 1 cup of the flour mixture with the nuts and fruit and set aside.
3. In a large bowl, cream the butter with the sugar until the mixture is light and fluffy. Add the eggs one at a time, beating well after each addition. Add the rum and buttermilk alternately with the flour and spice mixture. Blend well. Fold in the nuts and fruits.
4. Drop the dough by teaspoonfuls onto greased baking sheets. Bake until the cookies are firm and the edges begin to brown, about 10 minutes. Remove the cookies from the baking sheets and cool them on wire racks.

NOTE: If you do not have buttermilk, make your own by placing 1 teaspoon lemon juice or distilled white vinegar in a small bowl. Add ⅓ cup homogenized milk and let the mixture stand for about 5 minutes before using.

DATE BARS

Makes 1 dozen

Filling

2 cups pitted dates

½ cup sugar

Grated zest of 1 orange

¼ cup orange juice

½ cup chopped nuts

Crumb Base

1 cup flour

½ teaspoon baking soda

½ teaspoon salt

1 cup quick-cooking or old-fashioned rolled oats

1 cup firmly packed light brown sugar

½ cup butter, melted

1. Preheat the oven to 350°F.
2. To make the filling, combine the dates, sugar, orange zest, and orange juice in a saucepan. Cook over low heat, stirring occasionally, until the mixture has thickened. Cool, stir in the nuts, and set aside.
3. To make the base, sift together the flour, soda, and salt, add the oats and sugar, and mix well. Stir in the butter and mix until crumbly.
4. Firmly press two-thirds of the crumb mixture into a greased 8-inch square baking pan. Spread the filling evenly over the base, and top with the remaining crumb mixture. Using a spatula or spoon, lightly pack down the mixture. Bake until the center is set and the edges are golden, 30 to 35 minutes. Cool in the pan and cut into bars.

Chocolate walnut meringues

Makes 3 dozen

> 1 cup (one 6-ounce package) semisweet chocolate bits
>
> 2 egg whites, at room temperature
>
> Dash of salt
>
> ½ cup sugar
>
> ½ teaspoon pure vanilla extract
>
> ½ teaspoon white vinegar
>
> ¾ cup chopped walnuts

1. Preheat the oven to 350°F.
2. Melt the chocolate bits in the top of a double boiler over hot water, or in a small bowl in a microwave oven.
3. In the large bowl of an electric mixer, combine the egg whites and salt and beat them at high speed until they are foamy. Gradually add the sugar and continue beating until stiff peaks form. Beat in the vanilla and vinegar, and fold in the chocolate and nuts.
4. Drop the batter by teaspoonfuls onto a greased baking sheet and bake until the meringue is set, about 10 minutes, watching to make sure the meringues do not burn. With a spatula, immediately transfer the meringues from the baking sheet to a wire rack to cool.

Toffee bars

Makes 5 to 6 dozen

> 1 cup butter, softened
>
> 1 cup sugar
>
> 1 egg yolk
>
> 1¾ cups flour
>
> 1 teaspoon ground cinnamon
>
> 1 egg white, slightly beaten
>
> 1 cup chopped pecans
>
> 3 tablespoons milk
>
> 1 teaspoon instant coffee granules
>
> 2 ounces semisweet chocolate

1. Preheat the oven to 275°F.
2. In a large bowl, cream the butter. Gradually add the sugar and blend well. Beat in the egg yolk. Sift together the flour and cinnamon and gradually add to the creamed mixture.
3. Press the dough evenly into a buttered 15½-by-10½-inch jelly-roll pan. Brush the top with the egg white and sprinkle with pecans. Lightly press the nuts into the dough. Bake for 1 hour, until the edges begin to brown.
4. Meanwhile, in a small saucepan, heat the milk, coffee, and chocolate together over low heat, until the coffee is dissolved and the chocolate is melted.
5. Drizzle the chocolate mixture over the baked dough and cut it into diamonds or bars. Let them cool in the pan on a wire rack.

Chocolate mint sticks

Brownies are perennial favorites, no matter what the season. This dressed-up holiday version will be a popular addition to your cookie tray.

Makes about 3 dozen

> 2 eggs
>
> 1 cup sugar
>
> ¼ teaspoon salt
>
> ½ cup butter
>
> 1 ounce unsweetened chocolate
>
> 6 tablespoons flour
>
> ½ cup chopped pecans
>
> ¾ teaspoon pure peppermint extract

Peppermint Glaze

> 1½ tablespoons butter
>
> 2 tablespoons light cream
>
> 1½ cups confectioners' sugar
>
> ½ teaspoon pure peppermint extract

Chocolate Drizzle

> 1 ounce unsweetened chocolate
>
> 1 teaspoon butter

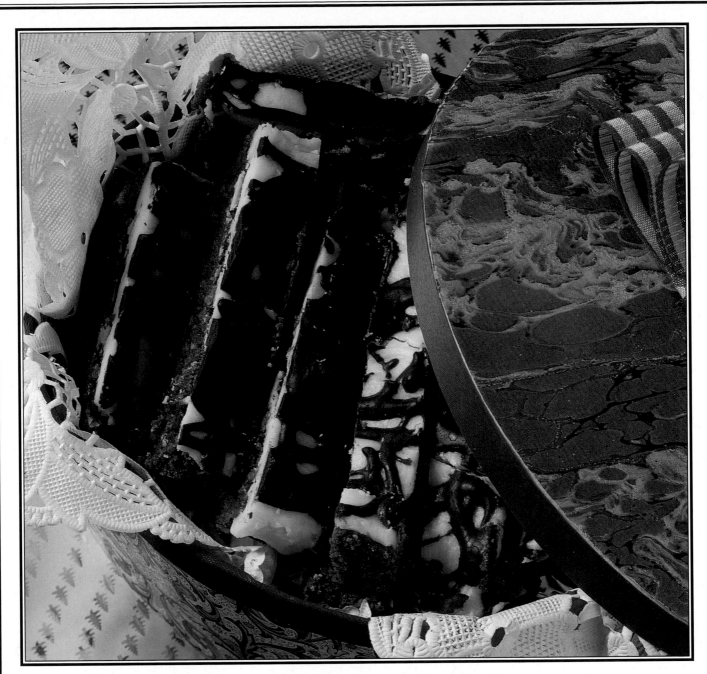

1. Preheat the oven to 350°F.
2. In a large bowl, beat the eggs with the sugar and salt until fluffy.
3. Melt the butter and chocolate together in a small, heavy skillet over low heat or in a small bowl in a microwave oven; blend into the sugar mixture. Stir in the flour, pecans, and peppermint extract. Blend well but do not beat.
4. Spread the batter in a greased 9-inch square baking pan and bake for 18 to 20 minutes (test for doneness in the center with a pick). Remove the brownies from the oven and cool in the pan on a wire rack.

5. To make the peppermint glaze, melt the butter in the cream in a small, heavy skillet or in a microwave oven. Remove the butter mixture from the heat and blend in the confectioners' sugar and peppermint extract. Spread the glaze over the cooled brownies and let it set.
6. To make the chocolate drizzle, place the chocolate and butter in a small skillet or in a microwave oven, and heat until melted. While it is hot and thin, drizzle the mixture over the glazed brownies in swirls.
7. Refrigerate briefly to harden the toppings, then cut into bite-size sticks.

BEATING AND BURNING

Overbeating and burning are two evil gremlins of the cookie-baking world. Because beating develops the gluten in the flour and thus toughens the batter, some cooks prefer to do all cookie-making procedures by hand. That way they are less likely to overmix the batter. Cookies burn because of the very nature of their Christmas appeal: The butter, the sugars, and the thinness combine to make them susceptible to scorching. To avoid the problem, test the accuracy of your oven temperature with an oven thermometer. Use heavy baking sheets, bake cookies on the middle oven rack, and time the baking period carefully with a reliable timer. Most important, check their progress frequently, especially when they begin to smell done—one's nose can be a valuable source of information about cooking and baking progress.

PECAN BRANDY BALLS

Makes 2½ dozen

> ½ cup butter, softened
>
> ¼ cup sugar
>
> ¾ cup flour
>
> 1 cup finely chopped pecans
>
> 1 tablespoon brandy
>
> ½ cup confectioners' sugar, or more

1. Preheat the oven to 300°F.
2. In a large bowl, cream the butter until fluffy and beat in the sugar, flour, and pecans. Add the brandy and combine well.

3. Press the mixture into an 8-inch square baking pan. Cut into 32 pieces. Dust your hands lightly with confectioners' sugar and form each piece into a ball (re-sugar your hands as needed). Place the balls on a greased baking sheet.
4. Bake the cookies for 30 to 35 minutes. They should brown only where they touch the pan. Remove from the oven. While they are still warm, roll the balls in confectioners' sugar. Cool them on wire racks and roll them again in confectioners' sugar. Store the cookies in an airtight tin between layers of wax paper.

CINNAMON STARS

The recipe for this chewy cookie, made with egg whites and ground nuts and topped with a delicate cinnamon meringue, comes from Germany. Because of the meringue, it is best to make these cookies on a dry day.

Makes about 2 dozen

> 6 egg whites, room temperature
>
> 2 cups confectioners' sugar, sifted
>
> 2 teaspoons grated lemon zest
>
> 2 teaspoons ground cinnamon
>
> 1 pound unblanched almonds, finely ground

1. Preheat the oven to 325°F.
2. In the large bowl of an electric mixer, place the egg whites and beat them until stiff peaks form. Slowly add the confectioners' sugar and beat continuously until stiff and shiny, about 7 minutes. Beat in the lemon zest and cinnamon until well blended.
3. Divide the mixture roughly in half and mix the almonds thoroughly into the slightly smaller portion, to make a dough. Reserve the remaining mixture for icing the cookies. On a lightly floured surface, gently roll out the almond dough to a ¼-inch thickness. The dough is delicate, and if it gets sticky add small amounts of flour to the sur-

face. Use a cookie cutter 2 to 3 inches wide to cut out stars, and place them on a greased baking sheet.

4. Ice the cookies with the remaining egg white-cinnamon mixture and bake for about 20 minutes, until the meringue icing is stiff and dry. Remove the stars from the baking sheets and cool on wire racks. Store in a cool, dry place in an airtight container.

LEMON LOGS DIPPED IN CHOCOLATE

Makes 15 cookies

    6 tablespoons butter, softened

    ¼ cup sugar

    1 egg yolk

    ½ teaspoon vanilla

    1 cup flour

    ¼ teaspoon ground cinnamon

    ¼ teaspoon salt

    3 tablespoons ground almonds

    4 teaspoons lemon curd

    Sugar for rolling

    3 ounces semisweet chocolate bits
      (½ cup)

1. Preheat the oven to 350°F.
2. In a medium-size bowl, cream together the butter and sugar until well blended. Beat in the egg yolk and vanilla.
3. In a small bowl, mix together thoroughly the flour, cinnamon, and salt. Add this flour mixture to the butter mixture and blend well. Stir in the ground almonds.
4. Cover the bowl with plastic wrap and chill in the refrigerator for at least 1 hour.
5. On a lightly floured board, roll out the dough to form a square about 7½ inches on each side (the dough will be about ³⁄₁₆ inch thick). Cut the dough into 15 rectangles about 2½ inches by 1½ inches. Spread ¼ teaspoon lemon curd lengthwise along the center of each rectangle. Roll the dough over the lemon curd to form a 2½-inch-long log; seal edges tightly.

6. Place the cookies on an ungreased baking sheet and bake until lightly browned on the edges, about 15 minutes.
7. Let the cookies stand on the baking sheet for about 2 minutes after removing them from the oven, then place them on racks. While they are still warm, roll them gently in the sugar.
8. Melt the chocolate bits in a pan over hot, but not boiling, water or in a small bowl in a microwave oven. Dip each end of the cooled cookies in the melted chocolate.

ALMOND CRESCENTS

Makes about 3 dozen

    1 cup unsalted butter, softened

    ⅔ cup sugar

    2 cups flour

    1¼ cups ground blanched almonds

    1 teaspoon pure vanilla extract

    ½ teaspoon salt

    ¾ cup confectioners' sugar

1. Preheat the oven to 350°F.
2. In a large bowl, cream the butter and sugar together until light and fluffy. Sift in the flour, ½ cup at a time, mixing well after each addition. Stir in the almonds, vanilla, and salt, and continue mixing until the ingredients are well blended. Shape the dough into a ball, wrap it in plastic wrap, and refrigerate for 1 hour.
3. For each cookie, pinch off enough dough to make a ball about 1¼ inches in diameter. Shape each cookie by rolling the ball between the palms of your hands into a strip about ½ inch thick and 3 inches long, with slightly tapered ends. Place the strips on two lightly greased and floured baking sheets and bend them into crescents.
4. Bake the cookies until light gold in color and lightly browned around the edges, 15 to 20 minutes.
5. Remove the crescents from the baking sheet and cool them on a wire rack. Sift the confectioners' sugar over the cookies while they are still slightly warm.

SANTA'S JELLY FINGERS

Makes 3 to 4 dozen

1 cup butter, softened

¾ cup firmly packed light brown sugar

1 egg, separated

2 cups flour

¼ teaspoon salt

1 cup quick-cooking rolled oats

1 cup finely chopped walnuts or pecans

Red currant or raspberry jelly

1. In a large bowl, cream the butter and sugar until light and fluffy. Add the egg yolk. Blend well and gradually mix in the flour, salt, and oats. Chill the dough for at least an hour.

2. Preheat the oven to 350°F.

3. Lightly beat the egg white. Shape the chilled dough in 1½-inch ovals, dip each in the egg white, and roll in the chopped nuts. Place the ovals on an ungreased baking sheet and press an indentation along the center of each one with your index finger.

4. Bake the cookies until golden around the edges, about 10 minutes. Remove them from the oven for a moment to press the indentations again. Return the cookies to the oven and bake them for about 5 minutes more. Allow them to cool slightly and then fill the indentations with jelly. Remove the cookies from the baking sheets and let them continue to cool on wire racks.

GINGER SHORTBREAD

Makes 12 wedges

- ¾ cup sifted cornstarch
- ⅔ cup flour
- ½ cup sifted confectioners' sugar
- ½ cup plus 2⅔ tablespoons unsalted butter, softened
- ⅓ cup very thinly sliced candied ginger, not longer than ¾ inch

1. Preheat the oven to 325°F.
2. Butter a 9-inch round springform or cake pan. In a small bowl, combine the cornstarch, flour, and confectioners' sugar.
3. In a medium-size bowl, beat the butter until light and creamy. Gradually beat in the dry ingredients until well blended. Gently stir in the ginger.
4. Press the dough evenly into the prepared pan. Using a sharp knife, score the dough into 12 pie-shaped wedges. With the tines of a fork, pierce the dough along the score lines, then use the fork to crimp the outer edges as you would for a pie crust.
5. Bake the shortbread until light golden, 40 to 45 minutes, rotating the pan after 20 minutes to ensure even baking. While the shortbread is still warm, again pierce the score lines with the fork. Run a sharp knife around the edge. Set the pan on a rack and let the shortbread cool completely.
6. Using a sharp knife, cut along the score lines and remove the wedges of shortbread from the pan. (If using a springform pan, remove the sides first.)

NOTE: Stored at room temperature in an airtight container, these shortbread cookies will keep for up to 2 weeks.

PRALINES

There is no need to send to New Orleans for pralines. They contain few ingredients and are easily made at home, if close attention is paid to the caramelizing process.

SANTA'S ORIGINS

Santa Claus may now live at the North Pole, but his origins lie elsewhere. He is a composite of the kindly gift-givers of many countries—the angel messenger Kris Kringle of Germany and Switzerland, the holy bishop St. Nicholas of Holland and Belgium, and the merry old elves Julenisse and Jultomte of Scandinavia. For generations, American children have set out cookies for Santa and carrots for his reindeer, as they wait expectantly—and impatiently—to see what the jolly old elf will leave them for Christmas morning.

Makes about 2 pounds

- 2½ cups sugar
- 1 cup light cream
- 1 tablespoon butter
- ½ pound pecan halves

1. In a heavy saucepan, combine 2 cups of the sugar with the cream and butter and bring to a boil over medium heat. Remove the pan from the heat.
2. In a separate heavy saucepan, cook the rest of the sugar over very low heat, stirring constantly, until it melts and turns a rich caramel color, 6 to 8 minutes.
3. Add the cream, butter, and sugar syrup to the caramelized sugar. Add the pecan halves and cook the mixture until it reaches the soft-ball stage, 235°F. on a candy thermometer.
4. Remove the pan from the heat and beat the mixture until it thickens. Drop spoonfuls of the mixture onto wax paper to form pralines about 2 to 3 inches in diameter. Let the pralines harden. Remove from the wax paper and store in an airtight container.

Peanut brittle

Makes about 2 pounds

  2 cups sugar

  1 cup light corn syrup

  ⅓ cup water

  2 tablespoons butter

  ¼ teaspoon salt

  2 cups roasted blanched peanuts

  1 teaspoon baking soda

  1 teaspoon pure vanilla extract

1. In a large heavy saucepan, combine the sugar, corn syrup, water, butter, and salt. Stir constantly over medium heat until the sugar dissolves. Continue cooking, stirring occasionally, until the syrup reaches the hard-crack stage, 300°F. on a candy thermometer. Remove from the heat and stir in the peanuts.
2. Combine the baking soda and vanilla and rapidly stir into the syrup (the mixture will foam). Quickly turn out the mixture onto a greased 15½-by-10½-inch jelly-roll pan. Spread the mixture to fill the pan. Let it cool completely, then break the brittle into pieces.

NOTE: Stored in an airtight tin in a cool dry place, the brittle can be kept for up to 4 weeks.

Chocolate truffles

Makes 3 dozen

  7 ounces bittersweet chocolate (Swiss or other high quality), cut into 1-inch pieces

  ½ cup heavy cream

  2 tablespoons butter

  ¾ cup confectioners' sugar, sifted

  2 egg yolks, slightly beaten

  2 tablespoons dark rum, or to taste

  Unsweetened cocoa powder or coarsely chopped toasted nuts

1. Combine the chocolate, cream, and butter in the top of a double boiler over hot water. Add the confectioners' sugar and egg yolks, stirring constantly, and whisk until smooth.
2. Remove the pan from the heat and add the rum. Mix well and pour the mixture into a flat dish and refrigerate it until the mixture is workable, about 2 hours.
3. Shape the chilled chocolate into small balls about the size of large olives and roll them in cocoa and/or nuts. Place the truffles in paper or foil candy cups and refrigerate them until they are firm. Store them in an airtight container in a cool place.

Kentucky bourbon balls

Makes about 3 dozen

  ¼ cup butter, softened

  1 pound confectioners' sugar, sifted

  2 teaspoons lemon juice

  ½ cup ground pecans

  ¼ teaspoon salt

  ¼ cup bourbon

  4 ounces unsweetened chocolate

  2 tablespoons vegetable shortening

1. In a large bowl, cream the butter until fluffy. Beat in half the sugar. Because this is a stiff dough, use your hands to work in the remaining sugar and the lemon juice, pecans, salt, and bourbon. Chill the mixture for 30 minutes.
2. Cover a baking sheet with wax paper. Shape the chilled dough into 1-inch balls, and place them on the wax paper. Chill them again for 30 minutes.
3. Melt the chocolate and shortening in the top of a double boiler over hot water, stirring occasionally, or in a small bowl in a microwave oven.
4. Dip the balls in melted chocolate, and place them on the baking sheet. Set aside until firm. Store in an airtight container in a cool place for 2 to 3 days before serving so the flavors can meld.

TOFFEE-BUTTER CRUNCH

Makes about 2½ pounds

½ pound almonds, blanched and peeled (about 1½ cups), half coarsely chopped, half finely chopped

1 cup butter

1½ cups sugar

3 tablespoons water

1 tablespoon light corn syrup

1 pound milk chocolate, broken into pieces

1. Preheat the oven to 350°F.
2. Spread the almonds on a baking sheet. Toast the nuts in the oven until they are lightly browned, about 5 minutes.
3. In a large saucepan, melt the butter over medium heat. Add the sugar, water, and corn syrup. Cook the mixture over medium heat, stirring occasionally, until it reaches the hard-crack stage, 300°F. on a candy thermometer. Quickly stir in the coarsely chopped almonds.
4. While it is still hot, spread the mixture onto a well-greased 9-by-13-inch baking sheet. Let the candy cool thoroughly, then turn it out onto wax paper.
5. In a bowl set in a saucepan of hot water or in a microwave oven, melt the chocolate. With a spatula, spread half of the melted chocolate over the candy and sprinkle it with half of the finely chopped almonds. Cover the top with wax paper, and turn the candy over. Spread the other side with the remaining chocolate and sprinkle it with the remaining almonds. Chill the toffee to firm it, then break it into about 24 pieces.

Cookies & Candies 🌿

COOKIE-BAKING WITH THE KIDS

What better way to include children in Christmas preparations than to give them a chance to mix dough, wield cookie cutters, decorate with icings and colored sugars, and, best of all, lick the bowl and sample the still-warm finished product. Both you and they will enjoy the project more if you are realistic and keep the following in mind:

* Depending on the age of the child, don't look for magazine-perfect creations. Encourage a reasonably edible result, but be flexible enough to allow youngsters to be creative and have fun.

* Plan ahead: make the dough as for Sugar Cookie Cutouts (page 136), a day before with or without your child's help, and chill it; the process of rolling, cutting, and decorating will go more smoothly when you both are fresh.

* Organize decorations—raisins, colored sugars, dragées, cinnamon red hots—in sturdy, nontippable containers.

* Keep your Christmas cookie cutters tucked away until needed; this will make them seem special and add to the once-a-year festivity of the whole process.

PENUCHE

Makes about 1½ pounds

  3 cups firmly packed light brown sugar

  1 cup light cream or evaporated milk

  1½ tablespoons butter

  1½ teaspoons pure vanilla extract

1. In a heavy saucepan, combine the sugar and cream or evaporated milk and cook slowly, stirring constantly, until the mixture boils. Boil without stirring until the mixture reaches the soft-ball stage, 235°F. on a candy thermometer.
2. Remove the pan from the heat and add the butter, but do not stir. Cool to lukewarm and add the vanilla. Beat until the mixture is creamy and holds its shape.
3. Pour the candy into a buttered 8-inch square pan and cool thoroughly. Cut into squares. Store in an airtight container.

DIVINITY DROPS

Makes about 1½ pounds

  2½ cups sugar

  ½ cup light corn syrup

  ¼ teaspoon salt

  ½ cup water

  2 egg whites, beaten until stiff but not dry

  1 teaspoon pure vanilla extract

  1 cup coarsely chopped nuts

  About 18 red candied cherries, halved

  About 18 green candied cherries, or pieces of angelica, chopped

1. In a medium-size saucepan, mix the sugar, corn syrup, salt, and water. Cook over medium heat, stirring, until the sugar dissolves. Continue cooking, without stirring, until it reaches the firm-ball stage, 248°F. on a candy thermometer.

2. Pour about half of the syrup over the egg whites, beating constantly. Cook the remainder of the syrup until it reaches the soft-crack stage, 272°F. on a candy thermometer.
3. Add the cooked syrup to the egg white syrup, and beat until the mixture forms stiff peaks. Add the vanilla extract and the nuts.
4. Drop tablespoons of the mixture onto sheets of wax paper. Decorate the divinity drops with the red cherry halves and the chopped green cherries or angelica. Let the drops stand until they are firm. Store in an airtight container.

MAMIE'S CHOCOLATE FUDGE

The Mamie in the title is none other than Mamie Eisenhower. It is probably safe to assume that this easy-to-make chunky fudge was one of the President's favorites.

Makes 64 small chunks

> 4½ cups sugar
>
> 2 tablespoons butter
>
> 1 12-ounce can evaporated milk
>
> Pinch of salt
>
> 1 12-ounce package semisweet chocolate bits
>
> 12 ounces sweet chocolate, grated
>
> 2 cups marshmallow cream
>
> 2 cups coarsely chopped pecans or walnuts

1. In a heavy saucepan, combine the sugar, butter, evaporated milk, and salt and bring to a boil over medium heat. Boil for 6 minutes, stirring occasionally, and remove from the heat.
2. Place the chocolate bits, grated chocolate, and marshmallow cream in a large bowl and cover with the hot sugar and butter mixture. Beat until the chocolate has melted and the mixture is smooth and creamy. Stir in the nuts.

3. Pour the fudge into a greased 8-inch square pan and let it cool completely. Cut into 1-inch squares. Store in an airtight container.

SUGARPLUMS

The original sugarplums were made in Portugal of fresh black figs or green plums, cooked and recooked for days on end in ever-thickening sugar syrups, to produce a sort of glacéed fruit. Prunes, figs, dates, and other dried fruits are now prepared as sugarplums. They can be wrapped in plain or colored foil, to be hung on the tree or given as small gifts.

Makes about 4 pounds

> 3 pounds combined pitted dates, figs, raisins, and dried currants, coarsely chopped
>
> ½ pound blanched walnuts or almonds, coarsely chopped
>
> ½ pound unsalted shelled pistachio nuts, coarsely chopped
>
> ½ pound crystallized ginger, coarsely chopped
>
> Grated zest of 2 oranges
>
> 3 tablespoons lemon juice or brandy, or as needed
>
> Confectioners' or granulated sugar

1. In a large bowl, combine the fruits, nuts, ginger, and orange zest. Add just enough lemon juice or brandy to enable the mixture to stick together.
2. With your hands, pinch off pieces of the mixture and shape into balls 1 to 1½ inches in diameter. Roll the balls in sugar, then wrap them in plain or colored foil.

NOTE: Vary the assortment of fruits and nuts to suit your own taste, using any one or all of those suggested.

MARZIPAN

Makes about 1 pound

    1 egg white, beaten

    1 cup almond paste (available at most
        grocery stores)

    1¾ cups confectioners' sugar,
        sifted twice

    Food coloring and flavorings such as
        almond extract, lemon juice, and
        orange extract

1. In a large bowl, whip the egg white until peaks form.
2. Gradually add almond paste, ⅛ cup at a time, until thoroughly blended.
3. Add confectioners' sugar, ¼ cup at a time, and knead mixture. The mixture will be sticky at first but will become easier to work with as you add more sugar.
4. Dust work surface with confectioners' sugar and place marzipan on it. Knead mixture so that it is pliable. If the mixture is too moist, add 1 to 2 tablespoons of confectioners' sugar. If the marzipan grows hard and cracks, add 1 or 2 drops of tepid water and knead mixture thoroughly until it becomes pliable again.
5. Divide the marzipan into portions and flavor and color to your liking. Use colors and flavors appropriate to the shapes you will be making. Traditional marzipan shapes include fruit and animals but any shape will do.
6. To create different fruit shapes, break off 1-inch balls and form appropriate shape. For lemons and oranges, press a fine grater against the shape to create a rough texture. Create stems for each fruit using cloves. For apples and pears, insert clove pointed end up. For oranges and lemons, insert clove, pointed end down, entirely into shape so only the flared end shows.
7. Place finished marzipan on a wire rack to dry overnight.

DATE-NUT CANDY

Makes 3 dozen

    7 ounces sweet, flaked coconut

    1 pound pitted dates, chopped

    2 cups firmly packed light brown sugar

    1 cup butter

    2 cups chopped nuts

    4 cups crisp rice cereal

    Confectioners' sugar

1. In a large saucepan, cook the coconut, dates, and brown sugar with the butter over low heat for 6 minutes, stirring constantly. Remove the mixture from the heat and let it cool for 15 minutes.
2. Add the nuts and the cereal. Roll the mixture into balls the size of walnuts, then roll the balls in confectioners' sugar. Store in an airtight container.

CANDIED GRAPEFRUIT PEEL

Makes about 4 dozen pieces

    3 large grapefruits

    2 cups sugar

    ¾ cup water

1. Wash and dry the grapefruits, cut them in half, and squeeze them of their juice; store the juice in the refrigerator for another use.
2. Cut each grapefruit shell into 4 pieces. With a paring knife, pull the white pith and remaining membranes from the peel and discard. Slice the peel into ⅓- to ½-inch-wide strips.
3. In a medium saucepan, combine 1½ cups of the sugar and the water. Cook over low heat until the sugar has dissolved. Bring the syrup to a boil and add half the grapefruit strips. Boil the peel for about 30 minutes, or until it is translucent.
4. Remove the saucepan from the heat and, with a pair of tongs, lift the

strips out of the syrup, letting the excess syrup drip back into the pan. Place the cooked peel on a rack over a jelly-roll pan. Cook the remaining peel in the same manner.

5. When all the strips of peel have been cooked and cooled to room temperature, roll the pieces in the remaining ½ cup of sugar. Store the candied peel in an airtight container.

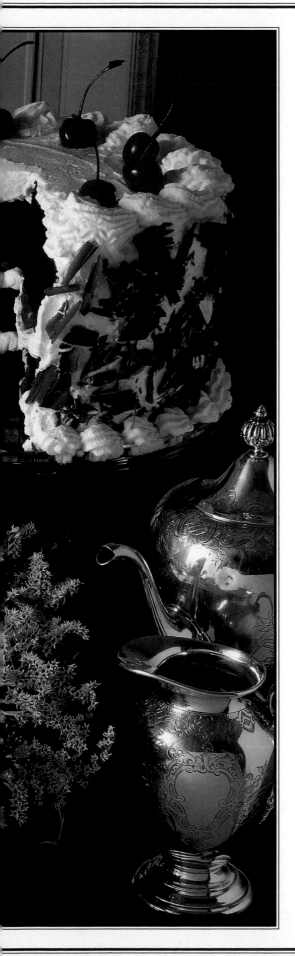

Cakes, Pies, & Desserts

 O MATTER HOW WONDERFUL THE MEAL OR how satiated people may feel after the main course, they always seem able to find room for dessert. Wherever Christmas is celebrated around the world, cooks have responded with some of the most spectacular of sweets. A roll call of favorites—running from the chocolate extravagance of that French work of culinary art, the *Bûche de Noël,* to the rich, fruity splendor of English Plum Pudding, complete with brandied hard sauce—makes a pleasurable difficulty out of deciding what to serve. Chestnuts and cranberries are uniquely seasonal and find especially tantalizing forms in the Candied Chestnut Roll and Frozen Cranberry Velvet Pie. Or for a light dessert after a particularly rich meal, try Tangerine Chiffon Cake with Lemon Glaze or Cranberry Sorbet. The fruitcakes offered here make excellent gifts, tucked in with a colorful cloth napkin in a pretty basket.

Ambrosia, Frozen Cranberry Velvet Pie, and Black Forest Cherry Cake

BÛCHE DE NOËL

The Yule log is an important symbol of Christmas in many countries. Lighting the Yule log marked the start of holiday festivities in medieval courts, and in northern Europe its fire was seen as the rebirth of the sun. The early French log-shaped cake, called *Bûche de Noël*—much plainer than the modern version—was thought to have powers of healing, and pieces of it were kept available all year for medicinal purposes.

Serves 10 to 12

2 tablespoons butter, softened, plus ½ cup unsalted butter, softened and cut into ½-inch pieces

2 tablespoons plus 1 cup flour

4 teaspoons cornstarch

1¼ teaspoons baking powder

¼ teaspoon salt

6 egg whites

1 cup sugar

½ teaspoon pure vanilla extract

4 egg yolks

3 tablespoons cold water

¾ cup crab-apple or red currant jelly

¾ cup maple syrup

1 ounce unsweetened baking chocolate, coarsely grated

Candied cherries

Green citron

1. Preheat the oven to 350°F.
2. Brush 1 tablespoon of softened butter over the bottom and sides of a 15½-by-10½-inch jelly-roll pan. Line the pan with a 20-inch strip of wax paper and let the extra paper extend over the ends. Brush 1 tablespoon of softened butter on the paper and sprinkle it with the 2 tablespoons of flour, tipping the pan from side to side. Turn the pan over and rap it sharply to remove the excess flour.
3. Combine the 1 cup of flour, the cornstarch, baking powder, and salt, and sift them onto a plate.

4. In the large bowl of an electric mixer, beat 4 of the egg whites until they begin to thicken. Slowly add ½ cup of the sugar, beating continuously until the whites are stiff enough to form unwavering peaks on the beater when it is lifted from the bowl. Beat in the vanilla.
5. In another bowl of the mixer, and with the unwashed whisk or beater, beat together the egg yolks, the remaining ½ cup of sugar, and the water. When the yolk mixture thickens enough to fall from the beater in a slowly dissolving ribbon, beat in the sifted flour mixture a few tablespoons at a time. Make sure each addition is completely incorporated before beating in more. Stir ½ cup of the beaten egg whites into the yolk mixture, then scoop it over the whites and fold the two together gently but thoroughly.
6. Pour the batter into the lined pan and spread it evenly into the corners with a spatula. Bake in the middle of the oven until the sides of the cake have begun to shrink away from the pan and the cake springs back instantly when pressed lightly with the tip of a finger, about 20 minutes.
7. Immediately after removing the cake from the oven, carefully invert the cake onto wax paper, peel the layer of paper from the top, and let it rest for 5 minutes, then spread the surface with crab-apple or red currant jelly. Starting at one long edge, roll the cake into a cylinder. Set the cake aside to cool.
8. To prepare the icing, bring the maple syrup to a boil over medium heat in a 3- to 4-quart saucepan. Cook, uncovered and undisturbed, regulating the heat to prevent the syrup from boiling over. When the syrup reaches a temperature of 238°F. on a candy thermometer, or when a drop spooned into ice water immediately forms a soft but compact mass, remove the pan from the heat. Add the chocolate and stir to dissolve it.
9. In the large bowl of an electric mixer, beat the two remaining egg whites until they are stiff enough to

stand in unwavering peaks on the beater when it is lifted from the bowl. Beating the egg whites constantly, pour in the maple syrup-and-chocolate mixture in a slow, thin stream and continue to beat until the mixture has cooled to room temperature. Then beat in the butter bits a few pieces at a time.
10. When the icing is smooth and thick, spread most of it over the top, sides, and ends of the cake roll with a metal spatula or knife. With fork tines, make irregular lines the length of the

roll to give the icing a bark-like look and the cake the appearance of a log. Decorate the cake with holly berries made from the cherries and with leaf shapes cut from the citron.

NOTE: To make the forked *Bûche de Noël* shown above, diagonally cut a third of the cake away from the cylinder (before frosting) and place it against the main log.

TANGERINE CHIFFON CAKE WITH LEMON GLAZE

Serves 16

 2 cups cake flour

 1 teaspoon baking powder

 4 eggs, separated, plus 3 egg whites

 ⅓ cup vegetable oil

 1⅓ cups sugar

 2½ tablespoons finely chopped tangerine zest or grated orange zest

 1 cup strained tangerine juice or orange juice, preferably fresh

 ½ teaspoon cream of tartar

Lemon Glaze

 ¾ cup confectioners' sugar

 1 tablespoon fresh lemon juice

 1 tablespoon grated lemon zest

 1 tablespoon sour cream

1. Preheat the oven to 325°F.
2. To make the cake batter, sift the flour and baking powder into a large bowl. Whisk in the egg yolks, oil, ⅔ cup of the sugar, and the tangerine or orange zest and juice, and mix them thoroughly.
3. To prepare a meringue, beat the whites and cream of tartar together in another large bowl until the whites hold soft peaks. Add the remaining ⅔ cup of sugar, 2 tablespoons at a time, beating continuously until the whites are shiny and hold stiff peaks.
4. Stir one-third of the meringue into the cake batter to lighten it, then fold in the remaining meringue. Rinse a 10-inch Bundt cake pan with water and shake it out so that only a few droplets remain. Spoon the batter into the pan and bake the cake for 50 minutes. Increase the oven temperature to 350°F. and continue baking the cake until a tester inserted in the thickest part comes out clean, 5 to 15 minutes more.
5. When the cake is done, remove it from the oven and let it rest for 10 minutes. Loosen it from the sides of the pan with a spatula and invert it onto a rack. Allow the cake to cool completely, about 1½ hours.
6. To prepare the lemon glaze, sift the confectioners' sugar into a small bowl, then stir in the lemon juice and zest. Continue stirring until a smooth paste results. Stir in the sour cream and pour the glaze over the cake, letting the excess cascade down the sides.

BLACK FOREST CHERRY CAKE

Kirsch, a clear, aromatic German brandy made from cherries, is the essential ingredient in this chocolate cake from the Black Forest region.

Serves 8 to 10

 6 eggs, at room temperature

 1 teaspoon pure vanilla extract

 1 cup sugar

 ½ cup sifted flour

 ½ cup unsweetened cocoa

 10 tablespoons unsalted butter, clarified and cooled *(see Note)*

Kirsch Syrup

 ¾ cup sugar

 1 cup cold water

 ⅓ cup kirsch

Chocolate Curls

 8 ounces semisweet bar chocolate, at room temperature but not soft

Cherry Filling and Topping

 3 cups chilled heavy cream

 ½ cup confectioners' sugar

 ¼ cup kirsch

 1 cup canned sour red cherries, drained

 Maraschino cherries with stems, rinsed, or fresh sweet red cherries with stems

1. Preheat the oven to 350°F.
2. With a pastry brush, spread a light coating of melted or softened butter

over the bottom and sides of three 7-inch round layer-cake pans. Sprinkle a spoonful of flour into each pan, and shake the pan to distribute it; tap out any excess.

3. In the large bowl of an electric mixer, beat the eggs, vanilla, and 1 cup of sugar together at high speed until the mixture is thick and fluffy and has almost tripled in bulk, at least 10 minutes. (By hand with a rotary beater, this may take as long as 20 minutes of uninterrupted beating.)

4. Combine the flour and the cocoa in a sifter. A little at a time, sift the mixture over the eggs, folding it in gently with a rubber spatula. Finally, add the clarified butter, 2 tablespoons at a time; do not overmix. Gently pour the batter into the prepared pans, dividing it evenly among them.

5. Bake the layers in the middle of the oven until a cake tester or toothpick inserted in the center of each cake comes out clean, 10 to 15 minutes. Take the cakes from the oven and let them cool in the pans for about 10 minutes. Then run a sharp knife around the edge of each layer, and turn it out onto a rack to cool.

6. Meanwhile, prepare the kirsch syrup: Combine ¾ cup of sugar and the cold water in a small saucepan, and bring it to a boil over medium heat, stirring only until the sugar dissolves. Boil, uncovered, for 5 minutes, then remove the pan from the heat. When the syrup cools to lukewarm, stir in the kirsch.

7. Transfer the cakes to a long strip of wax paper and prick each layer lightly in several places with the tines of a long fork. Sprinkle the layers evenly with the syrup and let them rest for at least 5 minutes.

8. For the decorative chocolate curls, hold the chocolate over wax paper and draw a sharp vegetable peeler along the wide surface of the bar for large curls, along the narrow side for small ones. Handle the chocolate as little as possible. Refrigerate or freeze the curls until ready to use.

9. In a large chilled bowl, beat the cream with a whisk or an electric beater until it thickens lightly. Then sift the confectioners' sugar over the cream and continue beating until the cream forms firm peaks on the beater when it is lifted out of the bowl. Pour in ¼ cup of kirsch in a thin stream, and beat only until the kirsch is absorbed.

10. To assemble the cake, place one layer on a serving plate. With a spatula, spread the top with ½ inch of whipped cream and strew the sour cherries over it, leaving a margin of about ½ inch around the edge. Gently set a second layer on top of the cherries and spread it with ½ inch of whipped cream. Then set the third layer in place. Spread the top and sides of the cake with cream. With your fingers, press chocolate curls into the cream on the sides of the cake. Arrange more curls on top, leaving a 1-inch margin around the edge. Put the remaining cream into a pastry bag fitted with a star tube, and pipe rosettes of cream around the top edge of the cake and around the base. Place a maraschino cherry, stem up, in the center of each rosette on the top of the cake.

NOTE: To make clarified butter, melt the butter in a small skillet or saucepan over low heat and skim off the foam that rises to the top. The remainder will separate into two parts: a clear yellow liquid and a white residue. Drain off the clear liquid (the clarified butter) and discard the white residue.

CRANBERRY SACHERTORTE

This variation on the famous Viennese chocolate cake strikes a definite American note with the addition of chopped cranberries.

Serves 12

> 8 ounces semisweet chocolate
>
> ⅓ cup flour
>
> 8 ounces walnuts, very finely ground
>
> 1 cup unsalted butter, softened
>
> 1 cup sugar
>
> ¾ teaspoon salt
>
> 2 teaspoons pure vanilla extract
>
> 8 eggs, separated
>
> 1½ cups coarsely chopped fresh cranberries
>
> 1 tablespoon grated orange zest
>
> Whole cranberries for decorating

Glaze

> ⅔ cup apricot jam

Icing

> ½ cup heavy cream
>
> 2 teaspoons instant coffee granules
>
> 6 ounces semisweet chocolate, chopped (do not use chocolate bits)

1. To make the cake, spread a light coating of softened butter over the bottom and sides of a 9-by-2½-inch round cake pan with a removable bottom, or a springform pan. Sprinkle a spoonful of flour into the pan, and shake the pan to distribute it; tap out any excess.
2. Preheat the oven to 350°F.
3. Melt the chocolate in the top of a double boiler over hot water or in a small bowl in a microwave oven, and cool it until it is lukewarm. In a small bowl, toss together the flour and walnuts.
4. In a large bowl, cream the butter with the sugar, salt, and vanilla. Add the egg yolks one by one to the butter-sugar mixture, beating after each addition. Stir the chocolate, floured nuts, cranberries,

and orange zest into the butter mixture.
5. In the large bowl of an electric mixer, beat the egg whites until they form soft peaks. Stir ¼ of the beaten whites into the chocolate mixture to lighten the batter. Fold in the remaining whites.
6. Pour the batter into the prepared pan and bake 1 hour. Let the cake cool in the pan for 20 minutes and push down the puffed-up sides so that they are flush with the middle. Remove the sides of the pan and invert the cake onto a rack set over wax paper. (The bottom has now become the top of the cake.) Cool it completely.
7. To make the glaze, heat the apricot jam in a small saucepan over low heat or in a small bowl in a microwave oven. Push the jam through a sieve, and brush it over the top and sides of the cooled cake. Let the glaze set for about 30 minutes before icing the cake.
8. To make the icing, in a metal mixing bowl or saucepan over medium heat, scald the cream. Whisk in the coffee and add the chocolate. Stir for 1 minute over the heat, then remove the pan from the heat and continue to stir until the chocolate has completely melted. Cool the mixture to warm and pour it over the cake. With a spatula, spread the icing evenly over the top and sides of the cake, rotating the cake as you work.
9. Chill the cake on its rack until the icing is completely set. Transfer it to a serving plate, decorate it with whole cranberries, and refrigerate it. Bring the cake to room temperature before serving. Garnish it with sprigs of fresh holly (not to be eaten) and serve with whipped cream.

NOTE: The cake can be made in advance and freezes beautifully, even iced. Freeze unwrapped first to set the icing, then wrap well.

White fruitcake

Serves 8

- 1½ cups butter, softened
- 2 cups sugar
- 6 eggs
- 1 teaspoon ground nutmeg
- 1 teaspoon pure vanilla extract
- ½ cup bourbon
- 2 teaspoons baking powder
- 4 cups flour
- 1 pound candied cherries
- 1 pound candied pineapple, cut into ½-inch pieces
- 1 pound shelled pecans

1. Preheat the oven to 275°F.
2. In a large bowl, cream together the butter and sugar. Add the eggs, one at a time, beating well after each addition. Add the nutmeg, vanilla, and bourbon. Sift together the baking powder and 3 cups of the flour and fold it into the batter.
3. In a medium-size bowl, dredge the cherries and the pineapple with the remaining flour. Spread the fruit mixture in a pan and place it in the oven for about 5 minutes. Add the flour-coated fruit and pecans to the batter. Pour the batter into a greased 10-inch tube pan and bake until the cake is lightly browned at the edges, about 3 hours.
4. Cool in the pan for 30 minutes before removing to a wire rack to cool completely.

NOTE: The great benefit of fruitcake is that it improves with age. It can be made months ahead, sprinkled with extra bourbon or brandy, wrapped tightly in cheesecloth, and then tightly sealed in plastic or foil.

ENGLISH CHRISTMAS CAKE

In England, Christmas Cake always means a large, rich dark fruitcake. Though in northern counties the cake is simply decorated with toasted almonds or marzipan, in the south the adornment is more festive and elaborate, as it is in this recipe.

Serves 16

1 cup plus 4 tablespoons butter, softened

2 cups finely chopped mixed candied fruit peel (about 10 ounces)

1½ cups dried currants

2 cups golden raisins

1 cup dark raisins

½ cup candied cherries, cut in half

½ cup finely chopped candied angelica

2 cups flour

½ teaspoon baking powder

½ teaspoon salt

1 cup firmly packed dark brown sugar

1 cup shelled almonds (about 6 ounces), pulverized in a food processor or blender or with a nut grinder or mortar and pestle

4 eggs

¼ cup pale dry sherry, rum, or brandy

Glaze

¼ cup red currant jelly

Marzipan

2 cups almond paste

1 teaspoon pure almond extract

½ teaspoon salt

1 cup light corn syrup

7 cups confectioners' sugar (2 pounds), sifted

Icing

6 cups confectioners' sugar, sifted

4 egg whites

1 tablespoon strained fresh lemon juice

⅛ teaspoon salt

1. Preheat the oven to 275°F.

2. Using a pastry brush, coat the bottom and sides of a 12-by-3-inch springform cake pan with 2 tablespoons of the softened butter. Coat one side of a 20-inch piece of wax paper with 2 tablespoons of butter, and fit the paper, greased side up, over the bottom of the pan with the excess extending up the sides.

3. In a large bowl, combine the fruit peel, currants, raisins, cherries, and angelica. Sprinkle the fruit with ½ cup of the flour, tossing it with a spoon to coat the pieces evenly. Set it aside. Then sift the remaining 1½ cups of flour with the baking powder and salt. Set it aside.

4. In another large bowl, cream the 1 cup of butter with the brown sugar by mashing and beating them against the sides of the bowl until they are light and fluffy. Add the almonds, then beat in the eggs one at a time. Add the flour-and-baking-powder mixture, a half cup or so at a time, then beat the fruit mixture into the batter. Finally, add the sherry and pour the batter into the springform pan. It should come to no more than an inch from the top. If necessary, remove and discard any excess.

5. Bake in the middle of the oven until a cake tester inserted in the center of the cake comes out clean, about 2 hours. Let the cake cool for about 30 minutes before removing the sides of the springform pan, then slip the cake off the bottom of the pan onto a cake rack to cool completely. Carefully peel off the strip of wax paper.

6. To make the glaze, heat the red currant jelly in a small saucepan over medium heat until it reaches a temperature of 225°F. on a candy thermometer or is thick enough to coat a wooden spoon lightly. With a small metal spatula, spread the hot glaze evenly over the top and sides of the cake.

7. To make the marzipan, use an electric mixer, preferably one equipped with

A SPARKLING DESSERT BUFFET

A dessert buffet offers you the chance to show off to advantage an array of your finest sweets. You can be sure that guests will want to sample a little of each, so provide half again as many servings as their number. Offer sparkling wines or dessert wines, as well as nonalcoholic wines and sparkling cider, and, of course, plenty of good coffee— mocha, spiced, or liqueur-laced. Since most of the work will be done beforehand, this is a party you will enjoy as much as your guests do. (See suggested menu on page 217.)

a paddle. Crumble the almond paste in small pieces into the bowl, add the almond extract and salt, and beat at medium speed until well blended. Gradually add the corn syrup in a thin stream, beating constantly until the mixture is smooth. Then beat in the 7 cups of confectioners' sugar, ½ cup at a time. As soon as the mixture becomes so stiff that it clogs the beater, knead in the remaining sugar with your hands. From time to time it will be necessary to soften the marzipan as you add the sugar by placing it on a surface and kneading it for a few minutes. Press the ball down, push it forward, and fold it back on itself, repeating the process for as long as is necessary to make it pliable.

8. On a clean surface, roll out half the marzipan into a circle about ½ inch thick. Using a 12-inch pan or plate as a pattern, cut a 12-inch disk out of the circle with a pastry wheel or a small, sharp knife. Roll and cut the remaining marzipan into a 36-by-3-inch strip. Gently set the disk of marzipan on top of the cake and press it lightly into place. Wrap the strip of marzipan around the sides of the cake, pressing it gently to secure it. If the strip overlaps the top, fold the rim down lightly.

9. Wrap the cake in foil or plastic, and let it stand at room temperature for at least 48 hours before icing. The cake

may be stored for longer periods; it improves with age, and can be kept for several months.

10. On the day you are serving it, ice the cake. Combine the confectioners' sugar, egg whites, lemon juice, and salt in a large mixing bowl. With a whisk or an electric beater, beat until the mixture is fluffy but firm enough to stand in soft peaks on the beater when it is lifted out of the bowl. With a small metal spatula, spread the icing evenly over the sides and top of the cake. Then decorate the cake to your taste with swirls of icing, artificial holly and mistletoe, candied fruits, or even small china reindeer, people, and houses.

NOTE: Packaged marzipan is available in some supermarkets and in specialty foods stores. If you decide to use it, skip step #7.

TWELFTH NIGHT CAKE

The twelfth night after the birth of Jesus traditionally marks the end of the festive Christmas season and the time when we take down the decorations and dispose of the tree.

There is a special cake to have on this evening—the French call it a *Galette des Rois*—and given below you will find a simple version. One custom is that hidden treasure (a new coin or a small charm or trinket) is baked inside. The person who finds the treasure is king for the night.

Another custom is to bake the cake with a bean and a pea (dried) in the batter. The one who finds the bean is the king and the one who finds the pea is the queen. They rule over the party, wearing crowns, and leading the games.

Serves 10 to 12

1 cup butter, softened

2 teaspoons grated lemon zest

1½ cups sifted confectioners' sugar

¾ cup flour

¾ teaspoon salt

1½ teaspoons baking powder

½ cup rice flour (available in natural foods stores)

3 eggs, separated, plus 3 yolks, the whites at room temperature

Confectioners' sugar for topping

Little figures of three kings or crowns or stars for decoration

1. Preheat the oven to 350°F.
2. In the large bowl of an electric mixer, cream the butter with the lemon zest. Add the confectioners' sugar and beat until the mixture is fluffy.
3. Sift the flour with the salt, baking powder, and rice flour.
4. Add one-third of the flour mixture to the creamed mixture. Add 2 of the egg yolks and beat until smooth. Repeat the procedure twice with the remaining flour and egg yolks.
5. In another bowl of the electric mixer, beat the egg whites until stiff peaks form. Stir one-third of the egg whites into the batter until well mixed. Gently fold the remaining egg whites into the batter.
6. Pour the batter into a greased 9-inch tube pan and bake until the cake is springy and a skewer comes out clean, about 1 hour. Cool the cake for 10 minutes in the pan.
7. Remove the cake from the pan and cool it completely on a rack. Sprinkle it with confectioners' sugar and decorate it with the figurines.

CANDIED CHESTNUT ROLL

This is one of the most impressive looking desserts and—with candied chestnuts, or *marrons glacés*, to flavor it—one of the most delectable. Yet it takes just an hour or so to put together and is close to being foolproof.

Makes one 15-inch roll

¾ cup sifted cake flour

1 teaspoon baking powder

¼ teaspoon salt

4 eggs

¾ cup sugar

1 teaspoon pure vanilla extract

Confectioners' sugar

Chestnut Butter Cream

3 egg yolks

½ pound unsalted butter, softened

½ cup sugar

⅓ cup light corn syrup

¼ cup dark rum

12 ounces *marrons glacés* (available at some supermarkets and in specialty foods stores), 5 chestnuts reserved for garnish and the rest cut into small bits

Chocolate curls, shaved from unsweetened chocolate with a vegetable peeler

1. Preheat the oven to 400°F.

2. Use a pastry brush to coat the bottom of a 15½-by-10½-inch jelly-roll pan lightly with melted or softened butter. Line the pan with parchment baking paper or wax paper trimmed to fit, and butter the paper.

3. Sift the flour, baking powder, and salt together, and set them aside.

4. In a large bowl, beat the eggs with a wire whisk or an electric beater until they are light and foamy. Adding the ¾ cup sugar slowly, continue beating until the mixture thickens and almost triples in bulk, at least 10 minutes.

5. Sprinkle the sifted dry ingredients over the batter, and use a rubber spatula to fold them in gently. Fold in the vanilla. Pour the batter into the prepared pan.

6. Bake the cake until it is springy and delicately browned, about 12 minutes.

7. Loosen the cake around the edges with a knife, and turn it out onto a clean cloth towel sprinkled evenly with confectioners' sugar. Working quickly while the cake is still warm, carefully peel away the paper. Cut off the crisp edges of the cake with a sharp knife. Starting at one long side, gently roll up the cake along with the towel, which will keep the cake from sticking to itself. Place the roll, towel and all, on a cake rack to cool.

8. Meanwhile, prepare the butter cream in a medium-size bowl by first beating the egg yolks with a wire whisk or rotary or an electric beater until they are foamy and lemon colored, 2 to 3 minutes. In another bowl, cream the butter by beating it vigorously against the sides of the bowl with a spoon until the butter is light and fluffy; refrigerate briefly.

9. Combine the ½ cup sugar and the corn syrup in a small heavy saucepan. Stirring constantly, cook over medium heat until the mixture comes to a boil. Then, beating the egg yolks constantly, add the hot syrup to them in a thin stream; continue to beat until the mixture cools, 10 to 15 minutes. Beat in the butter, a spoonful or so at a time. Stir in the rum and chestnuts. Cover the bowl with plastic wrap and refrigerate the butter cream until it is firm enough to spread easily, about 30 minutes.

10. When the cake is cool, unroll it and remove the towel. Spread the top with half of the chestnut butter cream. Reroll the cake, place it on a serving plate, and frost the outside of the roll with the rest of the cream. Cut each of the reserved chestnuts in half. Decorate the sides of the roll with the chestnuts and the top with the chocolate curls.

Pear and cranberry flan

Serves 6

- 1 cup sifted flour
- 2 teaspoons sugar
- ¼ teaspoon salt
- 2 tablespoons cold unsalted butter, cut into pieces
- 1 teaspoon cold unsalted margarine, preferably corn oil margarine, cut into pieces
- 3 tablespoons cold water
- ½ teaspoon pure vanilla extract
- 3 cups cranberries, picked over
- ¼ cup fresh orange juice
- 5 tablespoons sugar
- 3 ripe but firm pears, peeled, cored, cut into ¼-inch-thick slices, and tossed with the juice of ½ lemon
- 1 tablespoon chopped hazelnuts (filberts) (optional)

1. To prepare the flan pastry, combine the flour, sugar, and salt in a medium-size bowl. Use a pastry blender or two knives to cut the butter and margarine into the dry ingredients, then mix in the vanilla and water with a wooden spoon or your hands. Shape the dough into a ball.

2. To make the pastry with a food processor, put the flour, sugar, salt, butter, and margarine in the bowl and process with the steel blade attachment until the mixture resembles coarse cornmeal. With the motor running, add the vanilla and gradually add the water until the dough forms a ball.

3. Wrap the dough in plastic wrap and chill until it is firm enough to roll, about 20 minutes.

4. Meanwhile, put the cranberries into a small saucepan with just enough water to float the berries; bring the liquid to a simmer and cook the cranberries until they burst, about 4 minutes. Drain the cranberries to remove any excess liquid and put them in a food processor or blender; add the orange juice and 3 tablespoons of the sugar. Process the cranberries just until they are puréed.

(Take care not to overprocess the cranberries. Crushing the seeds can make the purée bitter.) Strain the purée through a fine sieve to remove the seeds and skins; chill the purée.

5. To form the flan shell, set the chilled dough on a floured surface. Using a rolling pin, flatten the ball of dough into a round, then roll the dough into a 10-inch circle. Transfer the dough to an 8-inch tart pan with a removable bottom by rolling the dough around the rolling pin and then unrolling it onto the tart pan. Gently press the dough into the corners and up the sides of the tart pan. Fold any excess dough back into the pan and press it well into the sides. Chill the flan shell for 10 minutes.

6. Preheat the oven to 425°F.

7. To prebake the flan shell, put the tart pan on a baking sheet. Prick the bottom of the dough several times with a fork. Line the flan shell with a round piece of wax paper and fill it with dried beans; this helps the pastry keep its shape. Bake the pastry for 10 minutes, remove the beans and wax paper, and continue baking until the flan shell is dry and just begins to color, about 5 minutes more. Remove the shell from the oven and let it cool in the tart pan.

8. Meanwhile, make a sugar syrup: Heat the remaining 2 tablespoons of sugar with 2 tablespoons of water in a small saucepan over medium-low heat until the sugar is dissolved, 3 to 4 minutes.

9. To assemble the flan, fill the bottom of the cooled flan shell with the cranberry purée. Arrange the pear slices on top in a circular pattern, overlapping the pieces slightly. Brush the pears and the edge of the pastry with the sugar syrup. Sprinkle the top with the hazelnuts, if you are using them. Bake the flan until the pears are soft and glazed, about 10 minutes. Remove the flan from the tart pan and serve it warm or cold.

PUMPKIN PIE

Serves 8 to 10

- 1 10-inch pie shell, unbaked
- 2 cups fresh or canned unsweetened pumpkin purée
- 1 tablespoon cornstarch
- 1 teaspoon ground cinnamon
- ½ teaspoon ground ginger
- ½ teaspoon grated nutmeg
- ⅛ teaspoon ground cloves
- Pinch of mace
- ½ teaspoon salt
- 1½ tablespoons butter, melted
- 1 12-ounce can evaporated milk
- ¾ cup granulated sugar
- ¼ cup firmly packed dark brown sugar
- ⅛ cup molasses
- 2 eggs, beaten
- ¼ teaspoon lemon juice
- Freshly grated nutmeg
- Sweetened whipped cream, flavored with a dash of rum or brandy

1. Preheat the oven to 450°F.
2. Place the pumpkin purée in a large bowl. Sift the cornstarch, cinnamon, ginger, nutmeg, cloves, mace, and salt into the pumpkin, and stir to blend well.
3. Gradually add the melted butter and evaporated milk, and beat until they are well combined. Add the sugars, molasses, eggs, and lemon juice, and continue to beat until the filling is well blended.
4. Pour the pumpkin filling into the prepared pie shell. Grate fresh nutmeg over the top.
5. Bake the pie for 15 minutes. Reduce the heat to 350°F. and continue baking until a knife inserted in the center comes out clean, about 50 minutes more. Cool the pie on a rack.
6. Serve the pie at room temperature with the whipped cream.

CHRISTMAS PIES

Dame get up and
bake your pies
Bake your pies,
bake your pies.
Dame get up and
bake your pies
On Christmas day
in the morning.

OLD ENGLISH
NURSERY RHYME

FROZEN CRANBERRY VELVET PIE

Serves 10 to 12

- 1¼ cups fine vanilla wafer crumbs
- 6 tablespoons butter, melted
- 8 ounces cream cheese, softened
- 1 cup heavy cream
- ¼ cup sugar
- ½ teaspoon pure vanilla extract
- 1 16-ounce can whole-cranberry sauce

1. To make the crust, combine the crumbs and butter in a medium-size bowl and blend well. Transfer the mixture to a 10-inch pie pan, and press the crumb mixture evenly against the sides and bottom of the pan to form a crust. Chill the crust for 1 hour.
2. In a medium-size bowl, whip the cream cheese until smooth. In the large bowl of an electric mixer, place the cream, sugar, and vanilla, and beat until the mixture is thick but not stiff. Gradually add the cream cheese, and beat until the mixture is smooth.
3. Fold the cranberries into the cream cheese mixture, and spread the mixture into the chilled crust. Freeze overnight or until firm.

MINCEMEAT TARTS

These delicious pick-up tarts can be eaten like cookies.

Makes 8 tarts

- 1 cup flour
- ½ cup butter, softened
- 1 3-ounce package cream cheese, softened
- 1 cup mincemeat *(see Note)*
- Sweetened whipped cream for garnish

1. In a large bowl, place the flour, butter, and cream cheese, and work with a pastry blender until well combined. With your hands, form the dough into a ball, wrap it in plastic wrap, and refrigerate it for 2 hours.
2. On a floured surface, roll the dough to a ¼-inch thickness. Cut it into 8 circles, each about 2½ inches in diameter, and into 16 rings of the same size (use a doughnut cutter for the rings).
3. Moisten the edge of a circle with water and lay one ring on it. Moisten the edge of the ring and top with a second ring. Press the pastry around the edge of the ring with the tines of a fork. Repeat the procedure until all of the pastry is used.
4. Preheat the oven to 450°F.
5. Place the tart shells on an ungreased baking sheet and bake them until lightly browned, 7 to 10 minutes. Cool the tarts on a wire rack.
6. Fill each tart with 2 tablespoons of mincemeat and garnish it with a teaspoon of whipped cream.

NOTE: Prepared mincemeat is available in jars and packages. If you use the packaged variety, be sure to follow the instructions for reconstituting the mixture.

HONEY-WALNUT TART

Sweetened with honey and laced with rum, this delicious tart is similar to Southern pecan pie, but is made with walnuts rather than pecans.

Serves 6 to 8
Sweet Pastry

- 1½ cups flour
- ⅓ cup sugar
- Pinch of salt
- ½ cup chilled butter, cut into ½-inch pieces
- 1 egg yolk
- 1½ tablespoons cold water

Honey-Walnut Filling

- 1 cup walnuts
- 3 eggs
- ½ cup honey
- ⅓ cup corn syrup
- 1½ tablespoons dark rum
- 1½ tablespoons unsalted butter, melted
- ¼ teaspoon pure vanilla extract

1. To make the pastry, combine the flour, sugar, and salt in a bowl. Cut the butter into the dry ingredients with a pastry blender or work quickly with your fingertips until the mixture resembles coarse cornmeal with some pea-size pieces remaining. With a fork, blend in the egg yolk and add up to 1½ tablespoons of cold water, if necessary, to hold the dough together.
2. To make the pastry with a food processor, place the flour, sugar, salt, and butter in the bowl and process with the steel blade attachment until the mixture resembles coarse cornmeal. With the motor running, add the egg yolk and, if necessary, gradually add the cold water until the dough forms a ball.
3. Press the dough into a disk. Cover it with plastic wrap and chill the dough for at least 20 minutes before rolling

out. (It can be refrigerated for a couple
of days but should be brought almost to
room temperature before rolling out.)
4. On a floured surface, roll out the
disk to measure slightly larger than a
10-inch tart pan. Line the pan with the
dough. Gently press the dough on the
bottom of the pan toward the middle.
Press down the dough around the sides
so that just a fraction of an inch
extends above the rim. Roll the rolling
pin across the top of the pan to cut off
the excess dough. Chill the dough in
the pan for 20 minutes or overnight.
5. Preheat the oven to 425°F.

6. Press a double thickness of aluminum foil against the pastry to hold it
in place. Bake the pastry until it begins
to brown, about 10 minutes. Reduce
the heat to 350°F., remove the foil, and
continue to bake until the crust is lightly browned, about 10 minutes.
7. To make the filling, break the walnuts
into pieces. In a large bowl, mix together
the eggs, honey, corn syrup, rum, butter,
and vanilla. Add the walnuts.
8. Pour the filling into the prepared tart
shell. Bake the tart until the filling is
puffed and the pastry is golden, about
30 minutes. Cut into wedges and serve.

UPSIDE-DOWN CRANBERRY PUDDING

Serves 6

- 2 tablespoons butter, softened, plus 6 tablespoons butter, melted and cooled
- 1½ cups firm, fresh, unblemished cranberries, rinsed, picked over, and patted dry
- ¼ cup coarsely chopped walnuts
- ⅓ cup plus ½ cup sugar
- 1 egg
- ½ cup flour
- ½ cup heavy cream, chilled

1. Preheat the oven to 325°F.
2. With a pastry brush, spread the 2 tablespoons of softened butter over the bottom and sides of an 8-inch pie pan. Spread the cranberries evenly in the bottom of the buttered pan and sprinkle them with the chopped walnuts and ⅓ cup of the sugar.
3. In a medium-size bowl, beat the egg and the remaining ½ cup of sugar together until the mixture thickens and clings to the beater. Beating constantly, add the flour, a few tablespoonfuls at a time. Then beat in the melted cooled butter and pour the batter over the cranberries and nuts.
4. Bake the pudding in the middle of the oven until the top is golden brown and a cake tester inserted in the center comes out clean, about 45 minutes. Cool the pudding to room temperature.
5. Meanwhile, in a chilled bowl, whip the cream until it is stiff enough to stand in unwavering peaks on the beater when it is lifted from the bowl. Refrigerate it, covered with plastic wrap, until ready to serve.
6. To unmold and serve the pudding, run a thin-bladed knife around the sides of the pan to loosen it. Place an inverted serving plate over the pudding and, grasping plate and pan together firmly, carefully turn them over. The pudding should slide out easily. Deco-rate the pudding as fancifully as you like by piping the whipped cream onto the top through a pastry bag fitted with a decorative tube, or simply spread the cream over the pudding and swirl it about with a small spatula.

PLUM PUDDING WITH BRANDY BUTTER

Though proper plum pudding at one time contained prunes (dried plums), raisins have become a common substitute. English tradition calls for every member of the family, beginning with the eldest, to stir the pudding before it is baked. The pudding is stirred from "east to west" in honor of the Magi's journey to visit the Christ Child.

To make four 1-pound puddings

- 1½ cups dried currants
- 2 cups seedless raisins
- 2 cups golden raisins
- ¾ cup finely chopped candied mixed fruit peel
- ¾ cup finely chopped candied cherries
- 1 cup blanched slivered almonds
- 1 tart cooking apple, peeled, quartered, cored, and coarsely chopped
- 1 small carrot, scraped and coarsely chopped
- 2 tablespoons finely grated orange zest
- 2 teaspoons finely grated lemon zest
- ½ pound finely chopped beef suet
- 2 cups flour
- 4 cups fresh soft bread crumbs
- 1 cup packed dark brown sugar
- 1 teaspoon ground allspice
- 1 teaspoon salt
- 6 eggs
- 1 cup brandy
- ⅓ cup fresh orange juice
- ¼ cup fresh lemon juice
- Brandy Butter
- ½ cup brandy, for flaming (optional)

1. In a large bowl, combine the currants, raisins, candied fruit peel, cherries, almonds, apple, carrot, orange and lemon zest, and beef suet, tossing them until well mixed. Stir in the flour, bread crumbs, brown sugar, allspice, and salt.

2. In a separate bowl, beat the eggs until frothy. Stir in the 1 cup brandy and the orange and lemon juice, and pour this mixture over the fruit mixture. Knead vigorously, then beat until all the ingredients are blended. Cover and refrigerate for at least 12 hours.

3. Spoon the mixture into four 1-quart pudding basins, deep stoneware bowls, or plain molds, filling them to within 2 inches of their tops. Cover each mold with a strip of buttered aluminum foil, turning the edges down and pressing the foil lightly around the sides to secure it. Drape a damp kitchen towel over each mold and tie with cord. Bring two opposite corners of the towel up to the top and knot them in the center of the mold; then bring up the remaining two corners and knot them.

4. Place the molds in a large pot and pour in enough boiling water to come about three-fourths of the way up their sides. Bring the water to a boil over high heat, cover the pot tightly, reduce the heat to its lowest point, and steam the puddings for 8 hours. As the water in the steamer boils away, replenish it with additional boiling water.

5. When the puddings are done, remove them from the water and let them cool to room temperature. Then remove the towels and foil and re-cover the molds tightly with fresh foil. Refrigerate the puddings for at least 3 weeks before serving. Plum puddings may be kept up to a year in the refrigerator or other cool place.

6. To serve, place the mold in a pot and pour in enough boiling water to come about three-fourths of the way up the sides of the mold. Bring to a boil over high heat, cover the pot, reduce the heat to low, and steam for 2 hours. Run a knife around the inside edges of the mold and place an inverted serving plate over it. Grasping the mold and plate firmly together, turn them over. The pudding should slide out easily. Serve with Brandy Butter.

A WELL-LOVED PUDDING

In days when desserts were less prevalent than today, a steamed Christmas pudding could elicit the highest praise, as in this breathless Victorian accolade: "And then when it is dished, when the pudding, in all the glory of its own splendour, shines upon the table, how eager is the anticipation of the near delight! How beautifully it steams! How delicious it smells! How round it is! A kiss is round, the horizon is round, the earth is round, the moon is round, the sun and stars, and all the host of heaven are round. So is plum pudding."

ILLUSTRATED LONDON NEWS, DECEMBER 1848

Brandy Butter

To make about ¾ cup

    4 tablespoons unsalted butter, softened
    ½ cup superfine sugar
    3 tablespoons brandy
    ½ teaspoon pure vanilla extract

Cream the butter until it is light and fluffy. Beat in the sugar, a few tablespoons at a time, and continue beating until the mixture is very white and frothy. Beat in the brandy and vanilla. Refrigerate at least 4 hours, or until firm.

NOTE: To flame the pudding, warm the ½ cup of brandy in a small saucepan over low heat, ignite it with a match, and pour it over the pudding.

TRADITIONAL OLD ENGLISH CAROL

We wish you a merry Christmas
We wish you a merry Christmas
We wish you a merry Christmas
And a happy New Year.

We all want some figgy pudding
We all want some figgy pudding
We all want some figgy pudding
So bring some out here.

We won't go until we get some
We won't go until we get some
We won't go until we get some
So bring some out here.

Good tidings we bring to you and your kin
We wish you a Merry Christmas and a Happy New Year.

FIGGY PUDDING
WITH COGNAC SAUCE

Serves 12

2 eggs
½ cup butter, softened
½ cup molasses
½ cup pure maple syrup
1 cup buttermilk
2 cups chopped figs
½ cup combined dark raisins and dried currants
½ orange (with its peel), ground
½ cup chopped walnuts
2⅔ cups flour
½ teaspoon baking soda
2 teaspoons baking powder
1 teaspoon salt
1 teaspoon ground cinnamon
½ teaspoon ground nutmeg
½ teaspoon ground mace

Cognac Sauce

⅔ cup butter, at room temperature
2 cups confectioners' sugar
⅓ cup cognac or brandy
4 egg yolks
1 cup heavy cream

1. Preheat the oven to 325°F.
2. In a large bowl, beat the eggs with the butter until the mixture is light and fluffy. Beat in the molasses and the syrup. Add the buttermilk, figs, raisins and currants, orange, and nuts. Mix well.
3. In a medium-size bowl, sift together the flour, baking soda, baking powder, salt, cinnamon, nutmeg, and mace. Stir the dry mixture into the fruit mixture.
4. Pour the mixture into a greased 9-inch tube pan and bake it until a cake tester inserted in the center comes out clean, about 1 hour.
5. To make the sauce, beat the butter and sugar together in a medium-size bowl or in the top of a double boiler

until the mixture is light and fluffy. Beat in the cognac.

6. Place the bowl or pan over simmering water. Beat the egg yolks into the sauce one at a time; then add the cream, stirring constantly until the sauce thickens. Pass the sauce in a separate bowl and serve with the pudding.

NOTE: Brandy is an acceptable substitute for the more expensive cognac.

RICE PUDDING
WITH RASPBERRY SAUCE

Serves 8

4 cups milk

½ cup long-grain rice

½ cup plus 2 tablespoons sugar

¼ teaspoon salt

1 egg yolk

3 tablespoons flour

½ teaspoon grated nutmeg

1 teaspoon pure vanilla extract

¼ teaspoon pure almond extract

¼ cup golden raisins

2 cups fresh raspberries or frozen whole raspberries, thawed

Freshly grated nutmeg (optional)

Fresh mint leaves (optional)

1. Bring 3 cups of the milk to a boil in a heavy saucepan over medium heat. Reduce the heat to low and add the rice, ¼ cup of the sugar, and the salt. Cook the mixture, stirring frequently, for 50 minutes.

2. Whisk together the egg yolk and ¼ cup of the remaining milk in a medium-size saucepan. Whisk in the flour and ¼ cup of the remaining sugar; then blend in the remaining ¾ cup of milk. Bring the mixture to a boil over medium heat, stirring constantly, then cook it, still stirring vigorously, for 2 minutes more. Remove the pan from the heat and stir in the nutmeg, vanilla, and almond extract.

3. When the rice has finished cooking, stir in the raisins, then fold in the egg

THE STORY OF JACK'S PLUM

Who does not know about Jack Horner and the plum he pulled out of his Christmas pie, but who knows the truth behind the nursery rhyme? It is said that it was not "Jack" but Thomas Horner, who bore a Christmas pie to King Henry VIII from the Abbot of Glastonbury. In the pie were hidden deeds to twelve English manors, former church property, intended as gifts to the king. On the way to London, Horner removed one of the deeds—a very excellent plum—for himself.

and milk mixture. Transfer the pudding to a clean bowl. To prevent a skin from forming on its surface, press a sheet of plastic wrap directly onto the pudding. Refrigerate the pudding until it is cold, about 2 hours.

4. To prepare the sauce, purée the raspberries and the remaining 2 tablespoons of sugar in a food processor or a blender. Rub the purée through a fine sieve with a plastic spatula or the back of a wooden spoon; discard the seeds.

5. To serve, divide the sauce among eight serving dishes. Top the sauce with individual scoops of pudding; if you like, sprinkle the scoops with some additional nutmeg and garnish each with a sprig of mint.

172

TRIFLE

Consisting essentially of sponge cake, custard, and fruit, this venerable English dessert has many versions.

Serves 10

　1 9-inch sponge cake layer

　¾ cup dry sherry

　2 10-ounce packages frozen raspberries, thawed and drained

　2 10-ounce packages frozen peaches, thawed and drained

　2 egg whites

　1 cup heavy cream

　1 tablespoon sugar

　½ cup toasted slivered almonds

Custard Sauce

　2 cups milk

　6 egg yolks

　¼ cup sugar

　Pinch of salt

　1 teaspoon pure vanilla extract

1. To make the custard sauce, scald the milk in the top of a double boiler over medium heat. Meanwhile, in a medium-size bowl, whisk the egg yolks until frothy, then add the sugar and salt. Pour a little hot milk into the egg yolk mixture, beating with a fork, and then stir the yolk mixture into the rest of the milk. Place the custard over simmering, not boiling, water and cook, stirring constantly, until the mixture coats a metal spoon. Pour the custard into a bowl and stir in the vanilla. Cover it and refrigerate it until it is thickened, about 1 hour, before adding it to the trifle.

2. To assemble the trifle, slice the sponge cake into three thin layers. Place one layer in the bottom of a flat-bottomed serving bowl, preferably glass, about 10 inches across and 5 inches deep.

3. Sprinkle the cake layer with ¼ cup of the sherry. Reserve and set aside 12 raspberries. Spread about one-third of the remaining raspberries and one-third of the peach slices on top of the cake. Pour one-third of the custard sauce over the fruit. Repeat cake, sherry, fruit, and custard for two additional layers.

4. Beat the egg whites until stiff in the large bowl of an electric mixer. In a separate large bowl, whip the cream until it forms soft peaks. Stir the sugar into the cream and gently fold in the beaten egg whites. Mound the cream-and-egg-white mixture over the top of the trifle. Garnish with the reserved raspberries and the toasted almonds. Refrigerate the trifle until you are ready to serve.

PEARS CARDINALE

Poaching in red wine colors, as well as flavors, the pears, turning them into a fine Christmastime dessert.

Serves 6

　¾ cup sugar

　2 cups dry red wine

　1 cup water

　4 whole cloves

　½ cinnamon stick

　Peel of ½ orange and ½ lemon

　1 teaspoon pure vanilla extract

　6 fresh pears, peeled and left whole, with stem attached

　½ cup red currant jelly

1. Put the sugar, wine, water, cloves, cinnamon stick, orange and lemon peels, and vanilla into a large enameled or nonreactive saucepan. Bring to a boil, reduce the heat to low, and simmer for 20 minutes.

2. Place the pears in the syrup and poach them over low heat, turning once, until they are tender but firm, 10 to 15 minutes. Using a slotted spoon, remove the pears from the pan and set aside.

3. Add the currant jelly to the pan, and stir well until it is dissolved. Return the pears to the pan, remove it from the heat, and cool the pears in the syrup. Chill the pears and serve in glass dessert dishes, with the syrup spooned over top.

AMBROSIA

Serves 6 to 8

- 1½ cups fresh pineapple, peeled, cored, and cut into 1-inch chunks
- 5 large seedless oranges, peeled and sectioned
- 1 cup freshly grated coconut
- 2 tablespoons sugar
- 3 tablespoons orange juice
- 2 bananas, peeled and cut into 1-inch pieces

1. In a large bowl, layer the pineapple, oranges, and coconut. Sprinkle the sugar and then the orange juice over the fruit, and stir the mixture gently to combine.
2. Cover the bowl with plastic wrap, and refrigerate the mixture for at least 2 hours, or overnight, if desired.
3. Just before serving, add the bananas. Gently stir again to mix. Serve the ambrosia in a large glass bowl.

ORANGE SLICES IN RED WINE AND PORT

Serves 6

- 6 large navel oranges
- 1 cup Beaujolais or other fruity red wine
- ¼ cup sugar
- 1 cinnamon stick
- ⅛ teaspoon ground cardamom or allspice
- ⅓ cup ruby port wine
- 2 tablespoons dried currants
- 2 tablespoons toasted sweetened shredded coconut

1. With a vegetable peeler, remove the zest from one of the oranges. Put the zest into a small saucepan with the wine, sugar, cinnamon stick, and cardamom or allspice. Bring the mixture to a boil and cook it over medium-high heat until the liquid is reduced to about ⅔ cup, approximately 5 minutes. Remove the pan from the heat; stir in the port and currants, and set the sauce aside.
2. Cut away the skins, removing all the white pith, and slice the oranges into ¼-inch-thick rounds. Arrange the orange rounds on a serving dish and pour the wine sauce over them; remove and discard the cinnamon stick. Refrigerate the dish, covered, for 2 hours.
3. Just before serving the oranges, sprinkle the toasted coconut over all.

NOTE: To toast the coconut, spread it on a baking sheet and bake in a preheated 325°F. oven, stirring every 5 minutes, until it has browned, about 15 minutes in all. Coconut also toasts well in a microwave oven. For 2 tablespoons, spread the coconut on a plate and toast on high for 3 minutes, stirring after 2 minutes to assure even toasting (larger amounts of coconut will take a longer time).

PEPPERMINT-STICK ICE CREAM

Serves 10

- ½ pound peppermint-stick candy, crushed
- 2 cups milk
- 1 cup light cream
- 1 cup heavy cream
- Shaved sweet chocolate

1. Place the peppermint candy and the milk in a medium-size bowl and refrigerate them, covered, for 12 hours.
2. Add the cream and heavy cream to the milk mixture and freeze in an ice cream maker, according to the manufacturer's instructions.
3. Serve with shaved sweet chocolate sprinkled on top.

CRANBERRY SORBET

Serves 8

¾ pound fresh or frozen cranberries (about 3 cups) (if fresh, rinsed and picked over)

2½ cups water

1½ cups sugar

2 tablespoons lemon juice

1 kiwi fruit, peeled and thinly sliced (optional)

1. Put the cranberries into a saucepan with the water. Bring the mixture to a simmer and cook it just until the cranberries pop, about 2 minutes.
2. Pass the mixture through a sieve, rubbing the cranberries through with the back of a wooden spoon. Stir in the sugar and lemon juice, and place the mixture in a large nonreactive metal bowl in the freezer. When a ring of crystals about half an inch wide has formed around the outside edge of the mixture, usually after an hour or two, whisk the mixture. Return the bowl to the freezer and allow another ring of crystals to form before whisking the mixture again. Repeat the whisking a few more times until the dessert is frozen through. After the final whisking, allow the dessert to freeze an additional 15 minutes, then serve it.
3. Serve the sorbet in scoops; if you like, garnish each portion with the kiwi slices.

NOTE: The cranberry mixture may also be frozen in an ice cream maker, according to the manufacturer's instructions.

Breakfasts & Brunches

 OUSE GUESTS AND UPTURNED HOLIDAY schedules often call for special breakfast and brunch dishes in place of the daily routine of cereal or eggs. The brunch dishes presented here offer such tastiness and variety that they might be considered year round for special occasions, as well as for light, quick, and nourishing family suppers. Breakfasts or brunches may begin with a first course of fruit and Granola, followed by a hearty dish, such as Baked Christmas Mushroom Omelet. If you prefer a sweeter main course, choose Norwegian Apple Pancakes or Pumpkin Waffles with Cider Syrup, which are easy and quick to make, and bound to be special favorites of the young in the house. Lots of steamy coffee, perhaps cinnamon- or hazelnut-flavored, and hot chocolate are essentials. Even more than for lunches or dinners, brunches that can be prepared partially or entirely in advance are particularly prized. You will find convenience and good flavor alike in Overnight French Toast and Curried Fruit Compote, which are actually improved by being made a day ahead.

Orange and Kiwi Fruit Slices and Overnight French Toast

BANANA-APPLE SALAD WITH DATES AND NUTS

Serves 4 to 6

  2 large eating apples, cored and cut into ½-inch pieces

  2 tablespoons lemon juice

  2 tablespoons water

  2 bananas, sliced

  1 cup pitted dates (not sugared), chopped

  ¼ cup chopped walnuts

  1 cup vanilla yogurt

  2 tablespoons honey

1. Place the apples in a large bowl and sprinkle them with the lemon juice and water. Toss to coat the apples.
2. Drain the juice from the apples and add the bananas, dates, and walnuts to the bowl.
3. In a small bowl, beat together the yogurt and the honey. Mix it with the fruit. Place the salad in a serving bowl and chill it until ready to serve.

CURRIED FRUIT COMPOTE

Serves 6

  1 cup apple cider or unsweetened apple juice

  2 tablespoons mango chutney, coarsely chopped

  1 teaspoon curry powder

  3 dried apricots, thinly sliced

  2 apples, preferably Granny Smith, cored and cut into 1-inch pieces

  ¼ cup dark raisins

  ¼ cup golden raisins

  1 cantaloupe, seeded and peeled, the flesh cut into 1-inch pieces

  1 large banana, peeled and cut into ¾-inch pieces

  ½ teaspoon cornstarch, mixed with 1 tablespoon water

1. Combine the cider or apple juice, chutney, and curry powder in a large saucepan and bring the mixture to a boil. Reduce the heat to medium and simmer the mixture, partly covered, for 5 minutes. Add the apricots, apples, and raisins and simmer them, covered, until the apples begin to soften, about 3 minutes.
2. Stir in the cantaloupe, the banana, and the cornstarch mixture and simmer them, stirring occasionally, until the liquid has thickened, about 2 minutes. Serve the compote warm.

GRANOLA

Serves 24

  4 cups rolled oats

  4 cups rolled wheat

  1½ cups unsweetened shredded coconut

  1 cup wheat germ

  1 cup chopped nuts (walnuts, pecans, or almonds)

  1 cup sunflower seeds

  ½ cup bran

  ½ cup sesame seeds

  ½ cup vegetable oil

  ½ cup honey or maple syrup

  1 to 2 teaspoons pure vanilla extract

  1 cup dark raisins or chopped dates

1. Preheat the oven to 375°F.
2. In a large bowl, mix together the oats, wheat, coconut, wheat germ, nuts, sunflower seeds, bran, and sesame seeds.
3. Combine the oil, honey or maple syrup, and vanilla in a small saucepan, and warm over low heat until they are well blended.
4. Pour the honey-oil mixture over the dry ingredients in the bowl and mix well.
5. Place the granola in a 9-by-13-inch pan and bake, stirring frequently, until golden, 20 to 30 minutes.
6. Remove the granola from the oven and stir in the raisins or dates. Cool and then store in an airtight container.

BAKED EGGS IN TOMATO SHELLS

This dish tastes as good as it looks. Prepare the tomato shells in advance.

Serves 12

    12 medium-ripe firm tomatoes

    Salt and freshly ground black pepper

    1½ teaspoons dried basil, crumbled

    12 eggs

    3 ounces processed Swiss cheese,
      shredded (¾ cup)

    ¾ cup fine dry bread crumbs

    6 tablespoons butter, melted

1. Preheat the oven to 350°F.

2. Cut a thin slice from the top of each tomato; scoop out the pulp. Turn the tomatoes upside down and let them drain for about 10 minutes. Turn them over again and sprinkle them with salt and pepper and the basil. Arrange the tomato shells in a greased baking dish, cut side up.

3. Break an egg into each tomato shell; sprinkle it with a little salt. Bake the shells until the egg whites have set, about 35 minutes.

4. In a small bowl, combine the cheese, bread crumbs, and butter; sprinkle the mixture on the eggs. Return the eggs to the oven and bake until the cheese melts and the crumbs are browned, about 2 minutes. Serve immediately.

ORANGE SLICES WITH POMEGRANATE SEEDS

Serves 6

> 3 navel oranges
>
> 1½ tablespoons finely chopped crystallized ginger
>
> ½ cup fresh orange juice
>
> 1 tablespoon dark rum
>
> 2 tablespoons sugar
>
> ½ teaspoon pure vanilla extract
>
> ¼ cup pomegranate seeds, or 1 kiwi fruit, peeled, quartered, and thinly sliced

1. Using a sharp, stainless-steel knife, cut off both ends of one of the oranges. Stand the orange on end and cut away vertical strips of the peel and pith. Slice the orange into ¼-inch-thick rounds.

Peel and slice the remaining oranges the same way.

2. Sprinkle the ginger into the bottom of a 9-inch nonreactive pie plate. Arrange the orange slices in a spiral pattern, overlapping them slightly, and set the pie plate aside.

3. Combine the orange juice, rum, and sugar in a small enameled or nonreactive saucepan over medium-high heat and boil the mixture for 5 minutes. Remove the pan from the heat and let the syrup cool slightly, then stir in the vanilla. Pour the syrup over the orange slices and chill the fruit thoroughly.

4. Invert a serving plate over the pie plate, quickly turn both over together, and lift away the pie plate. Sprinkle the orange slices with the pomegranate seeds, or scatter the kiwi fruit over the oranges, and serve at once.

LAYERED BREAD, TOMATO, AND ZUCCHINI CASSEROLE

Serves 8

2 eggs, plus 2 egg whites

1 cup milk

¼ teaspoon salt

Freshly ground black pepper

2 small zucchini, or 1 large zucchini, cut into ¼-inch-thick rounds (about ½ pound)

1 onion, chopped

4 ripe tomatoes, peeled, seeded, and chopped, or 14 ounces canned whole tomatoes, drained and chopped

¼ cup chopped fresh parsley

2 tablespoons chopped fresh basil, or 2 teaspoons dried basil

8 slices Italian or French bread, cut into ½-inch cubes (about 8 cups)

¼ pound mozzarella cheese, grated (about 1 cup)

1. Whisk the eggs, egg whites, milk, salt, and some pepper together in a bowl and set it aside.

2. Preheat the oven to 350°F.

3. Put the zucchini and onion into a nonstick skillet over low heat and cook them, covered, until they are soft, about 4 minutes. Add the tomatoes and increase the heat to high. Cook the vegetables, stirring continuously, until most of the liquid has evaporated, about 5 minutes. Remove the skillet from the heat and stir in the parsley and basil.

4. Spoon half of the vegetable mixture into an 8-by-12-inch baking dish; add half of the bread cubes and sprinkle half of the cheese over the bread. Repeat the process with the remaining vegetable mixture, bread, and cheese, then pour the egg mixture over all.

5. Bake the casserole until the egg mixture has set, about 20 minutes. Increase the oven temperature to 450°F. and continue baking the casserole until it is lightly browned, about 5 minutes more. Cut into eight squares and serve it hot.

BAKED CANADIAN BACON

Serves 6

3 pounds whole uncooked Canadian bacon, casing removed

½ cup firmly packed light brown sugar

1 tablespoon Dijon mustard

Dash of allspice

1 cup pineapple or orange juice

1. Preheat the oven to 325°F.

2. In a small bowl, mix the sugar, mustard, and allspice and spread it on top of the bacon.

3. Place the bacon on a rack in a roasting pan, and bake for 35 minutes to the pound. Baste often with the juice. Slice and serve warm.

NOTE: If you are using precooked Canadian bacon, bake only until the bacon is heated through and the glaze has browned, about 40 minutes.

Zucchini frittata

The Italian-style omelet, *frittata,* has two advantages over the French: It can be made for larger numbers of people and does not call for such precise timing. Endless vegetable, meat, and cheese combinations may be used as fillings.

Serves 6

3 tablespoons olive oil

2 tablespoons butter

6 to 8 small zucchini, scrubbed, trimmed, and cut into ¼-inch rounds

8 eggs

1 teaspoon salt

½ teaspoon freshly ground black pepper

½ cup grated Parmesan cheese

1. Heat the oil and butter in a large ovenproof skillet and sauté the zucchini slices over low heat until just tender, about 8 minutes.
2. In a medium-size bowl, beat the eggs with the salt and pepper and pour them gently over the zucchini. Cook the mixture over very low heat until just set, about 10 minutes.
3. Sprinkle the cheese on top and run the frittata under the broiler to brown it lightly. Let the frittata stand for a minute or two, and then cut into wedges and serve.

Broccoli and ricotta pie

Serves 6

1 envelope fast-rising dry yeast

2½ cups flour, preferably bread flour

¼ teaspoon salt

1 tablespoon olive oil

1½ cups chopped onion

½ teaspoon caraway seeds, or 2 teaspoons dried dill

1 egg, plus 2 egg whites

¾ cup part-skim ricotta cheese

¾ cup milk

Freshly ground black pepper

⅛ teaspoon grated nutmeg

1 ounce Canadian bacon, finely chopped

1 tablespoon cornmeal

1½ cups broccoli florets, blanched in boiling water for 1 minute and drained

2 tablespoons freshly grated Parmesan cheese

1. In a large bowl, mix the yeast with 1 cup of the flour and ⅛ teaspoon of the salt. Heat ¾ cup of water in a saucepan just until it is hot to the touch (130°F.). Pour the hot water into the flour mixture and stir the dough vigorously with a wooden spoon. Stir in 1 teaspoon of the oil and 1 more cup of the flour. Transfer the dough to a floured surface and begin to knead it. If the dough seems too sticky, gradually add up to ½ cup of flour; if it seems too dry, add water, 1 teaspoon at a time, as required. Knead the dough until it is smooth and elastic, about 10 minutes. Transfer the dough to an oiled bowl, turn the dough once to coat it with the oil, and cover the bowl with a damp towel or plastic wrap. Set the bowl in a warm, draft-free place and let the dough rise until it has doubled in volume, about 30 minutes.
2. While the dough is rising, heat the remaining 2 teaspoons of oil in a heavy skillet over medium-high heat. Add the onion and the caraway seeds or dill and cook the mixture, stirring frequently, until the onion is lightly browned, about 10 minutes. Remove the skillet from the heat and set it aside.
3. Whisk the egg and the egg whites in a large bowl until well blended. Whisk in the ricotta, the milk, the remaining ⅛ teaspoon of salt, some pepper, the nutmeg, and the Canadian bacon. Stir in half of the onion mixture and set the bowl aside.
4. Preheat the oven to 400°F. After the dough has finished rising, punch it

down. Knead the remaining onion mixture into the dough.

5. Sprinkle an 8-inch-wide cast-iron skillet or an 11-inch glass pie plate with the cornmeal. Put the dough in the skillet or pie plate and, with your fingertips, gently work some of the dough toward the edge to form a 2-inch-high rim. Allow the dough to stand for 10 minutes.

6. Place the skillet or pie plate in the oven for 10 minutes to partially bake the dough. Remove the crust from the oven; if the edge is not ¾ of an inch higher than the flat surface of the crust,

gently push the dough down to form a depression. Pour in the ricotta-egg mixture. Place the broccoli florets one at a time, bud sides up, in the filling, then sprinkle the Parmesan cheese over the surface of the pie. Return the skillet to the oven and bake the pie until the filling is set and the top is lightly browned, 35 to 40 minutes. Let the pie stand for 10 minutes before cutting.

NOTE: This recipe uses fast-rising yeast, which requires a different method of preparation from compressed or active dry yeast.

RED-FLANNEL HASH

Serves 4 to 6

¼ pound bacon, cut into ¼-inch pieces

½ cup finely chopped onion

2 cups (about 1 pound) finely chopped cooked corn beef

1 cup diced cooked beets, fresh or canned

3 cups coarsely chopped cooked potatoes

4 tablespoons finely chopped fresh parsley

¼ cup heavy cream

Salt and freshly ground black pepper

1. In a 10- or 12-inch skillet, fry the bacon until brown but not too crisp. Then set it aside to drain on paper towels. Pour off all but 2 tablespoons of fat from the pan and reserve.
2. Add the onions to the pan and cook them over medium heat for 3 to 5 minutes, but don't let them brown. Scrape them into a large bowl. Add to the bowl the corned beef, the beets, the reserved bacon, the potatoes, 2 tablespoons of the chopped parsley, and the cream. Mix together gently but thoroughly and add salt and freshly ground pepper to taste.
3. Heat the reserved bacon fat in the skillet. Add the hash, and, with a spatula, spread it evenly in the pan and pat it down. Cook, uncovered, over medium heat for 35 to 40 minutes, shaking the pan occasionally to prevent the hash from sticking. As it cooks, remove any excess fat from the top or sides of the pan with a spoon or bulb baster. When the hash is done (it should be crusty brown on the bottom) slide a metal spatula around the inside edge of the skillet and as far under the hash as you can without crumbling it. Then place a large, round platter over the skillet, and, gripping platter and skillet firmly together, invert the hash onto the platter.

4. If any of the hash has stuck to the pan, lift it out with a spatula and patch it in place. Sprinkle with the remaining chopped parsley and serve with poached eggs, if desired.

LOUISIANA CHICKEN HASH

Serves 6

2 tablespoons butter

2 tablespoons flour

½ teaspoon salt

½ teaspoon white pepper

½ teaspoon freshly ground black pepper

½ teaspoon dried thyme

½ teaspoon paprika

½ teaspoon cayenne pepper or less

4 cups hot milk

2 pounds poached chicken meat, cut into ½-inch cubes

6 to 12 eggs, poached

1. Melt the butter in a heavy saucepan, add the flour, and cook over medium-low heat, stirring constantly, until the mixture is a light brown color, about 5 minutes. Add the salt, peppers, thyme, paprika, and cayenne, and cook for 1 minute, stirring constantly, to toast the spices. Whisk in the hot milk and cook over medium-high heat, stirring constantly, until the sauce is thick and bubbly, about 10 minutes. Remove the saucepan from the heat.
2. Adjust the seasonings and add the chicken.
3. Preheat the oven to 350°F.
4. Place the hash in individual greased baking dishes and bake until bubbly, about 10 minutes. Top with 1 or 2 eggs and serve immediately.

NOTE: Leftover cooked chicken may be used in this dish, but newly poached chicken meat is preferable.

OVERNIGHT FRENCH TOAST

Allowing the soaked bread slices to rest overnight yields soft and creamy centers.

Serves 6

> 2 eggs, plus 2 egg whites
>
> ⅓ cup sugar
>
> Grated zest of 2 lemons
>
> ¼ teaspoon salt
>
> 2 cups milk
>
> 2 tablespoons light or dark rum, or 1 teaspoon pure vanilla extract
>
> 1 loaf (about 1 pound) French or Italian bread, the ends trimmed, cut into 12 ¾-inch-thick slices
>
> Freshly grated nutmeg

1. In a large, shallow dish, whisk together the eggs, egg whites, sugar, lemon zest, and salt; then whisk in the milk and the rum or vanilla.

2. Dip the bread slices into the egg- and-milk mixture, turning them once or twice until they are thoroughly soaked with the liquid. Transfer the slices to a large plate as you work. Drizzle any liquid remaining in the dish over the slices, then sprinkle some nutmeg over them. Cover the slices with plastic wrap and refrigerate them overnight.

3. Preheat the oven to 400°F.

4. Heat a large griddle or skillet over medium heat until a few drops of cold water dance when sprinkled on the surface. Put as many prepared bread slices as will fit on the griddle or skillet and cook them until the undersides are golden, about 3 minutes. Turn the slices and cook them until the second sides are lightly browned, 2 to 3 minutes more. Transfer the slices to a baking sheet. Brown the remaining slices and transfer them to the baking sheet.

5. Place the baking sheet in the oven and bake the French toast until it is cooked through and has puffed up, about 10 minutes. Serve it hot with the syrup or topping of your choice.

Eggnog french toast

There couldn't be a more perfect or simple way to begin Christmas morning than with eggnog French toast. Because the eggnog can be made the day before, you'll have plenty of time to peek into stockings and open Christmas presents.

Serves 6

>2 cups prepared eggnog, with or without spirits *(page 24)*
>
>8 tablespoons unsalted butter
>
>12 thick slices stale firm white bread

1. Pour the eggnog into a shallow bowl and dip the bread slices into the eggnog, turning to coat both sides. Transfer them to a large plate as you work. Drizzle any liquid remaining in the dish over the slices.
2. Preheat the oven to 150°F.
3. Melt 2 tablespoons of the butter in a skillet over medium-high heat. Add 2 or 3 slices of the bread and cook them until the undersides are golden, 3 to 5 minutes. Turn the slices and cook until the second sides are golden, 3 to 4 minutes more. Transfer the cooked slices to a baking sheet and keep warm in the oven while you repeat the procedure with the remaining bread and butter.

Baked christmas mushroom omelet

Serves 4

>1 pound mushrooms, wiped clean and trimmed
>
>4 tablespoons butter, melted
>
>8 eggs, separated
>
>3 tablespoons flour
>
>2 cups hot milk
>
>¼ cup dry sherry
>
>Salt and freshly ground black pepper
>
>¼ teaspoon cayenne pepper

1. Place the mushrooms in a broiling pan. Brush the mushrooms with a little of the butter and broil them, turning once, until lightly browned and cooked through, about 4 minutes. Let them cool, then slice them.
2. Lower the oven heat to 350°F.
3. In the large bowl of an electric mixer, beat the egg whites until they are stiff but not dry. In a medium-size bowl, beat the yolks until they are light and lemon colored.
4. Place the flour in a large mixing bowl and gradually add the hot milk, stirring rapidly with a wire whisk or beater. Add 2 tablespoons of the melted butter, the egg yolks, sherry, salt and pepper to taste, cayenne, and the mushrooms. Fold in the egg whites and pour the mixture into a greased 6-cup baking dish. Pour the remaining butter on top and bake until puffy and brown, about 45 minutes.

Puffy fruit omelet

Serves 4

>2 eggs, separated, plus 2 egg whites
>
>2 tablespoons flour
>
>½ teaspoon baking powder
>
>⅛ teaspoon salt
>
>½ cup milk
>
>5 teaspoons sugar
>
>1 teaspoon vegetable oil
>
>1 sweet red apple, preferably Stayman or Winesap, quartered, cored, and cut into ½-inch pieces
>
>1 pear, preferably Bosc, quartered, cored, and cut into ½-inch pieces
>
>1 teaspoon lemon juice
>
>¼ teaspoon ground cinnamon
>
>2 tablespoons raspberry preserves
>
>2 tablespoons apple cider or unsweetened apple juice

1. Preheat the oven to 450°F.
2. In a medium-size bowl, whisk together the egg yolks, flour, baking powder, salt, and 3 tablespoons of the milk until the mixture is well blended,

5 to 7 minutes. Whisk in the remaining milk.

3. In the large bowl of an electric mixer, beat the egg whites with 3 teaspoons of the sugar until they form soft peaks. Stir half of the whites into the yolk mixture and then gently fold in the remaining whites just until the mixture is blended; do not overmix. Set the egg mixture aside.

4. Heat the oil in a large, ovenproof skillet over medium-high heat. Add the apple and the pear, the remaining 2 teaspoons of sugar, the lemon juice, and the cinnamon and cook the fruit,

stirring frequently, until it is tender, about 5 minutes. Remove the skillet from the heat and pour the egg mixture over the fruit; smooth the top of the mixture with a spatula. Place the skillet in the oven and bake the omelet until the top is golden brown, 10 to 15 minutes.

5. While the omelet is baking, mix together the raspberry preserves and the cider or unsweetened apple juice in a small dish. When the omelet is ready, drizzle this syrup over it, cut the omelet into quarters, and serve it immediately.

Norwegian apple pancakes

These crêpes are festive for brunch or dessert.

Serves 6 to 12

Apple Filling

4 tablespoons butter

4 cups very thinly sliced peeled apples

¼ teaspoon ground cinnamon

1 teaspoon grated lemon zest

5 tablespoons red currant jelly

Batter

2 eggs plus 1 egg yolk

1½ cups milk

¼ teaspoon pure vanilla extract

⅛ teaspoon ground cardamom

⅛ teaspoon salt

¼ cup unsalted butter, melted

1 cup flour

Topping

Sugar

Slivered almonds

1. To make the filling, melt the butter in a large skillet over low heat. When the foam subsides, add the apples, cinnamon, and lemon zest. Cook, stirring frequently, until the apples are soft, about 4 minutes. When the apples begin to get soft, add the red currant jelly and stir until it melts. Keep the mixture warm.
2. In a medium-size bowl, beat the eggs and egg yolk until they are light in color and thickened. Add the milk, vanilla, cardamom, salt, and butter and beat well. Sift in the flour and beat well to mix. The batter will be thin.
3. Preheat the oven to 150°F.
4. Lightly grease an 8- or 9-inch skillet, preferably one with sloping sides (which will make the turning easier), and place it over medium-high heat. Once the skillet is hot, pour in about ¼ cup of the batter. When the pancake is brown on the bottom, slide an egg turner under a corner of the pancake, maneuvering it to the middle, and flip the pancake over. Let the pancake cook until it is brown on the bottom.
5. Remove the pancake, put 2 to 3 tablespoons of apple filling in the center, fold one edge over and then the other to cover the filling, then gently turn the rolled pancake over so the seam is down. Sprinkle with sugar and slivered almonds. Serve at once or keep warm on a platter in the oven until the rest are done. It probably will not be necessary to grease the skillet for subsequent pancakes, but if the cakes stick, brush on a little more oil with a pastry brush.

NOTE: This quantity makes 12 to 14 pancakes. You should probably serve two per person for dessert; one might suffice for brunch if there are other dishes.

Ginger pancakes

Serves 4

2½ cups whole-wheat flour

½ teaspoon salt

1½ teaspoons baking soda

1 teaspoon ground cloves

1 tablespoon ground cinnamon

3 eggs, lightly beaten

¼ cup firmly packed light brown sugar

2 cups buttermilk

¼ cup freshly brewed coffee

1 tablespoon butter, melted

2 tablespoons grated fresh ginger

1. In a medium-size bowl, combine the flour, salt, baking soda, cloves, and cinnamon and mix well with your hands (sieve the baking soda if it is lumpy).
2. In a large bowl or a pancake pitcher, stir together the eggs, sugar, buttermilk, coffee, butter, and ginger. Add the flour mixture to the egg mixture

and stir just to blend; do not overmix.

3. Preheat the oven to 150°F.

4. Cook the pancakes over medium-high heat on a lightly oiled, sizzling pancake griddle or in a cast-iron skillet for approximately 5 minutes on the first side and 1 minute after flipping. Serve immediately, or keep warm in the oven until all are cooked.

PUMPKIN WAFFLES WITH CIDER SYRUP

Serves 4

2 cups flour

2 tablespoons sugar

4 teaspoons baking powder

¾ teaspoon salt

½ teaspoon ground coriander

1 tablespoon ground cinnamon

½ teaspoon grated nutmeg or ground mace

1½ cups milk

1 cup canned unsweetened pumpkin purée

4 eggs, separated

¾ cup butter, melted

1 tablespoon pure vanilla extract

Cider Syrup

1½ cups clear apple cider

1 cup firmly packed light brown sugar

1 cup light corn syrup

4 tablespoons butter

2 tablespoons fresh lemon juice

Grated zest of 1 lemon

⅛ teaspoon ground cinnamon

⅛ teaspoon freshly grated nutmeg

2 tart apples, peeled, cored, and thinly sliced

1. Preheat the waffle iron to hot.

2. Preheat the oven to 200°F.

3. To make the waffle batter, sift together the flour, sugar, baking powder, salt, coriander, cinnamon, and nutmeg or mace in a medium-size bowl. In

THE MEANING BEHIND HERBS

The lore of herbs is ancient, colorful, and fascinating, and many of the herbs used in Christmas cooking and decorating have special associations with various legends of the Nativity.

* Lavender, symbolizing purity, virtue, and cleanliness, was said to have been particularly loved by Mary.

* Rosemary was believed to have protected the Christ Child as its pliant leaves kept silent when the Holy Family slipped through fields of rosemary on its flight into Egypt. Placed in a baby's crib, rosemary was considered protection against nightmares.

* Thyme, symbolizing bravery, was thought to have lined the Christ Child's manger.

a large bowl, combine the milk, pumpkin purée, egg yolks, butter, and vanilla. Pour the milk mixture into the flour mixture and stir just to blend; do not overmix.

4. In the large bowl of an electric mixer, beat the egg whites until stiff but not dry. Fold them into the batter. Lightly oil the hot waffle iron and cook the batter until the waffles are browned, crisp, and come away easily from the iron. Keep the finished waffles warm in the oven while the rest cook.

5. To make the cider syrup, place the cider, sugar, corn syrup, butter, lemon juice and zest, cinnamon, and nutmeg in a 1½- to 2-quart saucepan. Bring to a boil, reduce the heat to low, and simmer, uncovered, until the mixture is the consistency of maple syrup, about 15 minutes. Just before serving, add the apple slices and heat several minutes. Serve, with butter, over the warm waffles.

NOTE: These waffles freeze very well. To reheat, warm them in a 350°F. oven for 3 to 5 minutes, uncovered.

Foods to Give

HE UNIQUENESS OF A HOMEMADE GIFT makes it all the more a treasure to the recipient, and gifts of food of every kind—from appetizers and relishes to breads and sweets—are especially welcome when Christmas guests place heavy demands on cooking and baking resources. The following pages contain some traditional favorites as well as some old standards with original twists to add to other food gift ideas suggested throughout this book. Begin Christmas gift preparations as early as seasonal foods become available. Tutti-Frutti is a summer-long project, beginning with strawberries in late spring. Gleaming jars and bottles of liqueurs and vinegars, jellies and preserves also store well. If gardening chores prevent you from carrying out the whole process of jelly-making at harvest time, at least extract the juice from the fruit and freeze it. You can then make the jelly at your leisure.

Baskets of gifts

BRANDIED WHITE GRAPES

Makes 2 pints

> 5 cups large white California grapes, washed, halved, and seeded (reserve the grape seeds)
>
> 2 cups water
>
> 2 cups sugar
>
> ½ cup brandy or cognac

1. Place the reserved grape seeds in a small saucepan. Cover with the water, bring to a boil, reduce the heat to low, and simmer for 15 minutes. Strain the cooking liquid.

2. Place the reserved liquid and the sugar in a large saucepan and bring the mixture to a boil over medium heat. Boil for 5 minutes.

3. Add the grapes to the pan and cook over medium heat until they are tender, about 10 minutes.

4. Remove the grapes from the pan with a slotted spoon and pack the fruit into sterilized pint jars. Pour ¼ cup of the brandy or cognac into each jar.

5. Continue to cook the syrup over medium heat until it is thick or registers 222°F. on a candy thermometer. Pour the hot syrup into the jars to within ⅛ inch of the top and seal them. Store the fruit in a cool, dark place.

NOTE: You may use dark sweet cherries instead of grapes. The procedure is the same, beginning with simmering the cherry pits.

APPLE MINT JELLY

A classic combination of flavors, this sweet jelly can be made slightly spicy by adding 1 teaspoon of cinnamon, ½ teaspoon of ground allspice, or ½ teaspoon of ground nutmeg to the apples while they are cooking.

Makes 4 to 6 four-ounce jars

> 3 pounds tart apples, peeled, cored, and cut into ½-inch pieces
>
> Juice of 2 lemons
>
> 1½ cups water
>
> ½ cup chopped fresh mint
>
> 2 cups cider vinegar
>
> 1½ to 2½ cups sugar
>
> 2 tablespoons finely chopped fresh mint

1. Place the apples in a large stainless-steel saucepan and add the lemon juice, water, and the ½ cup of mint. Bring the mixture to a boil, reduce the heat to low, cover the pan, and simmer until the apples are reduced to a pulp, 15 to 20 minutes.

2. Suspend a jelly bag or a sieve lined with a double layer of damp cheesecloth over a large bowl. Pour the apple pulp into the bag or sieve and let it drip overnight. For a clear jelly, do not squeeze the bag.

3. Measure the liquid. For every 2 cups of juice, add 1½ cups sugar. Pour the juice and sugar mixture into the stainless-steel saucepan. Cook it over low heat, stirring constantly, until the sugar has dissolved. Then boil the liquid until it begins to jell, or reaches between 220° and 222°F. on a candy thermometer, about 10 minutes. Skim the foam from the top of the jelly periodically.

4. Remove the jelly from the heat, add the 2 tablespoons chopped mint, and stir. Pour it into hot, sterilized 4-ounce jars. Seal them immediately. Store the jelly in a cool, dark place.

THYME GRAPE JELLY

Makes 12 to 14 four-ounce jars

- 4 cups unsweetened grape juice
- 10 fresh thyme sprigs, each 3 inches long
- 1 lemon, sliced but not peeled
- 1 orange, quartered but not peeled
- 4 whole cloves
- 8 cups sugar
- ½ cup dark raisins
- 1 6-ounce bottle pectin
- Fresh thyme sprigs for garnish

1. Pour the grape juice into a large non-reactive saucepan. Add the 10 sprigs of thyme. Bring the juice to a boil and boil it for 10 minutes. Add the lemon, orange, cloves, and sugar. Cook over low heat until the fruit is tender, about 15 minutes. Remove the pan from the heat.

2. With a slotted spoon, lift out the fruit and place it on a plate to cool. Then chop it in a food processor or a food chopper and return it to the liquid. Stir in the raisins. Bring the jelly to a boil, pour in the pectin, and boil the mixture for 1 minute. Skim the foam from the top.

3. Pour the hot jelly into hot sterilized jars, poking a sprig of fresh thyme into each jar with a spoon. Seal the jars. Store the jelly in a cool, dark place.

DRESSING UP BAKED GOODS FOR GIVING

If you are an avid baker, buy handcrafted baskets and brightly colored, handwoven cloths or finely embroidered napkins, tea towels, and kerchiefs in which to wrap your loaves of bread and dainty cakes as gifts. Search out decorative tins, old or new, for nuts and candies. Baked goods are intrinsically beautiful, so all you need do in many cases is simply to arrange them on circles of heavy cardboard and wrap your cake, bread, or cookies in clear plastic wrap, tied around with red or green satin ribbon, and bedecked with a sprig of fresh greens or flowers. Your friends will appreciate receiving a copy of the recipe—provided you're willing to share it!

RED PEPPER JELLY

Serve this festive jelly with cream cheese, or as an accompaniment to cold meats.

Makes 2 pints

- ½ cup finely chopped hot red peppers
- 2 cups finely chopped sweet red peppers
- 1 cup apple cider vinegar
- 1½ cups sugar
- 2 ounces liquid pectin

1. Combine all the ingredients in a heavy enameled or nonreactive saucepan. Bring the mixture to a boil, stirring often. Reduce the heat to low and simmer, stirring frequently, for 5 minutes.
2. Pour the jelly into hot sterilized jars and seal. Store it in a cool dry place.

CRANBERRY KETCHUP

Cranberry ketchup is served as an accompaniment to poultry, wild game, or other meats.

Makes 1 pint

- 1 pound fresh cranberries, rinsed and picked over
- ½ cup finely chopped onions
- ½ cup water
- ½ cup distilled white vinegar
- 1 cup sugar
- ¾ teaspoon ground cloves
- ¾ teaspoon ground cinnamon
- ¾ teaspoon ground allspice
- ¾ teaspoon salt
- ¾ teaspoon celery seed
- ½ teaspoon freshly ground black pepper

1. Combine the cranberries and the chopped onion with the water in a 2- to 3-quart enameled or nonreactive saucepan and bring to a boil. Reduce the heat to low, cover the pan tightly, and simmer until the mixture can be easily mashed against the side of the pan with a spoon, 10 to 12 minutes.
2. Purée the cranberry mixture, with its cooking liquid, through the fine blade of a food mill or rub it through a fine sieve with the back of a spoon, pressing down hard on the berries before discarding the skins.
3. Pour the purée back into the saucepan and stir in the vinegar, sugar, cloves, cinnamon, allspice, salt, celery seed, and pepper. Bring the mixture to a boil and cook it, uncovered, over medium heat until most of the liquid in the pan has evaporated and the ketchup is thick enough to hold its shape almost solidly in a spoon, about 15 minutes. Stir the mixture from time to time to prevent the ketchup from sticking to the pan.
4. With a slotted spoon, skim off and discard any foam that may appear on the surface of the ketchup and taste it for seasoning. Ladle the hot ketchup into hot sterilized jars, process in a boiling water bath for 10 minutes, and seal the jars. Store the ketchup in a cool, dark place.

TARRAGON MUSTARD

Makes 4 cups

- 1 4-ounce tin English dry mustard (8 tablespoons)
- 1 cup tarragon vinegar
- 6 eggs
- ⅔ cup sugar
- 1 teaspoon salt
- ½ cup butter, cut into ½-inch pieces

1. Place the mustard in a small bowl and pour the vinegar over it. Do not stir. Cover the mixture with plastic wrap and let it stand overnight, at room temperature.
2. Put the mustard mixture in the top of a double boiler over hot water. Add the eggs one at a time, whisking after each

addition and continuing to whisk until the mixture is smooth. Blend in the sugar, salt, and butter, and cook, stirring constantly, until the mixture begins to thicken, about 5 minutes. Do not overcook or the mustard will curdle. Remove it from the heat and let it cool.
3. Pour the mustard into containers and refrigerate. It will keep for up to a month.

SPICED RED WINE VINEGAR

Perfect for a tangy salad dressing, this vinegar can also be sprinkled over meat or fish before grilling.

Makes 2 pints

4 cups red wine vinegar

½ teaspoon grated lemon zest

½ teaspoon ground mace

½ teaspoon dry mustard

½ teaspoon ground cinnamon

½ teaspoon ground cloves

½ teaspoon white mustard seeds (optional)

½ teaspoon black mustard seeds (optional)

½ teaspoon onion salt

½ teaspoon dried thyme

½ teaspoon black pepper

½ teaspoon paprika

½ teaspoon cayenne pepper

1 teaspoon celery salt

1 garlic clove

2 bay leaves

1. Place all of the ingredients in a large enameled or nonreactive saucepan. Bring the mixture to a boil and remove it from the heat. Cool the vinegar mixture in the pan.
2. Strain the mixture through a sieve lined with filter paper or damp cheesecloth into a nonreactive bowl. Cover the bowl with a clean cloth and let the vinegar stand for 3 days.
3. Filter or strain the vinegar again. Pour it into sterilized bottles and seal.

RASPBERRY VINEGAR

Makes about 1 quart

1 cup fresh raspberries, washed, those with blemishes discarded

3 cups white wine vinegar

1. Place the raspberries in a clean quart jar. Add the vinegar.
2. Cover the jar tightly and store it in the refrigerator for 1 week.
3. Strain the vinegar into bottles or jars with tight-fitting lids. Add a few of the raspberries to each container. The vinegar will keep indefinitely, stored in the refrigerator.

CURRY POWDER

Package this bright orange curry in an apothecary jar and arrange it in a basket with a container of chutney, a can of peanuts, and a bag of raisins or coconut.

Makes 1 cup

¼ cup poppy seeds

¼ cup coriander seeds

2 tablespoons ground turmeric

1 tablespoon cumin seed

1 4- to 6-inch stick cinnamon

10 whole cloves

1 teaspoon ground cardamom

1 teaspoon black peppercorns

1 teaspoon ground ginger

4 bay leaves

12 small dried hot chili peppers

1. Preheat the oven to 200°F.
2. Place all the ingredients in a shallow baking pan and bake for 25 minutes, stirring occasionally. Place the mixture in a blender and process at high speed until it is pulverized, about 60 seconds. Transfer the powder to one or more jars with tight-fitting lids.

saucepan and bring it to a boil over high heat, stirring until the sugar dissolves. Then cook briskly, uncovered and undisturbed, until the syrup reaches a temperature of 240°F. on a candy thermometer or until about ⅛ teaspoon of the syrup dropped into ice water instantly forms a soft ball.

3. At once remove the pan from the heat and add the cinnamon, nutmeg, and walnut halves. Stir gently for a few minutes, until the syrup becomes opaque and creamy. While the mixture is still soft, spread it on the buttered baking sheet and, with two table forks, carefully separate the candy-coated walnut halves. Set the sherried walnuts aside to cool to room temperature, then remove them with a spatula and store in a tightly covered jar.

Spiced mixed nuts

Makes about 1 pound

    1 tablespoon butter, softened

    ¾ cup sugar

    1 teaspoon ground cinnamon

    ½ teaspoon ground cloves

    ¼ teaspoon ground nutmeg

    ¼ teaspoon ground ginger

    ¼ teaspoon ground allspice

    ½ teaspoon salt

    1 egg white, lightly beaten

    2 tablespoons cold water

    1 cup whole unsalted blanched almonds

    1 cup unsalted broken walnuts, preferably black walnuts

    ½ cup whole unsalted hazelnuts (filberts)

1. Preheat the oven to 275°F.
2. With a pastry brush, spread the tablespoon of softened butter over a large baking sheet. In a small bowl, combine the sugar, cinnamon, cloves, nutmeg, ginger, allspice, and salt, and mix well. Add the egg white and water and stir until the mixture is a smooth paste.

Sherried walnuts

Makes about ½ pound

    1 tablespoon butter, softened

    1½ cups sugar

    ½ cup dry sherry

    ½ teaspoon ground cinnamon

    ⅛ teaspoon ground nutmeg

    2 cups unsalted walnut halves

1. With a pastry brush, spread the tablespoon of softened butter over a large baking sheet and set it aside.
2. Combine the sugar and sherry in a heavy 1-quart enameled or nonreactive

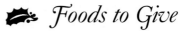

3. In a separate bowl, combine the nuts.
4. With a table fork, stir in about ½ cup of the nuts and, when they are evenly coated, transfer one at a time to the baking sheet. Coat the remaining nuts by the half cupful and arrange on the sheet in one layer.
5. Bake the nuts in the middle of the oven until the spice coating is crisp and golden brown, about 45 minutes. Cool the nuts to room temperature and store them in a tightly covered jar.

Ten bean soup

Here is a recipe to try at home and then share with friends. Tie the recipe to a bag of colorful assorted dried lentils, peas, and beans. To make several gifts, buy one pound each of 10 different legumes and prepare individual packages of the mix in plastic bags or jars, tied with a bright ribbon.

Makes about 4 quarts

¼ cup each of many beans (you may use any combination of lentils, green and yellow split peas, black beans, navy beans, lima beans, pinto beans, kidney beans, black-eyed peas, adzu beans, or any beans that are available), totaling 2½ cups, picked over

2 tablespoons barley

2 quarts water

1 ham bone or kielbasa sausage

1 bay leaf

2 garlic cloves

1 cup chopped onion

1 28-ounce can tomatoes, puréed in a food processor or blender

1 tablespoon chili powder

2 tablespoons lemon juice

½ teaspoon dried thyme

1 teaspoon dried savory (optional)

1 teaspoon salt

Freshly ground black pepper

1. Rinse the beans and barley and soak them overnight in enough water to cover them by about 3 inches.
2. Drain the beans and barley and rinse them under cold running water. Place them in a large, heavy enameled or nonreactive pot. Pour in the water. Add the ham bone or sausage, bay leaf, and garlic. Slowly bring the liquid to a boil over medium-low heat, reduce the heat to low, cover the pot, and cook gently for 3 hours, stirring occasionally.
3. Add the onion, tomatoes, chili powder, lemon juice, thyme, savory, if you are using it, salt, and pepper, and simmer for 30 minutes.
4. Remove the bone and bay leaf and serve. Extra soup may be frozen for another meal.

Herbed cheese

Makes about 3 cups

1 pound cream cheese or Camembert (rind removed), or ½ pound of each, softened

¼ cup butter, softened

2 tablespoons finely cut chives or green onion tops

2 tablespoons finely chopped fresh parsley

2 tablespoons chopped capers

1 tablespoon caraway seeds

Salt and black pepper

1. Place the cheese and butter in a large bowl. Add the chives or green onion tops, parsley, capers, and caraway seeds. With a wooden spoon, mix the ingredients, blending thoroughly. Add a little salt and pepper if desired.
2. Pack the cheese mixture into small containers and cover them with foil tops or lids. Store the cheese in the refrigerator.
3. For gift-giving, tie a ribbon on each container and place it in a basket with a package of thinly sliced pumpernickel bread or a small box of crackers.

READYING COOKIES FOR CHRISTMAS MAILING

To mail your gifts of cookies safely, line a stiff container with foil and cushion the bottom with a bed of gaily colored, crushed tissue paper. Wrap freshly baked, sturdy cookies individually or back to back in plastic wrap, place the heaviest on the bottom, and stuff the spaces in between with shredded tissue paper. Top with a layer of foil, put the lid in place, and tape it. You may want to include an address inside the box so that if the outer wrapping becomes torn or lost, the inner address may still assure delivery. Now take a slightly larger box, and place the gift box inside it, buffering the smaller box with popcorn or plastic packing materials. Use a waterproof marker for the outside address. Be sure to include the zip code, and place tape over the address to protect it further.

ORANGE-FLAVORED HONEY CAKE

This moist loaf cake keeps well and makes a nice change from gifts of quick bread or fruitcake.

Makes one 9-inch loaf cake

  3 tablespoons unsalted butter, softened

  ½ cup sugar

  2 egg yolks

  ½ cup honey

  1½ cups flour

  ½ teaspoon baking soda

  ½ teaspoon baking powder

  ½ teaspoon ground cinnamon

  ¼ teaspoon salt

  ¼ cup strained freshly squeezed orange juice

  2 tablespoons grated orange zest

  ½ teaspoon pure vanilla extract

  ½ cup finely chopped walnuts

  2 egg whites

1. Preheat the oven to 350°F.
2. With a pastry brush, coat the bottom and sides of a 9-by-5-by-3-inch loaf pan with 1 tablespoon of the butter.
3. In a large bowl, cream the 2 remaining tablespoons of butter and the sugar together by mashing them against the sides of the bowl with a wooden spoon. With a wire whisk or a rotary or an electric beater, beat in the egg yolks, one at a time; then, beating constantly, pour in the honey in a slow, thin stream.
4. In a large bowl, sift together the flour, baking soda, baking powder, cinnamon, and salt. Beat ½ cup of this mixture into the batter, then beat in the coffee. Beating constantly, beat in another ½ cup of the flour mixture, then the orange juice, then the remaining flour mixture. Stir in the orange zest, the vanilla, and the nuts.
5. With a clean dry whisk or beater in a separate bowl, beat the egg whites until they form unwavering peaks when the beater is lifted from the bowl. With a rubber spatula, gently but thor-

oughly fold the beaten whites into the batter, using an over-under cutting motion rather than a stirring motion.
6. Pour the batter into the prepared loaf pan and bake the cake in the center of the oven until a cake tester inserted in the center comes out clean, about 1 hour. Cool it in the pan for a few minutes, then run a sharp knife around the edges and turn the cake out on a rack. Cool it completely before slicing.

NOTE: Tightly wrapped, honey cake can be stored for several weeks.

WALNUT CRANBERRY BREAD

Makes 1 loaf

  2 tablespoons butter, softened

  1 cup sugar

  1 egg, lightly beaten

  Grated zest of 2 oranges

  ¾ cup orange juice

  2 cups plus 1 tablespoon flour

  ½ teaspoon salt

  ½ teaspoon baking soda

  1½ teaspoons baking powder

  1 cup whole cranberries

  ¾ cup chopped walnuts

1. Preheat the oven to 325°F.
2. In a large bowl, cream the butter and sugar together until they are light and fluffy. Add the egg, then the orange zest and juice, and mix until well blended.
3. Sift the 2 cups of flour, salt, baking soda, and baking powder onto wax paper.
4. Place the cranberries and nuts in a small bowl and dust them with the 1 tablespoon of flour.
5. Add the sifted dry ingredients to the sugar-orange mixture and stir to blend. Stir in the cranberries and nuts.
6. Pour the batter into a greased and floured 9-by-5-by-3-inch loaf pan. Bake it until a cake tester inserted in the center comes out clean, 1 to 1¼ hours.

Cool the bread in the pan on a wire rack for 10 minutes before removing from the pan.

DATE NUT BREAD

Makes 2 loaves

1½ cups chopped dates

1½ cups boiling water

2 teaspoons baking soda

1 tablespoon vegetable shortening

1½ cups sugar

½ teaspoon salt

2 teaspoons pure vanilla extract

1 egg, slightly beaten

2¾ cups flour

1 cup chopped walnuts

1. Preheat the oven to 350°F.

2. In a small bowl, combine the dates with 1 cup of the boiling water, and let them stand for 10 to 15 minutes while proceeding with the recipe.

3. In a large bowl, mix the baking soda with the remaining ½ cup of boiling water. Add the shortening, sugar, salt, vanilla, and egg, and beat until well combined.

4. Add the flour and nuts to the egg mixture and stir to blend. Add the dates and water and stir just until the dates are evenly distributed in the batter; do not overmix.

5. Pour the batter into two greased 9-by-5-by-3-inch loaf pans and bake until browned on top, about 45 minutes. Cool the loaves on a wire rack for 10 minutes before removing from the pans and continuing to cool.

COINTREAU CHOCOLATE SAUCE

This simple-to-make sauce may be served over fresh strawberries, poached pears, or a vanilla soufflé. Grand Marnier, cognac, Amaretto, or any liqueur can be substituted for Cointreau. If no liqueur is desired, increase the cream by ⅓ cup.

Makes 2 cups

1 cup heavy cream

10 ounces semisweet chocolate, chopped

3 tablespoons butter

⅓ cup Cointreau

1. In a heavy saucepan, bring the cream to a simmer over low heat. Remove the pan from the heat, add the chocolate and butter, and whisk until the mixture is smooth. Stir in the Cointreau.

2. Pour the sauce into warmed jars and store it in the refrigerator; the sauce will keep for several months. To serve, reheat the sauce in a double boiler, or place the jar in a small saucepan with about 1 inch of simmering water. The sauce can also be reheated in a microwave oven.

TUTTI-FRUTTI

What better way to show your friends that you think of them all year than by capturing summer's bounty in a jar and beginning to make this preserved fruit mixture in early summer for Christmas giving. Suggest that they eat it plain, drink the sauce as a cordial, or use the preserve as a topping for ice cream or pound cake, an embellishment for ham, or an enhancement for the stuffing for a holiday goose. Though it will keep for a long time, the tutti-frutti should be eaten up by the following spring.

Makes about 1½ gallons

    1½ pounds hulled ripe strawberries, wiped but not washed, enough cut in half to make 1 cup

    6½ pounds sugar

    1½ fifths, approximately, good quality brandy or rum

    1½ pounds fresh pineapple, peeled and cut into ¼-inch cubes, or ¾ pound each pineapple and orange meat free of skin, membrane, and seed, cut into ¼-inch cubes

    1½ pounds sweet or sour cherries, each pricked several times with a needle, or plums, quartered and pitted, or a mixture

    1½ pounds peeled, sliced peaches or apricots, or a mixture

    1½ pounds raspberries or ¾ pound raspberries and ¾ pound gooseberries (tipped and tailed), currants (pricked with a needle), or melon balls (honeydew or cantaloupe, not watermelon)

1. In a large bowl, combine the strawberries and 1½ pounds sugar, and stir well. Cover the bowl with plastic wrap and allow it to sit overnight at room temperature.
2. Make sure a crock, plate, and lid are very clean, then rinse each twice with boiling water and let them drain dry.
3. Pour 1 fifth of liquor into the crock and stir in the strawberry mixture. Set the plate on top of the berries to hold them under the liquid. Cover the crock and set it in the refrigerator.
4. For at least 1 week, but not more than 3, stir the mixture each day until the sugar dissolves. Remove and replace the plate each time.
5. In a large bowl, combine the pineapple or pineapple and oranges with 1½ pounds sugar, stir well, cover with plastic wrap, and allow to sit overnight. Remove the plate from the crock of strawberries. Stir in the pineapple mixture and check the liquid level; it should be at least ½ inch higher than the weighted fruit. Add more liquor if necessary. Replace the plate, cover the crock, and return it to the refrigerator.
6. Again, for at least 1 week, but not more than 3, stir the mixture each day until the sugar dissolves, removing and replacing the plate each time.
7. In a large bowl, combine the cherries or plums with 1½ pounds of sugar and repeat steps 5 and 6.
8. Using the peaches or apricots and 1 pound sugar, repeat steps 5 and 6.
9. In a large bowl, combine the raspberries or raspberries and gooseberries, currants, or melon balls with 1 pound of sugar; let the mixture sit overnight, then add it to the crock as before. Be sure the liquid level is at least 1½ inches above the fruit.
10. When all the sugar has dissolved, remove the plate and replace it with a floating layer of plastic wrap. Cover the crock, place it in the refrigerator, and allow the tutti-frutti to mature undisturbed for 4 to 6 weeks.

ORANGE AND COFFEE BEAN CORDIAL

Makes 1 pint

    1 extra large orange, washed

    44 coffee beans

    44 sugar cubes

    1 pint brandy or cognac

    1-inch length of vanilla bean

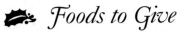

1. With a small, sharp-pointed knife, make as many small slits in the orange as possible. Stick a coffee bean in each slit and place the rest of the beans in a widemouthed quart jar. (Make sure the orange will fit in the jar.). Add the sugar cubes and the orange. Pour in the cognac and add the vanilla bean.

2. Let the cordial mature in a cool, dark place for 1½ to 2 months. Strain the cordial through a sieve lined with cheesecloth, squeezing the juice from the orange. Filter the cordial through a funnel lined with a coffee filter into a clean, attractive bottle, and tie with a holiday ribbon.

NOTE: Vodka or rum may be substituted for the brandy or cognac.

OLD-FASHIONED HOREHOUND CANDY

The bittersweet flavor of this candy is not to everyone's taste, but to some it is delightful, conjuring up memories of childhood joys. Horehound is a silvery-leaved herb that is easy to grow. In dried form it is often available at herb shops and natural foods stores.

Makes about 25 candies

    3 quarts water
    1 ounce dried horehound leaves,
        flowers, and stems (¼ cup)
    3 cups firmly packed light brown sugar
    1 teaspoon cream of tartar
    ¼ cup rum, or 1 teaspoon lemon juice
    1 teaspoon butter
    Superfine sugar

1. Bring the water to a boil in a large saucepan. Remove the pan from the heat, add the horehound, and let the mixture steep for 30 minutes. Strain the liquid into a bowl and let it settle.

2. Pour 2½ cups of the liquid into a heavy saucepan. (The rest of the liquid may be reserved for additional batches of candy.) To the liquid add the brown sugar, cream of tartar, and rum or lemon juice, and bring it to a boil. When the syrup reaches 240°F. on a candy thermometer, add the butter. Continue boiling over low to medium heat without stirring until the syrup reaches 312°F.

3. Pour the candy into a shallow buttered pan. Let it cool until you can handle it, then shape it into small oval candies. Roll the candies in superfine sugar, wrap each one in wax paper, and store them in airtight containers.

HAZELNUT LIQUEUR

Makes 1 pint

    6 ounces hazelnuts (filberts), chopped
    1-inch length of vanilla bean
    Pinch of allspice
    1½ cups vodka
    ⅓ cup sugar syrup (optional), made
        from 1 cup sugar and ½ cup water
        (see Note)

1. Place the hazelnuts in a widemouthed quart jar. Add the vanilla bean, allspice, and vodka.

2. Store the mixture for 2 weeks in a cool, dark place, shaking the jar occasionally. Strain the mixture through a sieve lined with cheesecloth, then pour it through a funnel lined with a coffee filter into a bowl as many times as necessary to produce a clear liquid.

3. Add the sugar syrup, if desired, return the liqueur to the quart jar, and age for 3 weeks more before bottling it.

NOTE: If you want a sweeter liqueur and decide to add sugar syrup, combine the sugar and water in a small saucepan and bring the mixture to a boil. Boil it for 5 minutes, or until the sugar is completely dissolved. Cool the syrup before adding it to the alcohol mixture, since heat will cause the alcohol to evaporate.

Decorations from the Kitchen

THE SIMPLEST CHRISTMAS DECORATIONS are often the loveliest. Indeed, a tree trimmed with items you have prepared—Christmas cookies, garlands of popcorn and cranberries, herb ornaments, and brightly polished apples—can be just as striking as the most lavishly decorated tree full of expensive store-bought trinkets. (Just be sure all the apples and cookies are not on one side of the tree or the sheer weight of them will bring your wonderful tree crashing to the floor!) Don't forget the importance of scent—it can be as much of an ornament to your home at Christmastime as any other decoration. A Christmas-cent Simmer is one way you can fill the air with delicious spiciness that will mingle delightfully with the familiar and welcoming fragrance of Christmas greens.

Gingerbread Carousel

GINGERBREAD CAROUSEL

A Gingerbread Carousel makes a delightful alternative to the gingerbread houses that have long been great favorites in many families—and it is quite easy to assemble, involving only a few simple cookie construction techniques. The conical roof is baked on a foil-covered posterboard form, which is left in place to support the roof on the candy stick posts. For the animal figures that are glued onto the carousel with icing, use cookie cutters in the shape of horses, or better still, circus animals. You may wish to place your carousel on a lazy susan so that the whole thing really can revolve.

1⅓ cups firmly packed light brown sugar

⅔ cup molasses

2 teaspoons ground cinnamon

2 teaspoons ground ginger

¼ teaspoon ground cloves

¾ cup butter

1 tablespoon baking powder

8 cups flour, sifted

Pinch of salt

2 eggs, lightly beaten

6 to 8 tablespoons water

1 18-by-24-inch piece of 6-ply posterboard

Aluminum foil

Empty bread crumb container, or similar container, 3½ inches in diameter, cut to 6½ inches high

Peppermint candies, candied fruit, raisins, candied angelica, almonds, colored sugars, paper flags as desired, for trimming

Thick Royal Icing

2 egg whites

4 cups confectioners' sugar

1½ teaspoons lemon juice

1. To make the gingerbread dough, in a heavy saucepan over low heat, dissolve the sugar with the molasses, spices, and butter. Slowly and carefully bring the mixture to a boil, cool it to room temperature, then mix in the baking powder. Place the flour and salt in a bowl and make a well in the center. Pour in the cooled syrup mixture and the eggs, and add the water gradually, stirring from the center to blend in the flour until a stiff dough is obtained. Turn the dough out onto a floured surface and knead about five times, then wrap it in wax paper and refrigerate for 30 minutes or so.

2. To make patterns for the various carousel pieces, mark a 1-inch grid on the posterboard and copy to scale the shapes shown here. With scissors, or a sharp knife and ruler, cut out templates for the base, roof, and center post slabs. Use commercial cookie cutters (approximately 3½ inches by 3½ inches) for the animals. Cut out at least 10 animal figures, in case some break in baking or handling.

3. Preheat the oven to 325°F.

4. To make the roof, roll out about one-third of the gingerbread dough to a ¼-inch thickness. Place the roof template on the rolled-out dough and, with a sharp knife, carefully cut away the dough from around it; set the roof piece aside and save the scraps. To form the posterboard template into a conical support, cut a slit on the radius of the circle as indicated on the pattern. Overlap the cut edges by about 1 inch and staple them securely in place. Cover the entire posterboard roof form, inside and out, with aluminum foil, smoothing the foil to avoid lumps, especially along the bottom edge.

Next, carefully lift the circle of gingerbread that you have cut for the roof, and lay it on top of the foil-lined cone. There will be excess dough because of the manner in which the roof was formed. Cut away dough as necessary, pinch the seam together, and smooth it with a finger moistened with cold water. Be sure that the dough extends to and covers the bottom edge. Place the dough-covered form on a baking sheet. Bake it until the roof is slightly browned at the edges, 15 to 20 minutes. Place the baking sheet on a rack to cool undisturbed.

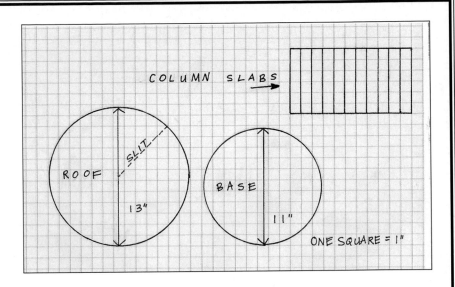

5. Roll another one-third of the dough to a ¼-inch thickness and cut out the base and as many animal figures as possible with the extra dough. Place these on greased baking sheets. You will want all the animals to "follow" one another around the carousel, so be sure that when they are right side up on the baking sheets, they face in the same direction. Bake the base and animal figures until they are slightly browned around the edges, about 15 minutes. Carefully remove the smaller shapes and place them on racks to cool, but leave the large base on the baking sheet and put the sheet on a rack to cool.

6. Roll out the remaining dough to a ¼-inch thickness and cut a large rectangle for the center column slabs. Do not cut this main piece into smaller slabs until after baking. Cut more animal figures from the remaining dough and scraps. Place these on greased baking sheets and bake as before, about 15 minutes. While the large slab for the center column is still warm, cut it into 11 smaller slabs, as indicated on the pattern piece, and transfer these and the cookies to racks to cool.

7. To make the center column support, cover the empty bread crumb container or cylinder completely with aluminum foil.

8. When the cookies are completely cool and you are ready to assemble the carousel, make the icing. Place the egg whites and 2 cups of the confectioners' sugar in a large mixing bowl. Beat with an electric mixer until the mixture is thoroughly blended, about 2 minutes. Add the remaining sugar, a little at a time, and the lemon juice, continuing to beat until the icing is thick and smooth, about 10 minutes. Use the icing immediately or cover it with a clean, damp cloth until needed. But take note: If kept longer than 30 minutes, the icing will begin to set.

9. To assemble the carousel, place the base on a flat surface, preferably on the plate or tray upon which the carousel will be displayed. Spread layers of icing on each of the center column slabs, and press them in place around the foil-covered cylinder. You may leave slight spaces between the slabs, allowing the foil to show through to give the impression of mirrors, or if you prefer, you may abut the slabs and later decorate the seams with stripes of icing. Use as many of the slabs as you have room for. Spread a layer of icing on the bottom edge of the column and press it in place at the center of the base cookie. Spread a thick layer of icing on the top edge of the column and put the roof and its posterboard support in place, centering it carefully.

10. Mark eight evenly spaced points on the base, each about 1 inch from the edge, for placement of the candy sticks under the roof. Dip both ends of the candy sticks in the icing, and carefully put them in place, keeping them as straight as possible. This is the trickiest step in assembling the carousel. If they are too long, cut the sticks to fit under the roof properly.

11. Before mounting the animal figures on the carousel, decorate the cookies with icing, candy, and raisins, as desired. Remember, all the animals should face in the same direction on the carousel, so be sure to decorate the correct side of the cookie. Place a small dab of icing on the back of each figure, and press it gently in place against a candy stick post.

12. Using a pastry tube, pipe icing in decorative patterns on the roof and base of the carousel. Pipe icing trim along the bottom edge of the roof to hide the foil-covered posterboard support. Decorate the icing with peppermint candies, candied fruit, candied angelica, and almonds as desired. The icing hardens quickly, so if you wish to sprinkle it with colored sugars, do so immediately or the sugar will not adhere. Affix flags or other decorations to the peak of the roof.

CANDY CANE COOKIES

Makes about 4 dozen

½ cup butter, softened

½ cup vegetable shortening

1 cup sugar

1 egg

1 teaspoon pure vanilla extract

½ teaspoon pure peppermint extract

2½ cups flour

1 teaspoon salt

¾ teaspoon red food coloring

Topping

½ cup sugar

½ cup crushed peppermint stick candy

1. Preheat the oven to 375°F.

2. In a large bowl, cream the butter, vegetable shortening, and sugar until light and fluffy. Add the egg, vanilla, and peppermint extract.

3. Sift the flour and salt into the butter mixture and beat just until the flour is blended in well.

4. Divide the dough in half. Stir the food coloring into one-half of the dough and blend thoroughly.

5. Roll 1 heaping teaspoon of each color dough into a 4-inch rope that is slightly thinner than a pencil. Lay the ropes side by side, press them lightly together, and twist. Place the twisted ropes on ungreased baking sheets. Curve the top of each to form a cane. Bake the cookies until they are lightly browned, 8 to 10 minutes.

6. To make the topping, combine the sugar and peppermint candy in a small bowl. Sprinkle the mixture over the cookies while they are still warm. With a spatula, remove the canes from the baking sheet and cool them on wire racks.

CHRISTMAS COOKIE ORNAMENTS FROM INEDIBLE DOUGH

Inedible dough, or modeling material, is as indispensable in a home with young children as crayons and blocks. At Christmastime, it is adaptable to more sophisticated skills and, in fact, can be the ideal medium for a family ornament-making session.

4 cups flour

2 cups salt

1½ cups water

1 tablespoon vegetable oil

Food coloring (optional)

¼-inch ribbon or No. 24-gauge wire

White shellac, polyurethane, or clear lacquer spray

1. In a large bowl, combine the flour, salt, water, and oil. Knead the ingredients with your hands until the mixture is smooth and very well blended.

2. Divide the dough into several portions. Dye each portion a different color by mixing a few drops of food coloring into the dough. You may omit this step and, after the ornaments have hardened, add color to the completed ornaments with poster paints or marking pencils. *(See step 6 below.)*

3. On a floured surface, roll out the dough to a thickness of ⅛ to ¼ inch. With Christmas cookie cutters, cut out shapes and place them on foil-lined baking sheets. If you wish to hang the ornaments, poke a hole in the top of each shape with a toothpick or drinking straw.

4. For three-dimensional ornamentation, roll fine "worms" of dough and press small pieces onto the cutout shapes to form eyes, mouths, bows, garlanding, and other kinds of trim. Use a garlic press or spaghetti maker to produce fine strands for fur or hair. To make these decorations adhere to the cutouts, brush a thin coat of water on the pieces before pressing on the ornamentation.

5. Air-dry the ornaments in a warm place for several days, or bake them in a very low oven (225° to 250°F.) until they are completely hardened and dry, about 2 hours.

6. Use poster paints or marking pencils to add color and additional detail. For shiny ornaments, paint them with one coat of white shellac or polyurethane, or spray them with clear lacquer.

7. Thread a 6- to 8-inch length of rib-bon through the hole in each ornament and tie it to make a loop for hanging. Alternatively, thread a 6-inch length of wire through the top of each shape and twist the ends of the wire together to fasten them securely.

NOTE: The dough keeps well in the refrigerator if stored in a tightly closed plastic bag.

FOIL-WRAPPED
COCOA MINT HEARTS

Makes about 3 pounds

- 9 cups confectioners' sugar
- 1 cup unsweetened cocoa
- ½ cup unsalted butter, softened
- ½ cup water
- 2 teaspoons peppermint extract
- Colored foil (available in stores where candy-making supplies are sold)
- Tapestry needle
- Lightweight silver or gold cording, cut into 6-inch lengths

1. In a large bowl, combine the sugar, cocoa, butter, water, and peppermint extract. Mix the ingredients with your hands or a spoon until they are well blended. (If necessary, add more water, ½ teaspoon at a time, until the mixture holds together.)

2. Shape the mixture into a ball. Place it between two sheets of wax paper and roll it out to a ¼-inch thickness. With a heart-shaped cookie cutter, cut out heart shapes. Place the hearts on foil-lined baking sheets. Chill for several hours.

3. Wrap the hearts in colored foil. Store them in an airtight container in a cool, dry place until it is time to hang them on your Christmas tree. Thread a tapestry needle with a 6-inch length of cording and carefully draw the cording through the top of the center of the heart, about ¼ inch from the edge. Tie ends securely to form a loop for hanging.

INSTANT
CHRISTMASCENT SIMMER

For a lovely gift, make up a package of the dry ingredients of this mixture, along with instructions on how to use it. The simmering spices will perfume the entire house.

- 3 tablespoons ground cinnamon
- 2 tablespoons ground cloves
- 1 tablespoon ground nutmeg
- 1 tablespoon anise seed
- 1 teaspoon ground ginger
- 1 quart water

1. Place the cinnamon, cloves, nutmeg, anise, and ginger in a 2-quart saucepan. Add the water and bring the mixture to a boil, stirring occasionally. Do not cover.

2. Reduce the heat to low, and keep this brew simmering on your stove or on your woodstove.

NOTE: The mixture can be stored in the refrigerator to use again and again until the scent has diminished.

POPCORN BALLS

Makes about 10 popcorn balls

- 1 cup popping corn
- 1 cup light corn syrup
- ½ cup molasses
- ½ cup sugar
- 1 teaspoon white vinegar
- 2 tablespoons butter
- Narrow, bright-colored ribbon

1. In a popcorn popper, pop the corn in batches to make 4 quarts of popcorn. Put the popcorn into a large bowl and set aside.

2. In a large heavy saucepan, combine the corn syrup, molasses, sugar, and vinegar. Bring the mixture to a boil. Remove the pan from the heat, and stir in the butter.

3. Pour the syrup mixture over the popcorn, stirring rapidly to coat it completely. Let the mixture cool enough to handle.

4. Rub your hands with butter. Working with about ½ cup at a time, form the popcorn into balls, pressing the mixture tightly together. Place the popcorn balls on a buttered pan to cool, arranging them so they do not touch.

5. When the popcorn balls are completely cool, tie them package fashion with ribbon, forming a loop at the top for hanging.

CRANBERRY AND POPCORN CHAINS

1 cup popping corn

Sewing needle

Button or quilting thread, cut in 3-foot lengths

Large buttons

1 pound cranberries

1. In a popcorn popper, pop the corn in batches, to make about 4 quarts of popcorn. Put the popcorn into a large bowl.

2. Thread the needle with the button or quilting thread, and tie a button onto one end of the thread.

3. String cranberries and popcorn in any pattern you wish: for example alternate them evenly one by one or in pairs, or string ten cranberries, followed by three pieces of popcorn. When you get to the end of the thread you may tie on another piece of thread and continue stringing to make one long garland. When the string is as long as you want it, tie another button on the end.

NOTE: Once the cranberries have been pierced they will not last as long as whole berries, so this decoration is best made close to Christmas. Cranberry and popcorn chains are beloved by birds and squirrels. When the indoor tree comes down decorate your outdoor trees and bushes with these edible remnants of Christmas.

TWELFTH NIGHT

At the turn of the century, an orange was often the only edible treat many American children received at Christmas, but among affluent families, trees were decorated with sweets. Lucky youngsters thus actually looked forward to Twelfth Night, the end of the Christmas holidays, for on that day all the cookies and candies were shaken off the tree and eaten at last.

FRUIT PLAQUE

This elegant over-door decoration is quite simple to make.

½-inch plywood, cut in a half circle or half ellipse, the base of which is slightly smaller than the door or window over which the plaque will be hung

Dark green paint

Hardy fruits, such as apples, pears, pomegranates, citrus, and pineapple

White chalk

Heavy-duty screw hooks and eyes

3-inch finishing nails

Fresh greens, cut into 4-inch sprigs (optional)

1. Paint one side and the edges of the plywood dark green and allow it to dry thoroughly.

2. On the painted side of the board, beginning at the top, arrange fruit in even rows, following the curvature of the board. Fill in the entire space, with fruit just touching. You may use one kind of fruit, or a variety. A pineapple, the symbol of hospitality, is traditionally placed at the bottom center of the fanning fruit. With a piece of white chalk, mark the center of each piece of fruit on the board. Set the fruit aside.

3. To provide hooks for hanging, screw hooks into the back, or unpainted, side of the plaque about 1 inch from the edge and about halfway up the plaque. Screw eyes into the wall to correspond to the hooks on the plaque.

4. Using the chalk marks as guides, drive nails into the painted side of the board (pound the nails into but not all the way through the board). If you are using a pineapple, because of its weight, drive at least three nails into the board to hold it. Impale fruits on the nails with the stem ends facing in. The pineapple should be upright. You may tuck fresh greens in among the fruits if you desire.
5. Hang the plaque over the doorway on the screw eyes.

NOTE: The fruit will remain fresh longer if this ornament is used outdoors.

DRIED HERB ORNAMENTS

The herb garden offers a wide variety of plant materials to dry for use at Christmastime. The challenge—and fascination—is to pick specimens at various stages of growth: some herbs are loveliest in bud, others in full flower, others when they form seed pods. Artemesia, bedstraw, calendula, chamomile, lavender, oregano, rosemary, tansy, and yarrow are only a few of the many herbs that can be used for scented Christmas decorations.

Fresh herbs, some in bud or flower

Sharp shears or clippers

Twine or rubber bands

A clothesline or rod from which to hang the herbs

Florist's wire and wire cutters (optional)

⅛-inch-wide satin ribbon (optional)

1. Harvest herbs throughout the growing season. Pick on a dry day, just after the morning dew dries, but before the sun becomes too hot. With the shears or clippers, harvest flowers with a foot or more of stem. If you are interested in preserving only the flower, strip the leaves off the stem. Using the twine or a rubber band, tie the herbs together in small bunches.
2. To dry the herbs, hang them upside down from a clothesline or rod in a dry, airy place out of the sun. Leave them until they are crisp, 2 to 4 weeks.
3. To use the herbs, as decorations for dried or live green wreaths, break off 3- or 4-inch sprigs and tuck them into the wreaths. Secure with florist's wire, if you wish. To create ornaments for the Christmas tree, make up small bouquets, twist a length of florist's wire around the stems to hold them together, and tie each bouquet again with the ribbon to hide the wire.

NOTE: Wait until after September 1 to cut artemesia. If you cut it too early, it will turn an ugly gray. If you wait, it will stay a lovely silvery color.

SUGAR-FROSTED FRUITS

Sugar-frosted fruits add old-fashioned elegance to Christmas centerpieces. If placed in a cool, dry place, the fruits will last about two weeks.

12 pieces of a variety of fruits, such as bunches of red, green, and purple grapes, lady apples (small yellow apples with a red blush), pears, plums, nectarines, cherries, any citrus fruits

2 egg whites

2 cups sugar

1. Wash and dry the fruit carefully.
2. In a bowl large enough to hold single pieces of fruit, lightly beat the egg whites. Holding the fruit with your fingers, dip the fruit into the egg white, allowing the excess to drip back into the bowl.
3. Put the granulated sugar on a plate and roll the wet fruit in it, coating the fruit well. Place the fruit on baking sheets lined with wax paper, making sure the pieces do not touch. Allow them to dry overnight.
4. Arrange the fruit in bowls or on a bed of greens, or use it to garnish platters of food for a buffet.

Menus for the Holidays

 O MAKE MENU PLANNING EASIER, THIS section offers traditional, as well as ethnic and regional, menu suggestions for a variety of sparkling entertaining, from an intimate get-together with best friends to a party for thirty-six. The numbers of people the food will serve are given with each menu, with the pages on which the recipes themselves appear noted after each selection. Hearty foods that will satisfy both children and adults are featured in menus for informal, energetic events like caroling, tree trimming, skiing, and skating. A Christmas Eve Buffet is more elegant and sophisticated—the occasion to bring out the finest linens, crystal, and china. The Christmas Cookie Swap is envisaged as a luncheon. The college-age group, looking for ways of getting together with hometown friends during the holidays, will enjoy a brunch. The New Year's Eve Open House brings friends and family together for a buffet with a Scandinavian theme. You can round out the season with a hearty Twelfth Night Dinner; in doing so, you may be initiating an event that in years to come will count as a regular family tradition.

Buttered Noodles, Chicken Marbella, Watercress and Bibb Salad with Parsley Dressing

CHRISTMAS TEA

For 12
Currant Scones *(page 120)*
Ginger Shortbread *(page 145)*
Fruitcake Cookies *(page 139)*
Cinnamon Stars *(page 142)*
Tangerine Chiffon Cake with Lemon Glaze
(page 156)
Sherried Walnuts *(page 196)*

TREE-TRIMMING PARTY

For 10
Apple Cheese Spread *(page 14)*
Potted Jack Cheese *(page 15)*
Assorted Crackers
Chicken Marbella *(page 82)*
Buttered Noodles
Watercress and Bibb Salad with Parsley
Dressing *(page 43)*
Peppermint-Stick Ice Cream *(page 174)*
Brownies

AFTER SLEDDING SUPPER WITH THE KIDS

For 6
Chicken Chili *(page 85)*
Mixed Vegetable Slaw *(page 42)*
Skillet Corn Bread *(page 118)*
Santa's Jelly Fingers *(page 144)*
Candy Cane Cookies *(page 206)*
Fresh Fruit

CAROLING PARTY

For 36
Mulled Wine* *(page 23)*
Raw Vegetable Platter with Curry Dip*
(page 18)
Chili for a Crowd *(page 67)*
Tossed Green Salad
Mexican Corn and Cheese Bread* *(page 118)*
Ambrosia* *(page 174)*
Assorted Christmas Cookies *(pages 136-151)*

SKATING PARTY

For 14
Hot Spiced Cider *(page 27)*
Country Bean and Cabbage Soup *(page 36)*
Grilled Sausages with Mustards and
Relishes
Cheeses and Apples
Winter Salad* *(page 38)*
Braided Cheese Bread Wreath *(page 116)*
Toffee Bars *(page 140)*
Chocolate Mint Sticks *(page 140)*

FAMILY CHRISTMAS EVE DINNER

For 8
Christmas Spiced Beef *(page 66)*
Purée of Celery Root and Potatoes
(page 54)
Salad of the Good Night *(page 42)*
Cardamom Muffins *(page 122)*
Figgy Pudding with Cognac Sauce
(page 170)

* This recipe can be made successfully
in larger quantities and will need to
be multiplied in order to make the
number of servings called for in
this menu.

SOUTHWESTERN CHRISTMAS EVE DINNER

For 6

Christmas Guacamole *(page 18)*

Green Chili and Chicken Enchilada
Casserole *(page 86)*

Sweet Red Peppers and Endive with Salsa
Vinaigrette *(page 38)*

Orange Slices in Red Wine and Port
(page 174)

New Mexican Hot Chocolate *(page 26)*

CHRISTMAS EVE BUFFET

For 12

Brie with Roquefort and Herbs* *(page 14)*

Oyster Stew* *(page 35)*

Beef Burgundy *(page 68)*

Buttered Noodles

Carrot and Orange Salad with Dill*
(page 38)

Bûche de Noël *(page 154)*

SCANDINAVIAN CHRISTMAS DINNER

For 8

Smoked Salmon Spread with Norwegian
Flatbread *(page 20)*

Roast Goose Stuffed with Apples and
Prunes *(page 96)*

Braised Red Cabbage* *(page 50)*

Caramelized Potatoes *(page 54)*

Rice Pudding with Raspberry Sauce
(page 171)

Almond Crescents *(page 143)*

CHRISTMAS EVE VISITORS

HOLIDAY DESSERT BUFFET

For 24

Black Forest Cherry Cake *(page 156)*

Cranberry Sachertorte *(page 158)*

English Christmas Cake *(page 160)*

Mincemeat Tarts *(page 166)*

Assorted Christmas Cookies *(pages 136-151)*

Eggnog* *(page 24)*

Dessert Wines

Demitasse

HOLIDAY BRUNCH

For 12

Hot Spiced Cranberry Punch* *(page 27)*

Baked Eggs in Tomato Shells *(page 179)*

Baked Canadian Bacon* *(page 181)*

Spoon Bread *(page 57)*

Holiday Vegetable Salad *(page 40)*

Bishop's Bread *(page 132)*

Menus for the Holidays 🍃

CHRISTMAS SUNDAY LONG AGO

CHRISTMAS BREAKFAST FOR THE FAMILY

For 8

Sliced Apples, Bananas, and Grapes
Granola with Honey-Sweetened Yogurt
(page 178)

Baked Christmas Mushroom Omelet*
(page 186)

Stollen *(page 129)*

WILLIAMSBURG CHRISTMAS DINNER

For 8

Roast Turkey with Corn Bread, Sausage,
and Pecan Stuffing *(page 88)*

Green Beans Tossed in Butter
Creamed Onions *(page 51)*

Candied Sweet Potatoes *(page 55)*

Cranberry Orange Relish *(page 58)*

Mulled Cranberries in Red Wine *(page 59)*

Watermelon Pickle, Celery, and Olives
Beaten Biscuits *(page 119)*

Plum Pudding with Brandy Butter
(page 168)

Candied Grapefruit Peel *(page 150)*

FIRESIDE DINNER WITH FRIENDS

For 4

Cream of Carrot Soup *(page 31)*

Mushroom-Stuffed Beef Filet *(page 62)*

Brussels Sprouts Tossed with Pecans
(page 50)

Wild Rice

Cucumber, Kiwi, and Pomegranate Salad
(page 40)

Pear and Cranberry Flan *(page 164)*

CHRISTMAS WEEK IN THE NORTHWEST

For 6

Savory Stuffed Mushrooms *(page 17)*

Braised Salmon in Red Wine *(page 100)*

Broccoli Soufflé *(page 48)*

Spinach and Apple Salad with
Lime Dressing *(page 40)*

Wheat Berry Bread *(page 116)*

Honey-Walnut Tart *(page 166)*

TWELFTH NIGHT DINNER

For 8

Chicken Liver Terrine with Melba Toast
(page 16)

Roast Beef with Yorkshire Pudding and
Horseradish Sauce *(page 64)*

Glazed Carrots with Red Grapes *(page 48)*

Peas Braised with Lettuce *(page 48)*

Watercress-Orange Salad *(page 43)*

Twelfth Night Cake *(page 162)*

CHRISTMAS COOKIE SWAP

For 24

Spicy Cream of Tomato Soup* *(page 30)*

Turkey Salad with Curry Dressing *(page 44)*

Muffins Crècy* *(page 121)*

Bunches of Grapes
Chocolate Truffles
(page 146)

NEW ENGLAND APRES-SKI DINNER

For 4

New England Clam Chowder *(page 37)*

Codfish Cakes with Ginger *(page 102)*

Stuffed Apple Salad *(page 41)*

Common Crackers

Brown Bread *(page 131)*

Upside-Down Cranberry Pudding
(page 168)

Mulled Cider

NEW YEAR'S EVE OPEN HOUSE

For 30

Champagne Punch* *(page 22)*

Mock Champagne Punch* *(page 27)*

Estonian Vinaigrette with Herring
and Beets* *(page 45)*

Assorted Danish Cheeses and Apple Slices

Gravlax with Dill Mustard Sauce *(page 20)*

Danish Meatballs *(page 68)*

Danish Christmas Fruit Loaf* *(page 133)*

Cardamom Cookies *(page 138)*

HEARTY SNACKS FOR NEW YEAR'S DAY BOWL GAMES

For 6 to 8

Texas Caviar *(page 17)*

Hot Crab Meat Appetizer *(page 18)*

Turkey Turnovers* *(page 92)*

Dill Shrimp Dip with Raw Vegetables
(page 21)

Bourbon Bread *(page 132)*

Penuche *(page 148)*

Mamie's Chocolate Fudge *(page 149)*

*This recipe can be made successfully in
larger quantities and will need to be
multiplied in order to make the number
of servings called for in this menu.

Index

Recipe Credits

Bailey, Lee, *Lee Bailey's Good Parties.* Copyright 1986 by Lee Bailey. Reprinted by permission of Clarkson N. Potter. Black-Eyed Peas, Sausage, and Monkfish (102), Seafood Risotto (113).

Brunner, Lousene Rousseau, *Casserole Treasury.* Copyright 1964 by Lousene Rousseau Brunner. Published by Harper and Row Publishers, Inc., New York. Curried Turkey (93).

Bullock, Mrs. Helen, *The Williamsburg Art of Cookery.* Copyright 1966 by The Colonial Williamsburg Foundation. Reprinted by permission of Henry Holt and Co., Inc. Fish House Punch (22), Oyster Stuffing for Turkey (97).

Butel, Jane, *Fiesta.* Copyright 1987 by Jane Butel. Published by Harper and Row Publishers, Inc., New York. New Mexican Hot Chocolate (26), Sweet Red Peppers and Endive with Salsa Vinaigrette (38), Green Chili and Chicken Enchilada Casserole (86).

Clairborne, Craig, *The New York Times Cookbook.* Copyright 1961 by Craig Clairborne. Published by Harper and Row Publishers, Inc., New York. Beef Burgundy (68), New England Stuffing (97), Shrimp Curry (106).

Clairborne, Craig, *The New York Times Menu Cookbook.* Copyright 1966 by The New York Times Publishing Company. Published by Harper and Row Publishers, Inc., New York. Beef Wellington (62).

Clancy, John, *John Clancy's Christmas Cookbook.* Copyright 1982 by John Clancy. Published by William Morrow & Company. Reprinted by permission of Virginia Barber Literary Agency, Inc. All rights reserved. Almond Crescents (143).

Cutler, Carol, *The Six Minute Soufflé and Other Culinary Delights.* Copyright 1976 by Carol Cutler. Reprinted by permission of Clarkson N. Potter, Inc. Country Bean and Cabbage Soup (36).

Hewitt, Jean, *The New England Heritage Cookbook.* Copyright

1977 by The New York Times, Inc. Reprinted by permission of The Putnam Publishing Group. Yuletide Wassail (23), White Fruitcake (159), Baked Christmas Mushroom Omelet (186).

Huste, Anne Marie, *Anne Marie's Cooking School Cookbook.* Copyright 1974 by Anne Marie Huste. Reprinted by permission of Houghton Mifflin Company. All rights reserved. Glazed Carrots with Red Grapes (48), Pears Cardinale (173).

Johnson, Ann Elizabeth, editor, *The Helen Corbitt Collection.* Copyright 1981 by Ann Elizabeth Johnson. Reprinted by permission of Houghton Mifflin Company. All rights reserved. Oyster Stew (35), Cranberry Mold (45), Wild Rice and Apples (56), Broccoli Soufflé (48), Lobster in Sherried Cream (107).

Lucas, Dione, *Dione Lucas Book of French Cookery.* Copyright 1947 by Dione Lucas; © reserved 1973 by Mark Lucas and Marion F. Gorman. By permission of Little, Brown and Company. Turkey Turnovers (92).

Ladies' Home Journal Cookbook. Copyright 1960, 1963 Meredith Corporation. All rights reserved. Used with the permission of Ladies' Home Journal®. Cornish Hens with Wild Rice Stuffing (93).

Lyren, Carl, *365 Ways to Cook Chicken.* Copyright 1974 Carl Lyren. Used by permission of Doubleday, a division of Bantam Doubleday Dell Publishing Group, Inc. Shaker Chicken Pudding (84).

Munger, George and Piret, *Piret's.* Copyright 1985 by George and Piret Munger. Reprinted by permission of Houghton Mifflin Company. All rights reserved. Brie with Roquefort and Herbs (14), Winter Salad (38), Leek and Sausage Pie, (75), Fettuccine with Scallop Sauce (111).

Myers, Barbara, *Christmas Entertaining.* Reprinted with permission of Rawson Associates/Scribner, an imprint of Simon & Schuster. Copyright

1980 Barbara Myers. Potted Jack Cheese (15), Panettone (128), Bishop's Bread (132), Chocolate Mint Sticks (140).

Nichols, Nell B., editor, *Farm Journal Country Cookbook.* Copyright 1972 by Farm Journal, Inc. Published by Doubleday and Company, Inc., New York. Mincemeat Tarts (166).

Olney, Judith, *Joy of Chocolate.* Copyright 1982 by Barron's Educational Series, Inc. Reprinted by arrangement with Barron's Educational Series, Inc., Hauppauge, New York. Curried Fruit Compote (178).

Pepin, Jacques, *A French Chef Cooks at Home.* Copyright Jacques Pepin. Published by Simon and Schuster, New York. Veal Scaloppini with Cream, Calvados, and Apples (79).

Plantation Cookbook, *The Junior League of New Orleans.* B.E. Trice Publishing. Louisiana Yam and Apple Stuffing (97), Pralines (145).

Poses, Steve and Rebecca Roller, *The Frog Commissary Cookbook.* Copyright 1985 The Commissary, Inc. Used by permission of Doubleday, a division of Bantam Doubleday Dell Publishing Group, Inc. Mixed Vegetable Slaw (42), Cranberry Sachertorte (158), Pumpkin Waffles with Cider Syrup (189).

Rosso, Julee and Sheila Lukins, *The Silver Palate Cookbook.* Copyright 1979, 1980, 1981, 1982 by Julee Rosso and Sheila Lukins. Reprinted by permission of Workman Publishing Company, Inc. All rights reserved. Chili for a Crowd (67), Chicken Marbella (82).

Rosso, Julee and Sheila Lukins, *The Silver Palate Good Times Cookbook.* Copyright 1984, 1985 Julee Rosso and Sheila Lukins. Reprinted by permission of Workman Publishing Company, Inc. All rights reserved. Chicken Chili (85), Eggnog French Toast (186).

Seranne, Ann, *The Joy of Giving Homemade Food.* Copyright 1978 by Ann Seranne. Reprinted by permission of David McKay Co., a division of Random House, Inc. Brandied

White Grapes (192), Curry Powder (195), Spiced Red Wine Vinegar (195), Herbed Cheese (197).

Sheraton, Mimi, *Visions of Sugarplums.* Copyright 1981 by Mimi Sheraton. Published by Harper and Row Publishers, Inc., New York. Sugarplums (149).

Vitz, Evelyn Birge, *Continual Feast.* Copyright 1985 by Evelyn Birge Vitz. Published by Harper and Row Publishers, Inc., New York. Christmas Eve Borscht with Polish Mushroom Pockets (32), Salad of the Good Night (42), Christmas Spiced Beef (66), Tortiere (76).

Rombauer, Irma S. and Marion Becker Rombauer, *The Joy of Cooking.* Copyright 1931, 1936, 1941, 1942, 1943, 1946, 1951, 1952, 1953, 1962, 1963, 1964, 1975 by the Bobbs-Merrill Company, Inc. Reprinted with permission of Simon & Schuster. Peppermint-Stick Ice Cream (174).

Woman's Day Collector's Cookbook, Hachette Filipacchi Magazines, Inc. Divinity Drops (148).

Picture Credits